# Positive Behavior Management Strategies *for* Physical Educators

**Barry W. Lavay, PhD**
California State University, Long Beach

**Ron French, EdD**
Texas Woman's University, Denton

**Hester L. Henderson, PhD**
University of Utah, Salt Lake City

**Human Kinetics**

**Library of Congress Cataloging-in-Publication Data**

Lavay, Barry Wayne.
    Positive behavior management strategies for physical educators  /
Barry W. Lavay, Ron French, Hester L. Henderson.
        p.   cm.
    Includes bibliographical references and index.
    ISBN 0-87322-880-4
    1.  Physical education and training—Study and teaching.
2. Classroom management.   3.  Reinforcement (Psychology)   I.  French,
Ronald W.   II. Henderson, Hester.   III. Title.
    GV363.L36   1997                                          97-18733
    613.7'071—dc21                                            CIP

ISBN: 0-87322-880-4

**Acquisitions Editor:** Scott Wikgren
**Developmental Editor:** Elaine Mustain
**Assistant Editors:** Susan Moore-Kruse, Sandra Merz Bott, Erin Cler, Melinda Graham
**Editorial Assistants:** Amy Carnes, Laura Majersky
**Copyeditor**: Bonnie Pettifor
**Proofreader:** Sue Fetters
**Indexer:** Craig Brown
**Graphic Designer:** Robert Reuther
**Graphic Artist:** Yvonne Winsor
**Photo Editor:** Boyd LaFoon
**Cover Designer:** Jack Davis
**Photographer (interior):** Deb McBee
**Illustrator:** Paul To
**Printer:** Versa Press

Printed in the United States of America      10  9  8  7  6  5  4  3

**Human Kinetics**
Web site: www.HumanKinetics.com

*United States:* Human Kinetics, P.O. Box 5076, Champaign, IL 61825-5076
800-747-4457
e-mail: humank@hkusa.com

*Canada:* Human Kinetics, 475 Devonshire Road, Unit 100, Windsor, ON N8Y 2L5
800-465-7301 (in Canada only)
e-mail: orders@hkcanada.com

*Europe:* Human Kinetics, 107 Bradford Road, Stanningley
Leeds LS28 6AT, United Kingdom
+44 (0) 113 255 5665
e-mail: hk@hkeurope.com

*Australia:* Human Kinetics, 57A Price Avenue, Lower Mitcham, South Australia 5062
08  8277 1555
e-mail: liahka@senet.com.au

*New Zealand:* Human Kinetics, P.O. Box 105-231, Auckland Central
09-523-3462
e-mail: hkp@ihug.co.nz

# DEDICATION

*I would like to recognize my parents Gabriel and Sylvia Lavay, who at an early age instilled the importance and power of receiving an education. I also dedicate this book to my family, Penny, Nicole, and Danielle, who continue to be supportive of what I do and who, most importantly, make life special.*

—B.L.

*I would like to thank Lisa Silliman-French for her practical guidance in editing several chapters of the book, based on her teaching experience in the public school setting. I would like to dedicate this book to her.*

—R.F.

*I would like to thank my parents, Hester and Tom Henderson, who always supported any educational endeavor I ever pursued. They instilled in me the value of learning at an early age, which is still a driving force in my life. I am grateful for the love they gave me, the lessons they taught me, and the role models they are for me. I would like to dedicate this book to them.*

—H.H.

# Acknowledgments

Many people supported and helped with our efforts to write *Positive Behavior Management Strategies for Physical Educators*. We would like to acknowledge the outstanding staff at Human Kinetics and their commitment to physical education. A special thanks to Rick Frey, past director of the academic division, and Scott Wikgren, acquisitions editor, for believing in our project from the beginning. A heartfelt thanks to Elaine Mustain, our developmental editor, who was a pleasure to work with. She provided the editorial assistance and organizational skills necessary to allow us to develop the initial manuscript into a polished text. Her persistence, diligence, and patience were infinite in seeing this book to completion. Finally, our thanks go to Dr. Tom McKenzie of San Diego State University and Dr. Melissa Parker of the University of North Dakota, who critically reviewed the original manuscript and gave us their thoughtful comments and suggestions.

Writing a book can be a tedious process, and we are grateful that we could keep our friendship and humor throughout the project. We also wish to recognize all the present and future physical educators who make a difference in the lives of the students they teach and who realize managing behavior is part of effective teaching.

Finally, Barry would like to acknowledge California State University, Long Beach, the College of Health and Human Services, and the Department of Kinesiology and Physical Education for their support of his scholarly endeavors.

# Contents

# Preface

Students have a basic right to learn and teachers have a right to teach! One of the greatest challenges educators face today is how to maintain appropriate student behavior in their classes so students can learn. Indeed, each year since 1969 in an educational poll conducted by Phi Delta Kappa, teachers and parents have cited a lack of discipline and control as one of the major obstacles educators face in teaching students effectively (Elam, Rose, and Gallup 1996). An inability to manage and motivate students is the reason most often given by beginning teachers for leaving the profession. And no wonder! A class that is unmanageable is unteachable. In such a class, learning does not occur.

Professionals who teach physical education are faced with a number of unique challenges. For example, it would be unthinkable to place 50 to 60 students in an English class and have them share one or two textbooks. Many physical educators, however, are placed in this difficult position every day. To make matters worse, they are expected to teach in outside facilities, a small gymnasium, or cafeteria with only a few pieces of equipment. Not surprisingly, it is difficult to teach effectively.

We have designed *Positive Behavior Management Strategies for Physical Educators* to give you—whether you are a current or future physical educator at the elementary, middle, or high school level—guidance in motivating students, managing behavior, and creating an environment that is conducive to learning. We have incorporated approaches from psychology, special education, and physical education and applied them to proven best teaching practices. This book is user-friendly and easy to read. We have tried to help remove the confusion you may feel about behavior management, empowering you to incorporate leading-edge behavior management theories into your everyday teaching.

We have illustrated the approaches we describe in this book with accounts of actual classroom incidents in which real teachers successfully applied the theories to real situations. These examples of successful use of behavior management methods will help you understand how to use them in your own teaching or coaching situation, increasing both the quality and fun of learning in your classes, teams, or groups.

Finally, we believe that no magical formula or set method for managing behavior to promote student learning exists. Behavior management is both a science and an art in which you must blend proven theories with your own personality and unique mix of students to produce effective down-to-earth teaching practices. Therefore, we'll show you how you can use different approaches in the same behavioral situations, depending on the dynamic interactions among the student, physical educator, and teaching environment. To this end we have woven vignettes of three common behavior management situations into chapters 4 through 7 and "One Last Look at the Vignettes" to give you a chance to see how to apply the material to concrete situations (see details in the introduction).

Is behavior management all about punishment? Certainly not! We strongly believe that you should address student behavior positively and constructively. First, as a professional in physical education, you need to be proactive, structuring your classes or activities so as to prevent behavior problems. Second, use positive methods to promote appropriate student behavior. Punishment is not a positive behavior builder nor is it conducive to student motivation and learning. Thus, use it only as a last resort after you have fully explored and applied proactive and positive methods. Then return to more positive methods as soon as possible. We hope our book will promote this process and philosophy, helping you create an environment more conducive to learning.

# Introduction

In general, the American public is skeptical about the quality of education and is calling for educational accountability. This is particularly true when it comes to student discipline, which is a major concern of many Americans (Elam, Rose, and Gallup 1996). Television programs such as *60 Minutes* and *20/20* often feature inappropriate behaviors of American students. And such shows often highlight model behavior management programs as well, asking the question "Why can't all schools be like this one?"

Ironically, the same television networks are also airing programs that glorify the very behaviors the news shows criticize. Consider, for example, the many negative social interactions of Roseanne Conner or Al and Peg Bundy with their children or the undesirable activities of the cartoon characters in *Power Rangers* and *Beavis and Butthead*.

## HOW BAD IS THE PROBLEM?

Learning cannot take place in an atmosphere of chaos. The ideal learning environment is safe, structured, consistent, and motivating. But what is happening in some of our schools? The severity of behavior problems seems to be escalating. In the past, teachers were primarily concerned with problems such as gum chewing, incessant talking, tardiness, swearing, and poor sportsmanship. Today, these behaviors are largely ignored while teachers focus on dealing with assault, murder, weapons possession, gangs, and illegal drugs. Today, students defy teachers and argue over any attempts at discipline. Even though these problems often originate in the family, society expects educators to manage and, indeed, permanently correct the bad behavior and attitudes.

How bad is the situation? Nearly 20 percent of 20,000 teachers surveyed in Texas reported experiencing a direct threat of personal violence. Today's teachers are increasingly confronted with fights, bullying, shoving, rapes on campus, the death of a student or teacher, and suicide (Taylor, Hawkins, and Brady 1991). As teachers today, we need special skills to cope with potentially explosive situations and violent students (Hughes 1994). Yet, at the same time, we may lack the legal, social, and practical support we need to effectively manage behavior. This dilemma may lead to situations such as in Texas, where murder now appears in the educational code as an offense for which a student may be expelled—a method of discipline teachers should be able to assume they inherently have!

## GOOD DISCIPLINE PRACTICES MUST BE TAUGHT

Many physical educators do not know how to design, implement, or evaluate a program to reduce behavior problems that will also increase appropriate conduct. Many have told us that in their teacher preparation programs, little time, if any, was devoted to behavior management. Others were told that the ability to manage behavior comes with experience and that they had to develop their own formulas to control their classes. This philosophy is clearly reflected in the limited amount of space given to this topic in elementary and secondary physical education pedagogy textbooks. Only recently have a few of these books included a complete chapter on behavior management.

Experiences are important, but we as physical educators can and must learn how to use management methods that solve discipline problems and motivate students to learn. Because learning cannot take place without control of the students, we must develop the skills to handle behavior problems.

## IMPORTANCE OF BEHAVIOR MANAGEMENT IN PHYSICAL EDUCATION AND SPORT

As physical educators and coaches, we are faced with unique conditions that negatively impact our abilities to manage behavior problems. First, many classroom teachers and school administrators regard physical education as an unimportant subject area. This attitude is often communicated to the students–who, as a result, fail to take physical education seriously. Second, physical education classes are held in a wide-open environment and often have more students than classes in other subject areas. Third, many students in the United States today have such low levels of fitness that they lack the basic motor skills required to participate fully in traditional games and sports (Pangrazi and Dauer 1995). Fourth, some children and youth in school sport activities are so unmotivated or anxious that their performances suffer significantly.

If we are to overcome these adverse circumstances, we must look first at ourselves. We must have expectations that go beyond students merely complying with the basic class and game rules. We must recognize that in an effective physical education program, students are engaged in the content, sometimes interacting with each other productively in cooperative pairs or groups and sometimes working independently toward lesson goals. But to create an environment conducive to learning, we must first have the knowledge and skills to both manage students' behavior and motivate them to succeed. Successful behavior management leads to less student hostility and frustration, less violent behavior, greater student achievement, and the development of life skills, including social skills and personal responsibility.

## RESPECTING CULTURAL DIFFERENCES

Physical educators need to be aware of, and also respect, cultural differences. The behavior of students from other cultural backgrounds could be perceived as disrespect, noncompliance, or lack of interest. In actuality, the behavior is totally appropriate in the student's culture. In some cases all encompassing rules could be violating the beliefs and practices of some cultures. For example, in some cultures girls are not allowed to wear shorts; so, girls in respecting their cultural heritage could be breaking a classroom rule requiring students to dress appropriately.

The key to understanding cultural differences is to make compromises as long as safety and hygiene are not sacrificed. Also, educators must guard against stereotyping behavior related to specific religious groups or societies. We need to respect the unique customs, values, and languages of smaller groups existing within the larger culture. Many districts offer sensitivity training workshops to assist in developing these skills to manage behavior effectively and fairly and in a just, ethical, and legally defensible manner. Johnson (1986) stated that though the approaches used to manage student behavior follow our knowledge of general human growth and development, we should understand that no one particular approach is superior. Further, the various cultural and ethnic backgrounds provide different ways of coping with and satisfying some basic needs. Because of this, all students do not look on each reward with equal satisfaction; the same applies to punishment. "Isolating one student to a chair outside the gym by the door is food for one and poison for another" (Johnson 1986).

## What Is to Come?

We have divided the eight chapters of this book into three parts. In part 1, which includes chapters 1 and 2, we'll introduce you to the general strategies, principles, and procedures you'll need to develop a positive and proactive management plan. In part 2, we'll examine various specific approaches to behavior management, including the behavioral approach (chapters 3 through 5), the psychodynamic approach (chapter 6), and nontraditional approaches (chapter 7). In part 3, which includes chapter 8 and two smaller sections, we'll apply all the concepts and methods we've covered in parts 1 and 2 to show you how to develop a program that works for you in your particular situation.

To help you review and assimilate the information in this book, we have included review questions at the ends of chapters 1 through 3. Then to help you apply the methods discussed to real-life situations, we have developed vignettes of three diverse behavior management situations for your consideration. You'll meet Hector, an overactive third grader, Ashante and Jim, two angry high school students, and Jill and Molly, two middle school students who refuse to dress for class (see page x). At the ends of chapters 4 through 7, we'll ask you to revisit these vignettes and apply the information covered in each chapter to each particular situation. So read the three vignettes and keep them in mind as you progress through each chapter. Then, we'll visit Hector, Ashante and Jim, and Jill and Molly one last time in "One Last Look at the Vignettes" in which we'll apply all the concepts and methods we've covered throughout the book as appropriate to their situations. But as you read our sample answers in chapters 4 through 7 and in "One Last Look at the Vignettes," keep in mind that they are simply that: samples, only some of the many creative ways you might effectively deal with similar situations at your school.

In "Increasing the Peace," we'll offer one more creative method for managing behavior as we discuss the "Increase the Peace" program. Finally, in appendixes 1 and 2, you'll find photocopy-ready checklists and worksheets to help you analyze your own and students' behavior and interests. Appendix 1 contains 18 checklists to help you assess your own use of several of the methods, concepts, and pointers this book contains. Refer to these often while you're studying this book and in the years to come to make sure you are on the right track. Remember, however, that you must ultimately tailor your behavior management approach to your personality, style, and situation. Simply being able to answer "always" or "yes" to each statement in these checklists will not make your program effective. In fact, trying to employ too many strategies at once may have a negative effect on your approach. So view the checklists as a way to review and assimilate the information covered in this book so that you can decide both what works for you and what you feel comfortable with. Appendix 2 includes eight worksheets to share with students, other teachers, and perhaps parents to collect information to help you assess how best to approach the particular student population you serve.

As you absorb all the information in this book, keep in mind that no one method will always be appropriate. This is because teaching styles, students, behavior management situations, and schools vary widely. Thus, we encourage you to develop a wide base of knowledge and a wide variety of skills and methods to call on in times of need. Then put together a "toolbox" of methods that work for you in the situations you face. One final note: Don't hesitate to ask for help in difficult or irritating situations. No teacher finds behavior management to be an easy task, and you should not feel inadequate if you call on the insights of other professionals. One day they'll call on you, too!

# The Practice Vignettes

The following vignettes are used in chapters 4 through 7 and "One Last Look at the Vignettes." At the end of each of these chapters, we'll ask you to think about how you would apply what you've learned to each of these situations. Then we'll give our own suggestions of how we would apply the principles discussed in the chapter to each of these cases. In "One Last Look at the Vignettes," we provide an extended discussion of how each of these situations might be handled, integrating all the material from the entire book.

## VIGNETTE 1

Hector is a third grader who is considered overactive. He is unable to stand or sit on his assigned spot in the gym for any length of time, and he runs when he should walk. In addition, for his age, Hector has difficulty following a series of directions, becomes easily upset and irritated, and has poor gross motor coordination. His behavior has reached the point at which the physical educator has requested that the classroom teacher not bring him to physical education class because he constantly causes chaos.

## VIGNETTE 2

Ashante, who is the president of his high school student council, has been dating Shannon for the last year. Jim, the captain of the school football team, has a crush on Shannon and has begun to telephone her at home and leave notes in her locker. She has asked Jim on several occasions to leave her alone, but he refuses. Finally, Ashante confronts Jim in the locker room. Then on the way out to physical education class, Jim pushes Ashante away and challenges him to a fight after physical education class in the locker room restroom. After class, the physical educator walks into the locker room to find the two boys fighting.

## VIGNETTE 3

Jill and Molly are two eighth grade students who are constantly coming to physical education class and telling their physical education teacher that they do not have their gym clothes for class. The physical educator immediately has them sit on the bleachers and gives them an "F" for the day. Neither of these students seems to care about the importance of physical activity or that they may receive a failing grade.

# Developing a Positive and Proactive Management Plan

In part 1, we'll introduce you to the general strategies, principles, and procedures you'll need to help you start developing your own positive and proactive management plan. In chapter 1, we'll explore how you can create a positive learning environment through examining your current teaching approach, getting to know your students as individuals, and avoiding negative approaches. In chapter 2, we'll examine ways you can take proactive steps in your planning and instruction to prevent problems before they have a chance to start. Specifically, we'll look at ways to develop and implement rules and routines to make each class run more smoothly.

## CHAPTER 1

# Creating a Positive Atmosphere

It was right after school and Mr. O'Brien, the middle school physical education teacher, and Ms. Truly, the school assistant vice principal, were walking to their cars. Shoulders drooping, Mr. O'Brien said, "I've had an awful day. During first period, I caught Billy and Shane fighting in the locker room and had to send them to the principal's office. It was the third time this month I've had to break up fights in the locker room!"

He continued, "That's not all: During third period I began a new unit on volleyball. Only a few of the students seemed interested, and I had to keep quieting the class because they were whispering while I was giving instructions. It went downhill from there. It looked like none of them had the basic volleyball skills—not that they would practice at the learning stations! To top it all off, I just got five students with mental retardation from Mr. Taylor's adapted physical education class added to my fifth period. I was not told that they were coming and had no idea what an impact they would have on my class."

"We all have days like this, sometimes," Ms. Truly said, trying to console him.

"But bad days are becoming a chronic problem!" Mr. O'Brien replied. "Teaching and coaching aren't fun anymore. I feel so burned out."

## CREATE A POSITIVE LEARNING ENVIRONMENT

As physical educators, we are the designers and managers of the physical education program. We must set the stage for learning by creating a positive, exciting class atmosphere. This is especially important today, when 20 percent of our students do not enjoy physical education and some consider it emotionally stressful (Carlson 1995). Most students want to listen, participate, and learn from physical educators who are competent and prepared for class. So we must be knowledgeable about the subject content, be able to perform the skills, and be able to manage behavior effectively.

In chapter 2, we'll give you a number of strategies for preparing the physical education setting in order to promote student learning. But because your first task is to provide a learning environment that is warm, supportive, and most importantly, encourages student performance and learning, we will begin by discuss-ing more general principles of creating a positive learning environment. Without such an environment, the best preventive management plan in the world will be far less effective than it could be. How, then, do you go about creating such a positive learning atmosphere?

## EXAMINE YOURSELF

Socrates' observation that "the unexamined life is not worth living" is as true now as when he originally said it. You might apply it to your own situation by rephrasing it like this: "If you don't examine yourself as a teacher, you might as well give up now!" Let's look closely, now, at some of the questions you should ask yourself (see figure 1.1).

### Am I "Tuned-In?"

Tuned-in teachers know what is going on during class at all times. Tuned-in teachers act immediately, stopping misbehavior before it spreads. For instance, William was up to bat

**Figure 1.1**  Self-evaluation is an important process for effective teachers.

for his third time during the class period; he had already struck out twice. The frustration could be seen in his eyes, and his teammates were starting to groan. Mr. Speckhardt, the physical educator, could see a problem coming. The teacher incorporated a new rule in the game: "Each team can use the batting tee each inning for one player." This both removed the peer pressure and allowed William to succeed.

## Am I Enthusiastic?

Enthusiasm is contagious. To be an effective teacher, you must be enthusiastic about what you're teaching. Your enthusiasm will spread to the students, helping to promote a positive, warm, and nurturing class climate. Take, for example, Mr. Angelo, a retired military officer, who now teaches physical education at a local junior high school. He believes that any show of enthusiasm (or any other emotion) is a sign of weakness, and so he teaches very matter-of-factly, giving the students no hint that he might be enjoying the class himself. Because Mr. Angelo is very firm, he has few "discipline prob-

lems": The students follow his instructions quietly and without question. But many of the students bring notes from home so they will not have to participate, and none of the students who are not already athletic are improving. That these problems are largely the result of Mr. Angelo's unenthusiastic attitude was clearly illustrated when he missed school for two weeks to meet his army reserve commitment. During this time, Mrs. Motta, a substitute physical education teacher with a buoyant personality, took over the class. While still using the basic command style of teaching, she incorporated music when she led the warm-ups and many times jogged with the students and participated in the games and activities. Not surprisingly, the number of excuses decreased, and students who had never tried to improve before began to show progress in both skill and fitness levels.

## Am I Flexible?

Adapt as well as adopt each behavioral strategy. For instance, if you have designed and

---

## LEARNING STUDENT NAMES

In a physical education class you typically have students constantly moving and sometimes looking away from you, so you must be able to get students' attention quickly for safety and behavior management reasons (Williams 1995). Naturally, it's easier to get confused or misbehaving students' attention if you know their names. But like many physical educators, you may have 30 to 60 students in a class and may be responsible for teaching every student in the school, making this quite a challenge.

The following are proven strategies for learning and using student names for different age groups (Cusimanio, Darst, and van der Mars 1993; Williams 1995):

- Greet each student by name as she enters the gym or during the warm-up. Similarly, dismiss each student by name at the end of class, commenting about her class participation for the day.

- Regularly include the students' names when giving feedback, when reinforcing appropriate behavior, and when reprimanding inappropriate behavior.

- Use name tags with younger students during the first few weeks of class.

- List the names of students you can remember. These students may be receiving a disproportionate amount of your attention. List the names of students you couldn't remember on an index card to use as a quick reference.

- Take and label a photograph of each class or photographs of students participating in physical activity to place on the bulletin board to use as references.

initiated a behavioral or performance contract with a student, you may need to renegotiate the contract if it proves insufficient. So write contracts in such a way as to allow you to modify them if unforeseen circumstances arise. For example, Mr. Zurel and Josh, an 11th grader, developed a behavioral contract to address Josh's frequent tardiness. Based on the contract, Josh could earn one bonus point per day for being on time, which Mr. Zurel promised to add to Josh's final physical education grade. For the first week, the contract seemed to work: Josh was on time every day. But the second week, Josh was late three times. At this point, the contract did not seem to be working, so Mr. Zurel called Josh into his office to renegotiate it. They decided that Josh could still earn bonus points by being on time, but every day that he was late he would owe Mr. Zurel 10 minutes after school to be spent cleaning up the equipment room. After modifying the contract, Josh was still occasionally tardy, but overall, his punctuality improved significantly.

## Am I Personable?

You must be personable: Learn the names of your students so you can greet them and say good-bye to them by name. For example, Mrs. Robert, an elementary school physical educator, makes it a point at the end of each class to shake the hand of each student, commenting to each one as she does so. Generally the comments are very positive, but if need be, this approach gives her a chance to express concern about a behavior and how the student can improve the next class period. While this takes Mrs. Robert approximately one to two minutes of class time, she believes interacting with her students on an individual basis saves time in the long run.

Even with our suggestions, if you have a number of very large classes, you may still have difficulty recognizing all your students. For example, you may spend so much time with one student in a given class period that you can only give your attention to a few other students. To minimize this problem, before class starts, identify a group of students on which to focus during class that day. Spend no more than 30 to 45 seconds with each student before moving to the next. The following day identify another set of students who will receive your attention and so on.

One final word about names: Always use a student's name respectfully. If you use it with sarcasm, he will most likely tune you out. Do these strategies sound like a lot of work? Keep in mind that all your efforts will pay off because students will know that you care. This, in turn, will help you develop a warm, stimulating learning climate in which students want to behave. Refer to checklist 1 in appendix 1, "Personal Inventory," often to keep you on track.

## USE POSITIVE APPROACHES

All students need to feel they belong, are special, and are an integral part of the class. It is important, then, for you to give equal attention to each student. This will help bring the class together as a unit as well as help develop class spirit among the students. This can be a challenge, especially with large classes. Incorporate the following positive practices into your teaching to meet this challenge.

## Catch Students Being Good

Too often we fall into the trap of calling attention to students who are off-task or acting out, inadvertently reinforcing and perhaps even increasing the inappropriate behavior we wish to stop. Unfortunately, students quickly learn they must act out to receive attention. So accent the positive by catching each student being good. This is particularly important when someone demonstrates a new positive behavior. Simply complimenting the positive behavior goes a long way toward reinforcing it.

Recognize students' successes. Advertise the success of your students by recognizing records, feats, and other accomplishments through the school newspaper, over the public address system, or on bulletin boards. Newspaper and bulletin board attention is especially motivating when you include students' pictures (see figure 1.2). For instance, Ms. Garcia began a new aquatics program with her students in cooperation with a local university. A reporter from a newspaper wanted to write a story about this program. In Ms. Garcia's class was a boy named George who often misbehaved. George would continually say, "No, I can't do it" when learning how to swim, then would disturb other students instead of trying. Ms. Garcia told him

**Figure 1.2** Using newspaper articles to recognize your students' accomplishments can be a powerful motivator.

that in the next two weeks if he participated in all the swimming activities, she would make sure that his picture was put in the local paper with the story about the aquatics program. His behavior immediately improved.

This is only one of many ways physical educators have accented the positive. Many more creative ways exist, so we'll look at these methods in more detail in chapter 2.

## Expect Students to Follow Your Directions

Give instructions once, twice if you believe the students are deeply involved in an activity and excited and simply did not hear the instruction, but no more! The more you give an instruction, the less likely your students are to follow it. It is more successful to give the instruction in a positive yet assertive voice, then remain silent, maintain eye contact, and wait for your students to comply. Generally after two to three seconds, you should employ a consequence for not complying. For example, Mr.

Jacino, a high school physical education teacher, had 60 students in his softball class, and none of them put the equipment away immediately after his requests. He became very frustrated. So he spoke with another physical educator about the problem. The other teacher said he used to have the same problem until he initiated a policy that stated "Each squad that is lined up within 15 seconds after a request will earn one additional point toward their daily grade." The next day Mr. Jacino tried this approach, and to his great surprise, the students lined up. Peer pressure and the earning of an additional point worked!

## Keep Your Cool and Address Problems Quickly

If you expect your students to behave, you must set a good example by being in control of yourself. When a student breaks a rule, you need to act, not react. So refrain from making on-the-spot judgments. Instead, make sure you know what happened before accusing a student of a violation. Moreover, remember that misbehaviors seldom start with bad intentions. Most importantly, however, don't allow behavior problems to continue, for they will often cause a ripple effect, spreading through the class, escalating into a major problem. Once misbehaviors occur, even the best corrective methods may disrupt learning and cause friction between you and your students (Charles 1992), so do not add to the problem by losing your self-control.

Instead, remain calm, take the student aside, and in a straightforward manner, explain the rule and the consequence for not following it, all the while keeping an eye on the rest of the class. When communicating with a student, use direct eye contact, which conveys a positive and assertive message (see figure 1.3). For example, "Nicole, I know you are capable of getting in your squad line on time because I have seen you do this many times before." Have the student repeat the rule and how she will follow it in the future. This procedure effectively reduces public confrontations between you and students.

## Focus on the Behavior to Be Corrected

When students misbehave, word your reprimands carefully. Describe the behavior rather than labeling or attacking the student. For example, instead of saying, "Cindy, you are unmotivated," specify the behavior that concerns you. You might say, "You are not participating during class exercises."

Develop a "we" attitude. The student needs to know that he is working in concert with you to solve the behavior problem. When you use the question "What can we do to solve this problem?" you focus on the behavior, not the student. Ultimately, this approach makes the student feel as if you care and really want to help.

**Figure 1.3**  When communicating with a student, use direct eye contact.

The negative behavior, not the student, must be the focus of your statements. If you put the student down rather than addressing the specific behavior, you may create major self-concept problems. Keep in mind that people who feel good about themselves are more likely to act appropriately. Some examples of dos and don'ts include the following:

### Dos

- I need you to stop talking when I am speaking.
- You will be expelled for fighting.
- It will help if you watch the ball going into your hands every time.

### Don'ts

- You will never make it in this sport.
- You have lost my respect.
- Can't you act like your brother?

Because focusing on the behavior instead of attacking the student personally is so difficult at times, we'll talk about this more in chapter 3.

## Be Consistent

Your students must know what they can expect from you and what you expect of them. Thus, your behavior and treatment of the students must be predictable and even-handed. Mrs. McCall, who is a first-year teacher, knew that she must post rules and explain them in detail to all of the students. But since she had befriended many of the students in her classes who were also members of her daughter's soccer team, the other students in class felt that many times she allowed her "class pets" to break many of the rules. This angered the excluded students, causing them to lose some respect for Mrs. McCall, which, in turn, led to their talking back to her.

### Your "Yes" Should Remain "Yes"

Turning "No" to "Yes" and "Yes" to "No" is a sure way to cause behavior problems. Say, for instance, you ask students to take a warm-up lap, and one student stubbornly says he does not want to warm up because he ran a lap during lunch time, two class periods ago. So you say, "Okay, you do not have to take a warm-up lap today." Or you tell a student she will be squad leader at the end of the week. She is very excited and cannot wait for Friday. But when Friday comes, you change the lesson plan and tell the class that they will be running an obstacle course. You tell the student she will be captain on Monday. In other words, you go from a "Yes" to a "No." No way—be consistent!

### Always Check for Compliance

Telling a student to do a task but not checking to see that he has done it can create an inconsistent approach to behavior management.

- Won Joon, please put away all the balls and bats properly in the equipment room.
- Class, since it's the end of the semester, I need you to clean out your lockers and turn in your locks.
- Class, please perform each activity at each station, recording your performances as you go.

It would only take a little time for you to follow up in each of these situations to make sure students have complied with your requests. In the first instance, you need only make a short trip to the equipment room right after class. In the second instance, you can simply have the students stand by their opened lockers for you to check. When you collect the locks, you can record this information on a form, instantly identifying the students who have not turned in their locks. In the last instance, you can randomly spot-check to see if students are performing the activities at each station and recording their performances. Praise those who are doing the activity correctly, using them as role models, so other students will be more likely to stay on-task. If this is not effective, you can provide other incentives, which we'll discuss later.

### Respond the Same Way to the Same Behavior

Depending on your mood, you may often unintentionally treat the same behavior by one student or another in different ways. What you punish a student for one day, you may ignore the next time the misbehavior occurs. But responding inconsistently to the same behavior makes your behavior unpredictable. So develop a reasonable and predictable consequence for each misbehavior.

### Ensure Consistency Among All Physical Education Staff

The physical education staff at your school must work as a unit, setting the same basic rules and expectations for student behavior. This structure prevents students' becoming confused when moving from teacher to teacher, semester to semester, because they can accurately predict what will be expected of them. Thus, the teachers in your physical education department must support each other; inconsistency undermines everyone's approach to behavior management, allowing students to play one teacher against another to get their own ways.

## Use Positive Tools

Be creative in finding new ways of motivating your students and helping them focus. Mr. Badashar noticed that during his first grade physical education class, many of the students walked during the jogging warm-up. So he decided to interact with each child when she completed each lap. He stood by the starting line, and as the student passed, he would give her a high-five if she had jogged that lap. If she had not jogged the lap, he would not physically interact with that student. Simply because he incorporated this positive social interaction, all of the students began jogging their laps.

### Vary Tasks

Generally students are clearly motivated when you introduce new drills and activities, but then their enthusiasm decreases, leading to off-task and inappropriate behavior. How do you keep student interest high? Vary the tasks! You don't always have to introduce new tasks when interest wanes, however, you can modify an "old" task or interrupt it to emphasize a learning cue or to give feedback. For example, if the students are practicing basketball drills and boredom begins to set in, introduce another drill that can be used to reach the same instructional objective or bring the students in to briefly illustrate a new skill to be added to the original

drill or briefly discuss a few tips to improve their skill performance.

### Play Music

Many times, you can increase student interest and motivation by introducing music into your classes. You can add music to warm-up exercises, fitness routines, and regular practice sessions. Or you can add it as a reward for successfully completing a task (Sariscsany 1991). Be sure, however, to select music that students like. You can have the students bring tapes in for you to play, but always preview them for appropriateness.

### Relax Students With Physical Activity

You can use physical activity itself to relax students. For instance, vigorous exercise, such as 10 minutes of jogging, may not only promote fitness, but may also reduce stress, give students more experience jogging, and improve their self-concepts (Allen 1980; Blue 1979; Doyne, Chambless, and Bentley 1983). Indeed, jogging can give students a form of time-out, removing them from external pressures or distractions. Other activities, such as bowling and racquetball, may also reduce anxiety. Relaxed students are more cooperative students.

## Use a Continuum of Styles

At the beginning of the school year, your style of instruction may need to be more controlling. Carefully weighing student ages and developmental levels as the school year progresses, you should lead your students toward making their own decisions more often. But first, you must establish a minimal level of class control. For example, at the beginning of the school year, Mr. Yu always uses a command style of teaching. He decides on the rules, the activity, the equipment, the location, and the consequences of all activities. As the semester progresses, he systematically allows students to begin to take charge during certain aspects of the class, such as leading exercises, taking roll, and otherwise assisting him. Then, if the students accept these responsibilities, he incorporates task cards, circuits, and obstacle courses into his classes. Next, if this approach is successful, he allows students to help select appropriate activities to meet the curriculum goals.

Focus on positive approaches to create the best possible learning atmosphere. Refer to checklist 2 in appendix 1, "Using Positive Approaches," often to see how you're doing, making sure negative approaches do not creep into your style.

# AVOID NEGATIVE APPROACHES

The choice is yours: You can approach your students in ways that are not very effective, possibly leading to more inappropriate behavior or you can use approaches that motivate students, leading to a positive learning environment. The following is a list of some ineffective methods you should never use with students; they are, indeed, the shortest route to becoming an ineffective teacher.

1. **Making comparisons:** Don't compare one student's behavior to another, making statements such as "Why aren't you as well-behaved as your older sister?" The child may not even like his sister, so she is not a role model that the child wants to emulate, or the child has heard this so often he doesn't listen to it and tunes you out. Even if it did work, it's a put-down and therefore not appropriate.

2. **Making idle threats:** Don't say you are going to send a student to the principal's office or call her parents when you have no intention of doing so. This will often increase behavior problems as the student challenges you by continuing to misbehave to see if you will follow through.

3. **Being sarcastic:** Making sarcastic remarks is very inappropriate. Many times, the student may not even understand the meaning you are trying to convey but will probably still understand that the remark is designed to hurt feelings.

4. **Humiliating:** Giving public reprimands is often humiliating. Never make fun of a student or use him as a negative example in front of peers. When possible, hold a private discussion with a misbehaving student, either in a separate area or to the side of the teaching area. Remember, when communicating with a student, use direct eye contact in order to convey a positive and assertive message.

5. **Overstating the situation:** Don't get angry and make a statement you can't, won't, or shouldn't follow through on.

- You will sit out of the activities for the rest of the week.

- I am going to drop you from the team.
- I'll have you clean the rest rooms for the next three weeks for snapping towels at other students.

Checklist 3 in appendix 1, "Avoiding Negative Approaches," offers a handy list to help you double-check your approach.

# APPLY COUNSELING TECHNIQUES

Often as a physical educator, you may find that students both respect you and perceive you as more approachable than other teachers. Because of this, you are in a good position to serve as a counselor if you choose to do so. But to more effectively help students, develop and practice basic counseling skills.

## Determine Who Owns the Problem

In attempting to resolve a conflict, it is helpful to analyze the situation to determine who owns the problem. If you are frustrated because a student is disrupting the class, this is your problem. If the student is frustrated because he does not have any friends, this is the student's problem. If each of you is frustrating the needs of the other, then both of you own the problem. For student-owned problems, you can try to understand and clarify the student's problem through "active listening" (Gordon 1994). This method involves your listening carefully to the student; trying to understand the student's point of view and feelings; then reflecting this information back to him. You could say, "What I hear you saying is that when your best friend, Jamal, gets around the older boys, he is mean to you, and that makes you sad. Am I correct in saying this or is something else going on?"

For teacher-owned problems, use "I messages," explaining to the student the effect that the behavior has on your needs and feelings. For example, you might say, "I feel frustrated when you come to class late because then I need to spend time explaining to you what we are doing after I have already explained it to the rest of the class. This wastes class time." Or when Jose is saying mean things to Brian because Brian took the soccer ball away from him in a game, you might say, "I am disappointed in your name-calling behavior. We just talked about being a good sport yesterday. Perhaps we need to talk again about possible solutions to this problem." I messages create a cooperative problem-solving attitude, minimizing blame and anger.

Once you identify the problem, work with the student to generate possible solutions. At this stage, avoid evaluating ideas: Let creative ideas flow freely. Then evaluate the possible solutions to determine which is best for the particular situation, allowing the student to contribute to this process as well. After agreeing on one solution, discuss specific ways to implement it. Next, actually implement the solution. Finally, assess the situation to determine the solution's effectiveness. If it is not working, negotiate a new solution following the same steps (Gordon 1994). Remember, involve the student at every stage, soliciting and respecting his input. He is more likely to follow a plan that he helped design.

## Choose Your Words Carefully

Use words like "will" and "can" instead of the guilt-producing word "should." For example, if LuYing says that she was late for class because she wanted to talk to Keesha about the dance tomorrow night, you might say, "LuYing, what can you do next time so you can talk to Keesha but not be late to my class?"

## Roadblocks to Effective Communication

Fronske and Birch (1995) make a number of suggestions you can use to enhance your communication skills. Avoid the following tactics:

- Giving advice: This occurs when one person tells another how to deal with a problem. For example, Maheshie comes to you with a problem, stating, "No one wants to be on my team." You may be inclined to give advice. For example, "Well, why don't you try to make friends with Sue?" When this happens, you take responsibility for the problem away from Maheshie. To help her take responsibility, you might say, "Maheshie, you seem concerned about no one wanting to be on your team. What can you do to change that?" When Maheshie offers a solu-

tion, you should reinforce her initiative, suggest other options if appropriate, and help her set a goal for making friends. Giving her your advice only takes away her responsibility.

- Passing judgment: This occurs when you evaluate what the student says whether favorably or unfavorably. This includes criticizing, blaming, and labeling. You may want to respond to Maheshie by saying, "You are popular, lots of students like you." But this undermines the student's confidence in her ability to solve her own problems, possibly causing her to rely on external judgments. Instead, it is better for you to listen carefully to what the student is saying and ask open-ended questions, such as "What could you do to make others want to be on your team?" This approach empowers the student to solve her own problems.

- Trying to persuade: Don't try to convince a student that a particular position or choice of action is correct, taking away the student's responsibility for finding a solution. It's tempting to think that our experience and wisdom will lead to the best choice of action. But allowing the student to make his own decision as to how to meet your expectations is more likely to engage his long-term cooperation.

- Playing psychoanalyst: Don't be tempted to suggest that only you know the cause of the student's behavior problem. Never assume reasons and always clarify what you think the student is saying, or you will take power away from the student.

- Using diversionary tactics: Don't divert the student's attention away from the behavior problem in any way. For example, you might tell Maheshie, "Just join in the game today, and we can discuss your problem some other time." This does not solve anything, except that it's more convenient for you for that day. But you are better off dealing with problem behaviors as they occur.

It is important for you to be aware of these common roadblocks to effective counseling so you can avoid them (see also checklist 4 in appendix 1, "Effective Counseling"). Then work to enhance your interactions with your students. We'll look more at specific strategies and examples for communicating with and counseling students in chapter 6.

## USE OUTSIDE RESOURCES

To create a positive atmosphere, you must use every available resource to ensure that inappropriate behaviors will not impact the learning or performance of your students. In most cases, you will be able to deal with behavior problems yourself without going outside your classroom or gym. But when a team approach is necessary, you should not feel that you are incompetent.

### Within the School

Most administrators are highly supportive. You should enlist their help as well as that of school psychologists and counselors. You should also consult other teachers who have experienced similar problems and have developed an effective program to solve or reduce the behaviors that were interfering with performance or learning. Other teachers also may have developed a behavior management program for the problematic student that you can modify for the physical education environment. This ensures a consistent behavior management program for the student from teacher to teacher.

Many school districts now employ special or adapted physical education specialists who can help you design a behavioral management program. Indeed, when a student with a disability receives his classroom instruction in a special education setting, often the special or adapted physical educator becomes an integral part of the behavior management program. One example is the special educator who uses a point system in his classroom for which the student may earn rewards. To participate, you send a note after each class period to the special educator, regarding the amount of points the student earned to be added to the total. Ask for or develop a brief form to simplify and standardize this process.

### Parents

Do not make the mistake of thinking you are only dealing with a group of students. Behind them stands a group of concerned parents you need to inform of your expectations. Therefore, you must effectively communicate with parents. Send a letter home to all parents at the beginning of the school year outlining the program policies and rules. You might include your teaching philosophy, expectations regarding class participation, and procedures for dressing in physical education. Use language that parents can understand, avoiding forbidding, technical, and complicated language. Be friendly and tactful. Encourage parents to contact you whenever they have concerns. After all, parents know their children best and can be both helpful resources for you and valuable support for the overall physical education program.

Other ways to effectively communicate your expectations to parents include sending written notes, making telephone calls, holding conferences, striking up conversations at PTA meetings (being sure to protect the family's privacy), and giving behavioral progress reports. In addition, a few parents may be willing to work with you to allow students to earn privileges at home for better behavior at school. But don't limit your communication efforts to the negative. Make an effort to select a few students from every class every week to send a positive note home with. A few words on a certificate recognizing good behavior and effort can go a long way toward engaging both student cooperation and parental support (see figure 1.4). Carefully rotate whom you select so that all students receive some positive recognition.

### When Behavior is Extreme

Although parents are among our best potential allies in the effort to create a positive atmosphere in our classrooms, we cannot ignore the reality that this is not always the case. We are seeing an increase in the number of parents, requested to come to school to discuss the behavior problems of their children, who verbally abuse, threaten, or even physically attack the teacher. It seems parents are becoming less willing to discuss problems in a calm and rational manner, preferring to settle issues with violence. Violent parents often mean violent children, and we must be prepared to handle them as well.

To deal with this problem, some schools have hired security guards to assist teachers by patrolling halls, playgrounds, and parking lots. Programs have also been developed between school personnel and police to deal with both violent parents and violent students. For instance, in Texas many school districts have

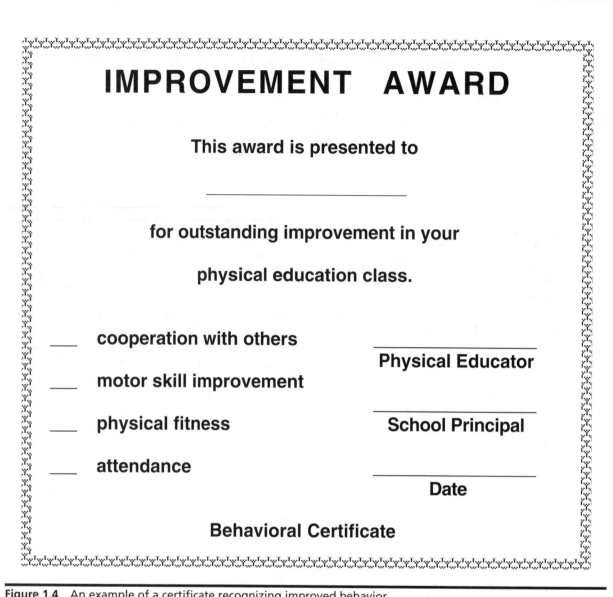

**Figure 1.4**  An example of a certificate recognizing improved behavior.

adopted a "no-tolerance" policy. Under this policy, the police are called on campus immediately when a problem occurs. In some cases, the student may be taken off the school grounds to the police station to wait for their parents' arrival.

## SUMMARY

The foundation that supports effective teaching is the ability to manage student behavior.

With this ability, your students' performance and learning will increase, which is, after all, your major responsibility. To create this foundation and the resulting positive learning environment, incorporate several general methods into your teaching approach. And don't hesitate to tap into the talents of those who can help you develop and implement a behavior plan. Remember, you are not alone. Finally, periodically use checklists 1, 2, 3, and 4 in appendix 1 to help you determine your own strengths and weaknesses.

# REVIEW

1. Analyze the behavior management methods you use with your students or athletes. Which ones are positive?

2. Physical educators may inadvertently use many negative methods in the physical education setting. Use checklist 3 in appendix 1 to analyze your high school physical education and athletic experience or your present teaching role. Which, if any, negative methods can you identify? What methods could replace them?

3. Rank the top five individuals you think can help you implement an effective behavior plan. Justify your choices.

## CHAPTER 2

# Proactive Management Techniques

Ms. Danielle was about to begin her second year of teaching at Kennedy Middle School. What a difference a year had made! When she began teaching, she had assumed all the students would enter her program motivated to learn. Because she had started the school year with no real management plan to promote learning, she got off on the wrong foot with her students. She spent the first three months of the school year struggling to gain class control. But over the summer she had taken a behavior management workshop at a local university. Based on what she learned in the workshop, she designed a proactive management plan that included strategies for students to enter and leave the locker room, to enter the gym and meet in designated squads, and to perform the warm-up routine with assigned squad leaders taking attendance. Ms. Danielle planned to discuss these new procedures during the first week's physical education orientation meeting and post them on the gym bulletin board. In addition, throughout the school year, she would review all management procedures with her students frequently. A proactive management plan would be even more critical this year than last, as the number of students in most of her classes had increased from 35 to 45. But this year, she was ready for them.

## AN OUNCE OF PREVENTION, A WORTHY INVESTMENT

Many times, you may be tempted to blame your students for off-task behavior and respond with punishment. Inappropriate student behavior, however, may be a function of poor planning, such as having students stand in long lines, not distributing enough equipment, making the activity too easy or too hard, failing to explain the relevance of an activity, or requiring students to continue practicing an already-mastered skill. Because these practices often cause boredom, low interest, and indifference to physical education, you must first examine your own procedures before looking further for causes of misbehavior.

Good teaching includes good management. Because you are more likely to encounter disruptive behavior during management time than instruction or activity time (Rink 1993; Siedentop 1991), you should develop a proactive management plan. An effective management plan will decrease behavior problems, increase learning time, and promote both the students' and your enjoyment of the physical education program. But effective class management does not just happen! You cannot control a class by simply hoping that behavior problems will not arise. You must proactively and properly plan and organize learning experiences. Indeed, planning and organization are the keys to preventing behavior problems (see figure 2.1). Therefore, spending time beforehand designing the program to prevent behavior problems is an important investment (Rink 1993; Siedentop 1991).

Proactive management works best if you carefully consider and integrate your own teaching style, unique student needs, and the environment in which you must teach. In order

**Figure 2.1** Without effective behavior management techniques, many teachers are desperate and feel they're about to go under.

to effectively manage behavior, you must organize, deliver, and monitor your instructional programs with these factors in mind (C.M. Charles 1992). In this chapter, we'll show you how to do this by providing you with a cadre of proactive management strategies you can incorporate into a plan that will meet both the unique needs of your students and the many teaching situations that may arise in your instructional environment.

## EVALUATION OF STUDENT BEHAVIORS AND TEACHER PRACTICES IN PHYSICAL EDUCATION

The first step in developing an effective proactive management plan is to identify the behaviors you want your students to exhibit and the behaviors you do not want your students to exhibit. You can start by asking yourself questions such as the following:

- What behaviors will bring order to my program?
- What behaviors will enhance student performance?
- What behaviors may possibly present problems?

Use these questions to help clarify your thinking and guide your development of a proactive behavior management plan.

To help you become more aware of how your program design may be a major cause of student problems and poor learning, use checklist 5 in appendix 1, "Evaluating Your Practices in Physical Education," to identify strong and weak areas in your teaching methods. After answering each statement, you may find that you need to make your teaching environment safer, more supportive, and engaging; or you may recognize that you are inconsistent in explaining to students your class expectations and consequences for not following class rules. By identifying problem areas on the checklist, you can begin to design a proactive management plan that works for you and your students. The key is to determine the problem or problems and then develop a plan. While this checklist will help get you started, examine the additional

examples provided in the evaluation section later in this chapter.

## PROACTIVE MANAGEMENT METHODS: PREINSTRUCTION, INSTRUCTION, AND EVALUATION

We can think of the design of the preventive class management plan as having three phases: preinstruction, instruction, and evaluation. During the preinstruction phase, you develop and mentally rehearse the management plan. During actual instruction you create a positive class atmosphere that promotes learning. At the same time, you implement your management plan, having students practice it in the same ways that they practice new motor skills. Finally, you evaluate the plan to determine its overall effectiveness. Keep in mind, however, that effective, preventive class management is an ongoing process never fully achieved. So once you establish a preventive class management plan, you must maintain and periodically review it (Rink 1993). In the upcoming sections, we'll discuss each of the phases of preventive class management in detail. Refer, also, to checklist 6 in appendix 1, "Proactive Planning During the Preinstructional and Instructional Phase," regarding proactive planning during the preinstructional and instructional phases.

### Planning Ahead: Preinstructional Phase

The preinstructional phase occurs before students start the class. For example, you can design routines for students entering the gym and for taking attendance that will minimize class disruptions from day one. By leaving nothing to chance, you can avoid potential problems. Let's look at how to plan for many of these procedures.

#### Facilities

Consider the space requirements you will need for each activity. Certain activities require more space than others. If you primarily instruct outdoors, you will need a rainy day backup plan. But facilities such as the school gymnasium, cafeteria, or multipurpose room may need to be shared among several teachers. At the secondary level, various physical education facilities, such as gyms and fields, are shared by all physical education teachers. Whatever the situation, it is important to designate in writing ahead of time who will use which facilities at what time and for what purpose. Everyone, including administrators, should be aware of this plan before school starts in the fall.

The physical education facilities and environment are unique educational settings requiring unique management. In the gym or outdoor area, traffic patterns are open, and students and equipment are constantly moving. Factors such as equipment use and proper spacing among students all have the potential to cause behavior problems. One way to control the environment during planning is to properly space equipment and students. Especially when equipment is potentially hazardous, for example, jump ropes and bats. This planning both helps maintain a safe environment and keeps students on-task (see figure 2.2).

The general condition or appearance of the teaching environment can affect student behavior as well. Hazardous, disorganized, and unclean facilities do not reinforce good work habits. Periodically check facilities for any potential hazards, such as glass on or holes in the playing field. Make sure that your facilities are neat and well-lighted and include interesting bulletin board displays (Dougherty and Bonanno 1987). For example, a bulletin board can attractively display the components of health-related physical fitness and how students can take their own pulse rates. Your efforts will help create a safe and positive atmosphere. We'll look at additional examples for proper planning of the physical education environment to enhance learning throughout this chapter.

### Equipment

To maximize practice time students should have their own equipment. This may not always be possible with large classes and a limited budget. But lack of equipment should not be an excuse for students to be off-task, which can lead to behavior problems (see figure 2.3). For example, during a basketball unit Mr. Knewitz has divided his 42 seventh graders into groups of three. In each group, one student practices dribbling a basketball, another member

**Figure 2.2** One way to control the environment is to space equipment properly before students arrive.

of the group practices basketball defensive sliding, and the third member skips rope. Every 5 minutes each member rotates to the next activity until they have completed all three activities, taking a total of 15 minutes to complete. This approach gives each student a specific task, creates variety, and effectively stretches a limited equipment supply—all of which work together to keep everyone on-task.

Don't be tempted, however, to use whatever equipment you have available. Carefully match the type of equipment to the ability level of each student. For example, young children who are in the initial stages of learning to catch a ball will feel more confident catching Nerf balls. Safety is also an important consideration. Damaged equipment may break while a student is using it, resulting in falls, cuts, or other injuries. Therefore, check all equipment periodically and fix or replace anything that is worn or broken. Develop a simple system for students

to check out and use equipment (see "Instructional Phase" section of this chapter).

To expedite setup and instruction, clearly identify and carefully store equipment for easy access. The storage area is also a good a place to keep first aid equipment available for an emergency. During class orientation discuss appropriate procedures for students accessing equipment from storage and periodically review and practice procedures throughout the school year.

### Curriculum

Curriculum selection needs to be student-centered. Specifically, base your selection of activities on students' chronological and developmental ages and pace increases in the degree of difficulty so as to challenge but not frustrate the children. Check with your school district's physical education administration regarding state and district physical education curriculum guidelines and policies. Discuss

**Figure 2.3** To minimize off-task time, students should have enough equipment.

your program with physical educators at the other levels in your school district to determine proper skill development sequencing from kindergarten through 12th grade to create continuity throughout the district.

Develop curriculum activities that students can relate to and find interesting. Use age-appropriate themes and interact with students to ascertain their interests. You might ask students what activities they enjoy during their free time or you might observe them during free play. At the early elementary level, you might introduce fitness concepts by having an exercise poster that states, "Mr. Muscle says, 'Do all your stretching exercises.'" At the high school level, you might introduce students to fitness concepts by having them complete laboratory assignments in a fitness workbook.

### Student Medical Needs

Both to better understand your students and to prevent management and safety problems, identify those who have medical problems, such as asthma, diabetes, or seizures. Be aware of who has special needs or is taking medication. Use this information not to place labels on students, but rather to be aware of any potential needs or emergencies. For example, students taking medication may experience side effects that adversely impact motor performance. To learn more about how you can help students with medical needs, contact the students' parents, check with the school nurse, ask other teachers who work with the students, or read the students' files (see also chapter 7).

### Student Expectations

Communicate your expectations clearly to the students. Expectations should be meaningful and success-oriented, yet challenging. Discuss class rules and routines with the entire class. We'll go into this later in the chapter. It may also be necessary to speak with a student individually about her unique needs. She may have a suggestion you didn't think of. For example, a student who has slight hearing impairment may ask to stay close to you during class instruction. Although getting to know a special needs student requires extra time, we guarantee it'll be worth the effort. We'll offer you more strategies for effectively communicating with students in chapter 6.

### Locker Room Procedures

Establish proper locker room procedures, including dressing before and after class, showering, and use of lockers. For example, instruct students not to slam lockers, to keep all their clothes in their assigned lockers, to keep their lockers locked at all times, and to be near their lockers when changing clothes. Tell students to shower and dry off in a designated area so floors do not become wet and slippery. Insist that while students are in the locker room they do not engage in horseplay, such as pushing other students or snapping towels.

### Excuse From Class and Nondressing

Your goal is for students to be as actively involved in physical education as possible. Try the following strategies to alleviate the problem of students sitting out, whether excused or not (Lavay and Bishop 1986):

- Discuss with students the reasons behind proper dress, including safety, personal hygiene, comfort, and enhanced performance.
- Post, discuss, and review rules regarding proper dress.
- Establish a policy regarding excuses from physical education class.
- Acknowledge those students who dress appropriately.
- Have gym clothes available for nondressers to borrow. Make sure you have a way to wash clothes.
- Make nondressers' time constructive by having them prepare a report specific to the day's activity or unit.
- Be an effective role model by dressing appropriately.
- If you have any input to uniform selection, make sure the uniform is attractive to the age group and/or fosters a team spirit, such as T-shirts with a catchy saying.

### Entering and Exiting

Establish routines for entering and exiting the physical education setting. For example, when students enter the gym, provide them with a familiar activity that requires little instruction, such as a warm-up routine. Assign students to a designated area determined by squad or warm-up number. Post information and directions regarding the initial class activity as well as the day's lesson on the bulletin board in the class setting or locker room. Start class on time and expect all students to promptly begin participating in the initial activity.

Relaxation activities are an effective way to end the class, not only from a physiological standpoint but also because they calm the students down after the day's vigorous lesson, helping them be more relaxed when they reenter their classrooms. Moreover, relaxation activities can help students deal with stress in a more socially acceptable manner—a skill they can use in all areas of their lives. During relaxation activities, ensure that the setting is quiet and free of any outside stimuli. To set the mood, dim the lights and play soft, soothing music (see also chapter 7).

Insist that students leave the physical education setting in an orderly fashion. For example, make sure that young elementary students are supervised on the way back to class, either by you or the regular classroom teacher, and that they walk, not run.

### Attendance

Don't waste precious instructional time taking attendance. Instead, for example, take attendance while students are warming up. Or have students report to their squad leaders or sign or check in as they leave the locker room. You might use a tag board on which students turn over their tags if present or areas with numbers for them to stand or sit on so you can look at the open spots to see who is absent. To keep accurate records and save time, you can use a number system in which, for example, a student who is number 24 on the roll call floor areas is also number 24 in the attendance book. You can use a handheld computer, such as the Sharp Wizard, PSION Organizer, and Apple Newton, to record and manage attendance. *Electronic Roll Book* software for the Wizard is available from Bonnie's Fitware to record attendance, grades, and fitness scores. Once you are back in your office, you can connect the Wizard to your desktop computer and place all necessary information in a spreadsheet (Mohnsen 1995). For further information regarding this software, contact Bonnie Mohnsen, 18832 Stefani Avenue, Cerritos, CA 90703, 562-924-0835.

### Time Frame

Planning the correct amount of time for each activity is critical to the success of a lesson. A well-developed lesson plan can help you keep in mind how much time to spend on each activity. With time and experience, this will come more naturally if you keep basic rules of thumb in mind. For example, be careful not to spend too much time discussing the rules before starting an activity or game. Students who are waiting to get started can become bored, possibly leading to behavior problems. Give basic rules only before starting the activity, then explain more rules as needed while students are participating.

## Insructional Phase

Once you've laid the groundwork so that class will run more smoothly, it's time to actually teach. The instructional phase includes procedures that occur once students enter the physical education setting so you can put all your plans into action.

### Orientation

Time spent early in the school year orienting students to your rules and routines is a good investment as it will save instructional time later. Begin orientation the first day of class and continue it during the first few weeks of school with periodic reviews. To deliver an effective orientation, inform students of what you expect of them. Cover class routines and rules of appropriate student behavior that are critical to the program's success (see next section). During this time, explain the who, what, where, when, and how to each student (Sanders 1989). For example, each student (who) must line up for warm-up exercises (what) in his squad line (where) five minutes after the bell rings (when) and wait quietly, keeping his hands and feet to himself (how).

### Class Rules

Rules are reminders of behaviors that you expect students to display. In general, rules are less specific than routines (see next section), and you will usually need to teach students what each rule means in specific situations.

Role-play or explain examples of appropriate and inappropriate responses to each rule. When you neglect to clearly communicate rules, the students only learn what you want when their actions are unacceptable (Charles 1992). Instead, create a more effective classroom climate by stating your rules clearly the first day of class and by reviewing the rules as needed throughout the school year.

### Designing rules.

When designing physical education class rules, consider district and school policies as well as the specific behaviors you need students to exhibit in the physical education setting:

- List acceptable and unacceptable behaviors in the program.
- Involve students in the development of the rules when possible.
- Keep the rules simple and to the point.
- Make no more than five or six rules as too many will only confuse students.
- State all rules in a positive, measurable, and age-appropriate manner.
- Develop general rules that are flexible, covering different class situations.
- Develop specific rules for specific situations as well.
- State consequences clearly.
- Be sure students understand the rules and the consequences.

Specific issues to keep in mind include safety, equipment usage, traffic patterns among activities, and student cooperation.

When possible involve students in the development of the rules. Students who feel ownership of the rules are more motivated to follow them. In addition, it is always a good idea to send the rules home with students to have the parents read, sign, and return. This involves parents in a positive way as members of your behavior management team right from the start.

### Implementing rules.

The following are helpful hints for you to remember when implementing class rules:

- Post rules in an area where all students can clearly see them, such as the locker room or on a bulletin board in the gym.
- Provide pictures of rules for nonreaders.

- Strictly enforce rules.
- Consistently enforce consequences for not following rules.
- Practice and review rules periodically.
- Inform fellow teachers and parents of the rules.

In general, design rules for the entire class to follow; do not single out one particular student. Moreover, do not establish rules and consequences that you cannot carry out. For rules to be effective, you must consistently apply them to all students, following through immediately with consequences for breaking rules. If students cannot count on consistency, they will consider it a game to see if they can get away with breaking the rules.

Design consequences along a continuum of least to greatest intervention. For example, for the first offense, warn the student and discuss your expectations with her and the consequences if she continues to misbehave. After the second offense, give the student a time-out, having her sit in a designated area for one minute while watching the class continue the lesson. For the third offense, hold a teacher-student conference.

It is important to document infractions of the rules. Some physical educators use a coding system to create a permanent record of rule infractions (Swager and Mante 1986). For example, a student making fun of another student, a violation of rule three, receives a minus three (-3) alongside her name in the attendance book. We'll give you more examples of instructional management methods in chapters 3 through 6.

Figures 2.4 and 2.5 provide examples of general rules appropriate for elementary students and secondary students, respectively. While specific rules are much easier to understand, they are not always applicable to different situations (Siedentop 1991). Figure 2.6 provides examples of more specific rules to promote active participation with elementary students. Figure 2.7 offers specific rules for secondary students who are squad leaders. Notice all rules are stated positively, telling students what they should do not what they shouldn't. Rules that start with "don't" are negative and convey a restrictive message

Thoroughly discuss the rules during class orientation. Provide clear and concrete examples of why each rule is necessary. For example, say

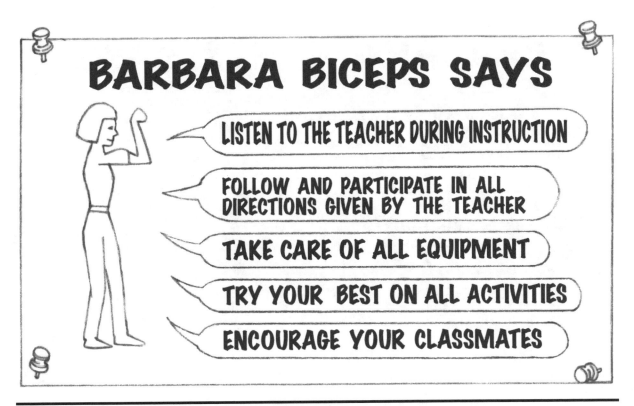

**Figure 2.4** General rules appropriate for elementary students.

1. Be dressed and in your squad 7 minutes after the bell
2. Listen and follow all teacher directions
3. Use proper language
4. Respect equipment
5. Respect the rights and be supportive of others

**Figure 2.5** General rules appropriate for secondary students.

"You must listen when I am giving instructions so you will know what to do" or "It is important to take care of equipment so that it will last for all of us to use."

Remember, you must post the rules for all to see and periodically review them. Younger students need more examples of appropriate and inappropriate behavior than older students (Rink 1993). For example, place a basketball on the floor between your feet and say, "While I am giving you instructions, any equipment you have should be right here [point at the basketball] on the floor between your feet." Then pick up the ball and bounce it while you are speaking, explaining to the class, "It's hard to hear my instructions over this noise. That is why we follow the rule." Finish by placing the ball back between your feet and remark, "Now, you see, it is so much easier to hear what I am saying."

To ascertain how well students understand the rules, quiz them about appropriate and inappropriate behaviors (Summerford 1996). To help younger students remember the rules, put them into a song or rhyme. Periodically have students state the rules as a part of lessons. For example, early in the school year, require that students recite a rule correctly before moving to the next skill station.

### Class Routines and Procedures

Routines or procedures are predetermined ways of handling situations that frequently occur in the physical education setting. As with class rules, define routines clearly and follow them consistently. You also need to practice them with students. Examples of student routines include the following:

**Figure 2.6** Examples of specific rules for elementary students to promote active participation.

- Rotate clockwise (to the right) when changing stations.
- Signal a group before entering their space to retrieve a ball.
- Walk directly to the squad area when you come into class.

- Face the students in your squad so they can all see you

- Provide hand signals to keep your squad organized

- Provide clear directions using a voice all can hear and understand

- Use correct form when modeling activities and sport

**Figure 2.7** Examples of specific rules for secondary students who are squad leaders.

When students follow established routines, you can devote more time to what is important: improving performance and increasing learning. But how do you engage student cooperation? Provide positive and specific feedback to students who follow routines properly. This reinforces students and creates a ripple effect, influencing other students to follow the routines properly as well. With praise and practice, eventually you'll find you only need to tell the students which routine to follow once before proceeding. Later on in the school year, students should follow certain routines automatically without being reminded, for example, quickly moving to their squads when entering the gym or playing field. Allow students to help with routines by making them responsible for various assignments, such as being a squad leader, spotter, official, or equipment monitor. Rotate helpers every few weeks.

Only you can decide which class routines to develop, depending on your situation. But no matter what routines you design, practice and reinforcement are the keys to establishing them as routines (Boyce and Walker 1991). Let's look at the most commonly used routines in the sequence in which they usually occur during a class period (see checklist 6, appendix 1).

### Signals.

Use signals to start and stop class or get the students' undivided attention. An effective signal eliminates the need to yell. But you must use signals consistently and employ a consequence for not paying attention to them consistently. In general, do not give students more than five seconds to respond to a signal before applying a consequence.

Signals are especially important for young students who have difficulty stopping an activity to listen to instructions or transitioning from one activity to the next. Without clear signals, the class may become confused. So establish age-appropriate signals with young students, teaching them to "freeze" when you say a certain word. For example, say, "When I say 'surfer,' freeze and stand like a surfer, ready to listen to instructions." You can even have each class vote on its own signal word. For secondary students, the signal may be hearing a hand clap and seeing your hand go up. The number of claps you give can correspond to the number of the squad you wish to signal. For example, one clap could mean squad one moves to the next activity and two claps could mean squad two moves. Whatever signal you choose, students must be able to easily hear and see it. This is especially important as students perform activities while turned away from your voice. Training students to listen for signals means not needing to shout or repeat directions.

### Initial activity.

Start each class promptly with a familiar activity. Choose an activity that students feel fairly comfortable performing and can do with little instruction. Routines that have been practiced and well-established are effective initial activities. For example, in Ms. Lee's middle school classes, students know without being reminded that they must enter the gym and get in their six assigned squads for attendance, and that while attendance is being taken, they must perform warm-up exercises in their squads at five different fitness stations. Ms. Lee has posted simple directions on a task card at each station. Students have one minute to complete each station and on signal jog around the gym for one minute before starting the next

station and after the last station. This initial activity takes a total of 10 minutes to complete. Each week, Ms. Lee changes the fitness activities or routines for the stations, based on student input and her own objectives.

### Equipment distribution and collection.

Establish procedures for equipment distribution, use, and collection. Poor distribution of equipment can lead to behavior problems. For example, you should never leave playground balls in a bag in the middle of the gym floor for students to argue over; instead, carefully distribute the balls around the gym, giving each student an equal opportunity to secure a ball. At the elementary level, you can place a ball for each student in a hula hoop. Spread the hoops around the blacktop or gym floor. Another strategy is to assign squad leaders who are responsible for securing, distributing, and collecting equipment for each member of their squads (see figure 2.8).

When students first receive a piece of equipment, they may be too excited to hold the equipment and listen to your instructions. So don't ask for the impossible when you introduce new equipment, especially on the elementary level. Give students time to practice with the equipment or provide them with a specific or open-ended task to complete, then give instructions for the lesson with the equipment on the floor beside them. To regain their attention, provide an incentive. For example, say, "The first three students who are on their poly spots with their equipment on the floor at their sides will get to demonstrate the next skill."

### Organization of students into partners, groups, or teams.

Not only does choosing or having students choose partners, groups, or teams waste time, it also embarrasses students, which does not make for a positive class climate. Divide younger students into groups by using such techniques as birth months, favorite colors, clothes (short sleeves or long sleeves, collars or no collars, and so on), or those who prefer plain or peanut M & Ms (Phillips and Carter 1985). A more sensitive approach with high school students is to select groups or teams ahead of time and post them. Keep each group small (no more than five students) in order to ensure more practice trials and change groupings

**Figure 2.8** Squad leaders can be responsible for securing, distributing, and collecting equipment for each member of their squad.

frequently—at least every month—to give students the opportunity to interact with other class members. For example, at Manzano High School at the beginning of each month's unit, teachers create new squads by rotating the names on the class rosters. They rotate two names into a different squad, making sure each squad includes an equal amount of males and females. At the same time, they choose a different squad leader, then post all updated information on the gym bulletin board. Occasionally for special events such as tournaments or to create variety, teachers change the squad members, based on a squad leaders' meeting with the teachers after class to select teams privately. Team selection is confidential with discussion ending once squad leaders leave the teacher's office.

### Movement Management Procedures

The amount of structure and teacher assistance you need to provide will vary from student to student and class to class. For example, a high school elective physical education class may include students who are more motivated than usual and are therefore able to handle less structure. But don't confuse or allow students to confuse less structure with less appropriate behavior; instead, expect students to behave properly with less direction from you (Rink 1993).

No matter how much structure and direction you provide, when your directions are unclear, confusion and behavior problems may develop. Strategies for managing the flow of activities during the lesson are helpful in reducing management time (Siedentop 1991). The key is to structure activities so they proceed smoothly, maintaining momentum from one activity to the next. This starts with making sure students know what you want them to do. If, for example, you use circle or line formations for certain drills or activities, clearly mark where you want students to stand and move with poly spots, cones, or flags. The movement management methods that follow are especially important for students with special needs who have difficulty following routines and directions but will help manage all students.

### Transitions.

Whether they occur within or between activities, a transition is a primary time to use a signal to reduce management time and allow the class to run smoothly. Younger students who may have difficulty remaining on one task for a long period of time may require more transitions to be successful.

Of course, effective transition signals and directions are clear and concrete. For example, establish clear boundaries and traffic patterns by using cones, poly spots, flags, arrows, and task cards. A good example of a clear transition within an activity is for a task card at station 1 to read "Perform volleys with your racket against the wall for two minutes and then power walk to station 2." A good example of a transition statement from one activity to the next is "While the music is playing, I want you to perform the aerobic routine we practiced this past week. When you hear the music stop, you have five minutes to jog outside and be on the soccer field in your teams, ready to play."

Certain students may require a cue a few minutes before you give the actual transition signal. For example, you may need to warn a student with a learning disability who has difficulty processing information that a transition is coming. To avoid singling out the student, you and the student can work together to develop a discrete hand signal to use as a cue.

When getting students to transition quickly from one activity to the next, praise only those students who move quickly to the next activity, rather than calling attention to those students who are moving slowly. Select the more responsive students to model the positive behavior in front of the class.

### Hustles and prompts.

Use verbal and nonverbal hustles or prompts to remind students to remain on-task or to quicken the pace. These should convey a feeling of high learning expectations. For example, say, "Each time you rotate to a new floor hockey skill station, you have 30 seconds to run a lap around the gym and be at your assigned station!" This statement conveys enthusiasm and is contagious, helping to energize students. An example of a nonverbal hustle or prompt is to wave or physically, but gently, guide a student over to the next exercise station.

### Teacher proximity.

Use this method to keep students on-task without saying a word. Casually move toward students who are being disruptive to help get them back on-task. Teacher proximity can eliminate the ripple effect through which the misbehavior spreads to other students. In addition, always keep the entire class in your field of vision.

### Formations.

Students who are actively involved and not standing in long lines are less likely to be disruptive. Keep lines short: No more than five students. Develop formations, such as lines or circles, to maximize active time, thereby increasing on-task behavior. For example, when the first student in line leaves to begin an activity and is five feet away or reaches a designated cone, the next student may begin. In a passing drill using a circle formation, for example, student one passes the ball to student two who passes the ball to student three. Once student three has caught the ball, student one passes another ball to student two. With five students per circle, two balls used simultaneously will keep all students continuously on-task.

## Handling Disruptions

It is important to remain focused on the lesson and simultaneously be able to deal with unforeseen situations. A student might act out or be injured or your class might be surprised with a fire drill. So expect the unexpected and plan for it! This feat often gets easier with experience and practice. But right from the start, train your students to continue with the lesson on their own while you are handling a problem.

Mr. Carmen has done this, and so when emergencies arise, his class carries on. One day, for example, 15 minutes into his ninth grade class, a student had a seizure. Mr. Carmen remained calm and assisted the student to a matted area as she began to collapse. One squad leader left to get the school nurse. While this was happening, the rest of the class, although concerned, continued the volleyball drill. After the seizure had run its course, Mr. Carmen stayed with the student but directed the squad leaders from the bleachers to continue with the series of volleyball drills they had been working on. It was not an accident that the class remained focused on the lesson since they had practiced this skill during the first week of orientation and periodically reviewed it throughout the school year. At the end of class, Mr. Carmen thanked all the students for continuing with the lesson and being responsible, then rewarded them with their choice of a game tournament to be held during Friday's class. He also briefly discussed what a seizure is and assured the class that the student would be fine.

### Developing Personal Responsibility

Enlist student help in establishing preventive management methods such as routines, rules, and other instructional procedures. Once students have mastered such skills as distributing equipment and meeting in their own squads, you can place them in situations that demand more responsibility. Because students must earn the privilege of more responsibility, this approach motivates and reinforces appropriate behavior. Ultimately, with time and practice, students learn to interact and work independently in pairs or groups productively. For example, you can ask older, more mature students how they would prefer to work and learn tasks. In chapter 6, we'll look more closely at Hellison's Teaching Personal and Social Responsibility Model, which includes strategies designed to help students learn to demonstrate self-directed, responsible, and caring behaviors. Also in chapter 6, we'll relate more information about and examples of how to teach students personal responsibility.

# EVALUATION PHASE: MONITORING CLASS TIME FOR LEARNING

Once you have designed, then implemented your preventive management plan for a while, you should evaluate its effectiveness. Use checklist 6 in appendix 1 of typical physical education class routines to help you determine how much time you are spending on various managerial tasks and episodes. Ask yourself, "Are my students spending more time practicing the lesson content so more learning can occur and less time is spent in behavior management episodes?" To find the answer to this question, videotape yourself teaching a lesson. You might choose a class for which you feel you are spending too much time on management. Next watch the video with a stopwatch. Each time your students are involved in a manage-

ment episode, start the watch. When the management episode is over, stop the watch. Do this throughout the entire lesson. Add up all the time you spent on management and calculate the percentage of the total lesson time it took. Do this several times during the year with the goal of reducing management time as the school year progresses. For more information on how to evaluate class time, the reader should see Siedentop's book *Developing Teaching Skills in Physical Education* (1991).

Mrs. Rodriguez used the following method of self-evaluation. After viewing a videotape of one of her middle school classes, Mrs. Rodriguez realized her students were spending too much time transitioning from the warm-up exercises to the first activity of the day. After keeping records with a stopwatch for a week, she determined that it generally took the majority of the students in the class 40 seconds to properly transition from the warm-up activities to the first activity. During the next week Mrs. Rodriguez told her class, "Each student who moves from the warm-up activities to the first activity of the day in 40 seconds or less will have her name publicly posted on the physical education bulletin board. Based on the number of times your name is posted, you can participate in fun physical education activities we select as a class." Almost immediately most of the students responded by getting to the first daily activity quickly. It was simple for Mrs. Rodriguez to note the few students who did not make it on time and to post the names of all the other students. Within a week, the majority of the students had greatly reduced their transition time and were standing and ready at the first activity of the day in well under 40 seconds! Many of the students remarked how they liked having their names posted on the board for all to see.

# SUMMARY

Be proactive and enter your physical education setting with a positive and consistent management plan. But remember that student needs vary and unforeseen circumstances occur, so temper consistency with flexibility, making your teaching both a science and an art. For example, you may use a more student-directed style of teaching for a mature or motivated class of students than for a class of less independent and more immature students. In fact, you may have to use different management styles with different students in the same class. Use checklist 5 in appendix 1 to help you assess your overall approach.

Critical to your program's success is the development and consistent implementation of class rules and routines with appropriate consequences if not followed. When designing the specifics of your rules and routines, keep in mind the general considerations we have discussed, but tailor them to meet your own unique teaching situation and student needs. Refer often to checklist 6 in appendix 1 to make sure you stay on track.

Once your plan is in place, take time to mentally rehearse, then verbally explain and physically practice your plan with your students. The initial time and energy you invest will pay off when students become engaged in appropriate educational endeavors, thereby fostering learning. One final point: View your management plan as an ongoing process of evaluation and refinement, continually tailoring it to better fit your situation.

Perhaps the best proactive management technique is to keep students on-task and excited about coming to physical education class. But even this will not guarantee that you will have no behavior problems. Coming up in this text, we'll explore strategies and more powerful methods for managing more difficult and challenging student behavior.

## REVIEW

1. Think about your own teaching and list ways you are preventing class disruptions. Now list ways you may be causing class disruptions, whether directly or indirectly. Are you preventing or reinforcing inappropriate behavior by bringing attention to the undesirable behavior?

2. Mentally rehearse or outline on paper the preventive management routines discussed in this chapter, relating them specifically to your own teaching situation. Use checklist 6 in appendix 1 to guide you. For example, develop specific class routines for entering and exiting the physical education setting, being a squad leader, exercising, transitioning from one activity to the next, dressing for class, using the locker room, handling disruptions, organizing students into partners, groups, teams, or formations, and getting student attention. Develop any other routines your teaching situation and student needs may require.

3. Develop a rules chart appropriate for your physical education program and student ages. Remember five or six rules is a good limit.

# Exploring Traditional and Nontraditional Approaches

In part 2, we'll examine several specific approaches to behavior management to help give you the concrete tools necessary for meeting your everyday teaching needs. In chapter 3, we'll give you an overview of the behavioral approach, including how to select, observe, and analyze a target behavior and how to implement an appropriate behavioral intervention. In chapter 4, we'll delve deeper into the behavioral approach as we explore ways to maintain and increase desirable behaviors using positive reinforcement methods. Also in chapter 4, we'll begin to examine the vignettes on page x in light of the information presented in the chapter. We will continue to revisit the vignette situations through chapter 7. In chapter 5, we'll conclude our examination of the behavioral approach by discussing how to decrease inappropriate behaviors through the prudent application of punishment methods. In chapter 6, we'll look at the psychodynamic approach, including responsibility models, reality therapy, the talking bench, and student self-evaluation. Finally, in chapter 7, we'll discuss what to do when all else fails as we examine several nontraditional approaches to behavior management, including how to deal with stress-related misbehavior, disabilities, students taking behavior-modifying medications, and nutritional issues.

## CHAPTER 3

# The Behavioral Approach

Mr. Cabraal, a student teacher, and Dr. Sumner, his university cooperating teacher, met to discuss a lesson Mr. Cabraal had just taught to one of his sixth grade physical education classes. Dr. Sumner told Mr. Cabraal, "Overall the lesson went very well today. Compared to the first time I observed your teaching eight weeks ago, student activity time has certainly increased and the time you spend on management is decreasing. You are addressing students a lot more by name and making more positive statements to them. I could tell the students in class understood and enjoyed the new drills and activities you incorporated into today's lesson. I attribute these positive changes to your increased organizational skills." Mr. Cabraal smiled and said, "Thanks, I've been working on getting my lessons better organized on paper, and this has helped me with my class management and the ability to flow from one activity to the next. I am also working hard to be consistent in having students follow the class rules. Things are starting to come together, and the students are feeling more comfortable with me."

Then, Dr. Sumner asked about Steven the student who was talking out of turn quite a bit during the lesson. Mr. Cabraal's smile quickly turned into a frown. "Yeah, Steven. I've told him repeatedly the rule that when I or others are speaking that he

*continued*

is to listen. Last week I even gave him a warning and a time-out! It didn't seem to matter. In fact, he started making faces at the class while he was in time-out. He's a real pain!"

Dr. Sumner responded, "Sounds like the strategy or plan you are using with the rest of the class is not working with Steven. Why don't you think back to the times he has talked out of turn and see if there is any pattern? Based on what you have told me and what I observed today, it seems like he is speaking out to get attention. As soon as you can, have a meeting with Steven, get to know him better and find out what kind of activities he likes. Perhaps have him tell you some of the rewards, class activities, or privileges he would like to earn. Remember, be positive but firm with him. Be sure to give him examples of the way he is speaking out of turn so he recognizes the problem behavior. From there, you can begin to map out a management plan or intervention package to reduce Steven's talking out of turn. After you've developed your plan, come by my office, and we can discuss it before you present it to Steven." Looking concerned, Mr. Cabraal replied, "Well, I guess it can't hurt."

In recent years, the behavioral approach has successfully helped teachers manage student behavior, thereby promoting student performance in physical education (French and Lavay 1990; Hellison 1995; Siedentop 1991). This approach is the most widely accepted method of intervention used in education today. It is based on the principles of operant conditioning, which involve systematically modifying the environment to develop, increase, maintain, or decrease a behavior.

Too often, however, we equate the behavioral approach with discipline used to reduce inappropriate behavior. Yet, many teachers have successfully used the behavioral approach to motivate student performance and increase desirable behaviors as well.

## WHAT IS THE BEHAVIORAL APPROACH?

In the behavioral approach, you link the behavior to be changed to actions occurring before the behavior, which are called the antecedents, and to the consequences that will occur after the behavior. For example, you might say, "Line up and get ready for physical education class (antecedent). The first student to be ready at his space and quiet (desired behavior) will be the exercise leader for today (consequence)."

Remember, we can define behavior as any observable, measurable act. It is a response or a movement such as a student throwing a Frisbee or not standing in her designated space during warm-up exercises. Advocates of the behavioral approach believe that behaviors are learned and, once clearly identified, they can be changed.

Antecedents can stimulate the behavior to occur, such as when you say, "Line up and get ready for physical education class." Antecedents can also prevent misbehaviors from occurring, such as when you stand next to a student who is being disruptive in order to get him to pay attention. Keep an eye out for a variety of examples of antecedents or preventive behavior management methods in chapters 2 through 4 you can tailor to your situation.

Consequences follow the behavior and affect the probability that the behavior will increase or decrease in the future. Use pleasant consequences, or reinforcers, to develop, maintain, and increase behaviors. Use unpleasant consequences, or punishments, to decrease inappropriate behavior. Moreover, we cannot emphasize enough that for consequences to be effective it is critical that you consistently apply them. Beyond this basic premise, make sure that a consequence only reinforces or punishes those students who actually performed the specific behavior. This ensures a fair and predictable class atmosphere.

In this chapter, we'll show you how to implement a plan to change your students' behavior using the behavioral approach. To help you see how to tailor this information to your situation, we'll give you specific examples of these concepts applied in various situations. Then, in the final section, we'll examine methods for evaluating the behavioral approach in order to help you determine if a behavior has actually changed.

The behavioral approach includes the following sequential steps:

1. Select and define the behavior.
2. Observe and record the behavior.
3. Implement the behavioral intervention.
4. Evaluate the behavioral intervention.

In the following sections, we'll look closely at each of these four steps. Checklist 7 in appendix 1 outlines the key points of each procedure for you to use as a guide.

## SELECT AND DEFINE THE TARGET BEHAVIOR

The critical first step in the behavioral approach is to identify the behavior you wish to develop, increase, maintain, or decrease. This is known as the target behavior. Naturally, you must identify it before you can measure it. Indeed, the target behavior must be measurable, meaning you can observe and objectively identify it. Saying that a student is "acting inappropriately" in physical education class is simply too vague. Instead, you must describe exactly what the student is doing to act inap-

propriately. For example, "The student does not stand on her designated number during warm-ups" or "She talks while I'm giving instructions" or "She dribbles the ball when instructed to pass." These are all examples of behaviors you can measure; they have clear beginnings and ends. For other examples of indefinable and definable behaviors often seen in physical education, see table 3.1.

But where should you start? You may want to change so many different behaviors exhibited by a student or a class that it may be difficult to decide which behaviors to work on first. Initially, target the most important. Identify all undesirable behaviors and then prioritize them from most to least important. Then make behaviors that cause harm to the student or that risk the safety of classmates your first priority. Other high priorities are to maintain class control so learning can occur and to increase behaviors that promote physical skills, such as listening to instructions, and social skills, such as the ability of the student to participate with peers. Based on your teaching philosophy, you may decide to prioritize these behaviors differently, but we find this list to be a good place to start.

Keep in mind, however, that you don't have to target a negative behavior to get positive results. Promoting a particular positive behavior may help to strengthen other desirable

**TABLE 3.1**

### Examples of Indefinable and Definable Behaviors

| INDEFINABLE BEHAVIORS | DEFINABLE BEHAVIORS |
|---|---|
| Paying attention | Going from the locker room to the playing field when the direction is given |
| Taking care of equipment | Putting equipment away in the equipment cart after completing an activity |
| Cooperating | Sharing a piece of equipment with a partner |
| Being responsible | Turning in a tennis skills worksheet with all skills completed |
| Proper throwing | Stepping with foot opposition when releasing a ball |
| Being a behavior problem | Hitting the student next to him during warm-up exercises |
| Misusing equipment | Kicking a basketball during a basketball drill |
| Not following directions | Not sitting in the designated area or watching class demonstrations |
| Interrupting | Not raising a hand and waiting for permission from the teacher to speak |

behaviors. For example, encouraging the student to listen and watch class demonstrations may help to improve skill performance. Other considerations to remember when identifying target behaviors include the type, frequency, duration, intensity, and the overall number of misbehaviors demonstrated by the student. Behaviors that occur infrequently do not warrant the time and energy it takes to fully develop a behavioral plan.

# OBSERVE AND RECORD THE BEHAVIOR

Not surprisingly, identifying the target behavior helps you determine the proper direction to take when designing the behavioral plan, but first you must gather information about the behavior and look for patterns that may help you develop an effective plan. Determining baseline information means observing and recording the targeted behavior as it occurs naturally in the program—before you intervene—changing the actual program in order to increase or decrease the observed behavior. For example, Ms. Danielle is concerned that Penny, a seventh grader, is not making enough effort in class, leading to inappropriate behavior, such as distracting her classmates, instead of concentrating on performing her fitness activities. After collecting baseline information for a week on the number of abdominal curl-ups (behavior) that Penny can perform during each warm-up session, Ms. Danielle calculates a baseline average of 19. And the scores are variable with a range of 29 for the high and 10 for the low score. Next, Ms. Danielle decides and explains an appropriate intervention: "You know, Penny, I think it's terrific that you can do 19 curl-ups on average, but I think you could be more consistent. If you perform at least 20 curl-ups each day during the next four days, you can select a physical education activity of your choice during Friday's class."

Notice that in this example, the teacher chose a measurable behavior to observe and manage for which she could praise the student while encouraging her to do even better. Nothing was said about the negative behavior that originally elicited the teacher's concern. But if Ms. Danielle had not taken a baseline measure, she may have set the number of curl-ups for Penny to complete to receive an award too high

or too low. A low number is too easy to obtain, while a high number is unattainable and possibly too frustrating. Either way, an inappropriate goal always fails to motivate. You may consider working with all students to help them set appropriate fitness goals to keep them focused on your objectives before problems can arise. Then follow up. You should also use your observations and recorded baseline information to ascertain if an intervention is working. In the example, when Ms. Danielle systematically applied the intervention of allowing Penny to select a physical education activity of her choice during Friday's class, Penny increased her average number of curl-ups completed during warm-ups to 27, an over 40 percent improvement. At the same time, a more focused Penny stopped distracting her neighbors. Of course, Ms. Danielle was pleased that the intervention was so effective!

## Observation and Recording Methods

A number of methods have been developed for observing and recording student or class behaviors. Which you use depends on the nature of the behavior. First you must ask yourself if you are determining the frequency (event, such as the number of abdominal crunches) or the duration (length of time, such as 15 minutes) of the behavior in a given period. In addition, how you observe and record data depends on what kind of behavior you're dealing with as well as the setting in which it occurs. At the same time, you must stay alert to what is going on with the rest of the class, always positioning yourself so that you can still keep an eye on them. As you read the following list of commonly used recording methods and examples of common practices stemming from these methods, think about how you might tailor the ideas to your particular situation.

- **Event recording:** Record the frequency, or number of times, a specific behavior occurs within a specific time period. For example, count the number of basketball layups a student correctly performs in two minutes during a basketball layup drill.

- **Duration recording:** Use this method when the length of time engaged in the behavior is the best way to determine performance. For example, measure the amount of time a student is on-task and correctly attempting layups during a four-minute basketball drill. Then you can convert duration recording results into percentages by dividing the total amount of time engaged in the desired or observed-for behavior by the total performance time available. For example, a student who correctly attempts layups for three minutes during the four minutes of the drill is on-task and correctly performing 75 percent of the time (180 seconds ÷ 240 seconds = .75).

• **Interval recording:** To use this method, observe the behavior for short intervals (6 to 20 seconds) periodically throughout a specific time period. Mark event behaviors during each observation interval. Calculate the percentage by dividing the number of intervals during which the behavior occurred by the total number of interval sessions. For example, observe once every 5 minutes if a student is on-task and correctly attempting layups in a 50-minute class for a total of 10 times. If you observed the student correctly attempting layups 8 out of 10 times, the student was on-task 80 percent of the time.

• **Group time sampling or placheck recording:** This method is used to measure the behavior of a group by scanning the entire class at regular intervals. For example, you might observe the number of students in a class of 30 students who are correctly performing the layup drill during a 30-minute basketball lesson once every 5 minutes. Next, determine the percentage of students in the class correctly performing the layup. For example, 25 out of 30 students are correctly performing the layup: 25 ÷ 30 = .83, or 83 percent of the students. Repeat this procedure every 5 minutes for a total of six times during a 30-minute lesson. Average the percentages you find for each interval to find the performance percentage for the entire class.

To save time, develop specific observational recording charts. Figure 3.1 is an example of a frequency recording chart with information Mr. Cabraal from the opening vignette has filled in for Steven. See worksheet 1 in appendix 2 for a blank you can photocopy for your own use. To use it, merely cross out a number each time the behavior occurs, then circle the total number of times the behavior actually occurs on a particular day.

## Reliability of Measurement

It is important to determine if the measurement is accurate and whether the observation is actually measuring the desired behavior. Unreliable measures can give you inconsistent information, leading you to make the wrong decisions when designing behavioral interventions and your overall program. Ask yourself, for example, "Is the behavior change specifically due to the behavioral intervention or is it the result of something else?" We can define reliability as the degree to which two or more independent observers agree on what they see and record (Siedentop 1991).

Specifically, to ensure your data are reliable, make sure the data collected by at least two observers in one session of observation or by the same observer in two sessions agree. When reliability is poor or low, it may be that you need to more clearly define the behavior (see also table 3.1). For example, in the previous discussion of recording behaviors, we defined on-task behavior as "The student correctly attempts layups." Correctly attempting a layup was clearly defined and agreed on by the observers. Observer 1, using the example of interval recording, recorded the student correctly attempting basketball layups eight times while observer 2 observed the student correctly attempting layups nine times. The formula to calculate this *interobserver reliability* is as follows: the lower frequency observation (observer 1) divided by the higher frequency observation (observer 2), or 8 ÷ 9 = .89, or 89 percent. Therefore, an 89 percent agreement, or interobserver reliability, exists between the two observers. Acceptable reliability is usually 80 percent (.80) or above, but this can vary, depending on the particular behavior you are measuring. But what if you don't have an assistant? Another effective strategy to enhance reliability is to videotape the observation and observe the lesson a second time to check your own data; this is known as checking for *intraobserver reliability*. You can also view a videotape for both observations so that during the lesson you can concentrate more on teaching. Or offer the videotape to a colleague to get a second set of data.

As we have defined it, intraobserver reliability is the agreement of one observer with herself. For example, the same person observes a student correctly attempting basketball layups

## Frequency Recording Chart

STUDENT NAME: *Steven Q.*          INITIAL DATE OF OBSERVATION: 3/24/97

MEASURED BEHAVIOR: *Number of times talking out of turn during 5th period P.E. class.*

DATES OF OBSERVATION: *M-W-F during a 4-week period*

| | WK 1 | | | WK 2 | | | WK 3 | | | WK 4 | | |
|---|---|---|---|---|---|---|---|---|---|---|---|---|
| | 3/24 | 3/26 | 3/28 | 3/31 | 4/2 | 4/4 | 4/7 | 4/9 | 4/11 | 4/14 | 4/16 | 4/18 |
| | 12 | 12 | 12 | 12 | 12 | 12 | 12 | 12 | 12 | 12 | 12 | 12 |
| | 11 | 11 | 11 | 11 | 11 | 11 | 11 | 11 | 11 | 11 | 11 | 11 |
| | 10 | 10 | 10 | 10 | 10 | 10 | 10 | 10 | 10 | 10 | 10 | 10 |
| | 9 | 9 | 9 | 9 | 9 | 9 | 9 | 9 | 9 | 9 | 9 | 9 |
| | 8 | 8 | 8 | 8 | 8 | 8 | 8 | 8 | 8 | 8 | 8 | 8 |
| | 7 | 7 | 7 | 7 | (7) | (7) | 7 | 7 | 7 | 7 | 7 | 7 |
| | 6 | (6) | 6 | (6) | 6 | 6 | 6 | 6 | 6 | 6 | 6 | 6 |
| | (5) | 5 | (5) | 5 | 5 | 5 | 5 | 5 | 5 | 5 | 5 | 5 |
| | 4 | 4 | 4 | 4 | 4 | 4 | 4 | 4 | 4 | 4 | 4 | 4 |
| | 3 | 3 | 3 | 3 | 3 | 3 | (3) | 3 | 3 | 3 | 3 | 3 |
| | 2 | 2 | 2 | 2 | 2 | 2 | 2 | (2) | (2) | 2 | 2 | 2 |
| | 1 | 1 | 1 | 1 | 1 | 1 | 1 | 1 | 1 | (1) | 1 | 1 |
| | 0 | 0 | 0 | 0 | 0 | 0 | 0 | 0 | 0 | 0 | (0) | (0) |

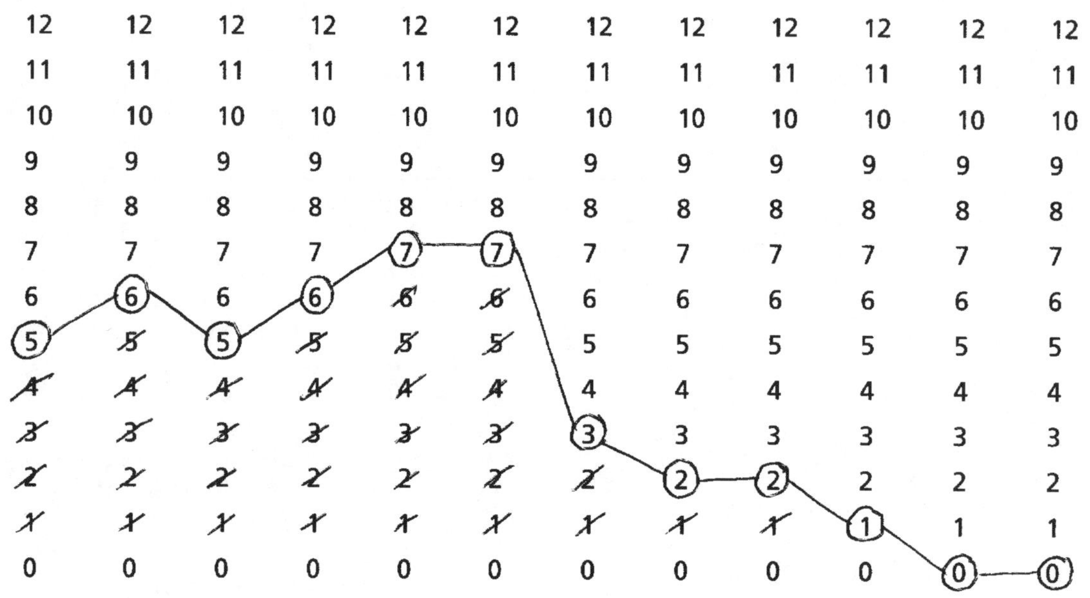

Cross out a number each time the behavior occurs.

Circle the total number of times the behavior actually occurs for that particular date.

Connect the circles to form a graph.

Modified from: Walker, J. E., & Shea, T. M. (1995). Behavior management: A practical approach for educators. (6th ed.) New York: Macmillan.

**Figure 3.1**   A frequency recording chart recording the number of times Steven spoke out of turn.

on two different occasions, perhaps first on Monday and then on Wednesday. You can use the same formula to determine interobserver reliability to calculate intraobserver reliability. The only difference is you substitute observation 1 (Monday) for observer 1 and observation 2 (Wednesday) for observer 2.

## IMPLEMENT THE BEHAVIORAL INTERVENTION

The behavioral intervention is the heart of the behavioral plan. In the basketball layup example, the physical educator effectively promoted student on-task behavior by reinforcing only those students who correctly practiced the basketball layup at their skill stations. You can select from a variety of behavioral methods to develop, maintain, or increase a desired behavior. For example, you can use prompts, a token economy system, or a contract. For an extensive discussion of these and other methods, see chapters 4 and 5.

Many behavioral interventions fail because the teacher does not give the plan sufficient time to take effect or does not implement it consistently. You must recognize that behavior change does not always occur immediately. In fact, some inappropriate behaviors may escalate at first as the student rebels against the change in your approach. Therefore, you must be consistent and patient when intervening, allowing at least a week for changes to begin to take place. In general, behavioral interventions are quite simple to design, but it is an art to successfully change a student's behavior and maintain the change over time.

## EVALUATE THE BEHAVIORAL INTERVENTION

You must periodically evaluate the situation to determine if the specific behavioral intervention is effective and is, in fact, actually contributing to the student's desired behavioral change. When evaluating, ask "Is the student or class now displaying the target behavior or not?" Another question to ask is, "Can the behavior change possibly be attributed to some other factor?" Use the data you have collected through an observation and recording method, such as event recording, duration recording, interval recording, or group time sampling, to evaluate the behavioral plan.

Graphs are another helpful evaluation tool. They clearly display data and the level of change of the behavior during the behavioral intervention, helping you detect small degrees of student change you may otherwise miss (figure 3.2). In addition, graphs can show if the targeted behavior did not change at all or worsened. They provide simple, effective, and unbiased feedback about the targeted behavior, performance, or learning. A simple way to create a graph is to connect the circled numbers on the frequency recording chart (see figure 3.1).

You must, however, keep graphs simple if they are to be useful. Remember Steven, the boy who often spoke out of turn in our opening vignette? Mr. Cabraal could draw a graph of Steven's behavior as illustrated in figure 3.2, which is based on data he recorded (figure 3.1). The graph shows Steven's baseline behavior followed by the change, which shows a decrease in the targeted behavior after the administration of the behavioral intervention. How did Mr. Cabraal entice Steven to improve? After meeting with Steven to discuss the situation, Mr. Cabraal determined that Steven wanted to be a class exercise leader and help collect equipment, so Mr. Cabraal selected these two privileges as reinforcements. To interpret the graph in figure 3.2, first examine the information collected on the frequency recording chart in figure 3.1. This shows the baseline data of how often Steven spoke out of turn during class in a two-week period (3/24 to 4/4). Steven averaged speaking out of turn six times a class period, and the behavior was escalating. With Dr. Sumner's help analyzing Steven's baseline data (figure 3.1), Mr. Cabraal determined that Steven may not be able to completely stop speaking out of turn immediately.

For this reason, Mr. Cabraal developed the following behavioral plan, which we can also call an intervention package. During the first week of the behavioral intervention (4/7 to 4/11), for each class session that Steven spoke out of turn three times or less, he was allowed to help collect equipment after class. During the second week of the behavioral intervention (4/14 to 4/18), for each class session that Steven did not speak out of turn at all, he was able to not only continue to help collect equipment but also to be the exercise leader at the beginning of the following class period. Throughout the intervention, Mr. Cabraal also complimented Steven for listening during class instruction and for not interrupting, thereby reinforcing the positive behavior even more frequently.

The graph shows that Steven's tendency to speak out of turn was greatly reduced the first week and completely stopped by the end of the second week of the behavioral intervention (figure 3.2). Specifically, during the first week of intervention, Steven spoke out of turn an average of less than three times per class session. Thus, at the end of each class period, he was allowed to help collect equipment. During the

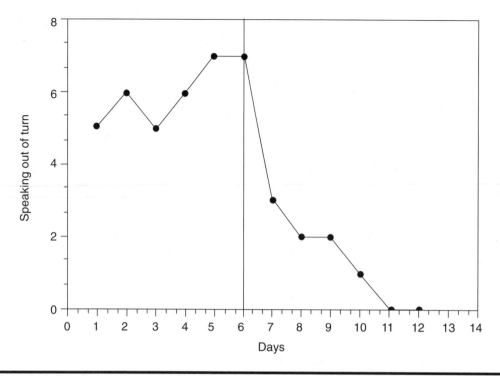

**Figure 3.2** A baseline-to-treatment graph of Steven's behavior based on data recorded on the frequency recording chart from figure 3.1.

first day of the second week of the behavioral intervention, Steven spoke out of turn once and therefore was not allowed to collect equipment or be the exercise leader. Immediately after that class session, Mr. Cabraal met with Steven to discuss his behavior, reminding him that he needed to stop speaking out of turn completely if he wanted to continue to collect equipment as well as be the exercise leader. During the next two class sessions, Steven was able to stop speaking out of turn completely (4/16 and 4/18) and was able to resume collecting equipment as well as become the exercise leader (see figure 3.2). Mr. Cabraal also noticed that since Steven stopped speaking out of turn, he was paying better attention to instruction and consequently his class performance was improving. He pointed out this improvement to Steven in a follow-up meeting.

Figure 3.2 is an example of a simple baseline-to-treatment graph, called an AB design, which includes measurements of baseline and treat-ment or intervention. The design includes graphing the baseline phase during which the intervention is absent (represented by A) and a treatment phase during which the behavioral intervention is introduced in order to change the behavior (represented by B). A reversal A-B-A-B design, which includes baseline, intervention, return to baseline, and reintro-duction of the intervention is the most straight-forward and powerful design for showing that the change in behavior was due to the inter-vention or behavioral method used. In this de-sign, Mr. Cabraal should stop the reinforce-ment for a week and merely collect baseline data again. Then if Steven's behavior deteriorated, Mr. Cabraal would reinstitute the reinforce-ments or design new reinforcements. Additional graphing procedures include alternating treat-ment design, multiple baseline design, and changing criterion design. For more informa-tion on these and other graphing procedures and designs that are available, see Cooper, Heron,

**Figure 3.3** If correctly applied, the behavioral approach almost always results in a reduction in undesirable behavior and a significant increase in desirable behavior.

and Heward's (1987) *Applied Behavior Analysis*. In addition, computer graphic programs such as Cricket Graph and Excel are available to make graphing data quite simple.

## SUMMARY

The behavioral approach is based on the principles of operant conditioning, which involves systematically modifying the environment to develop, increase, maintain, or decrease a behavior. In this approach, you take advantage of the fact that relationships exist between the behavior to be changed and both the actions occurring before the behavior and the consequences following the behavior. Remember to follow these steps to apply the behavioral approach:

1. Select and define the behavior.
2. Observe and record the behavior.
3. Implement the behavioral intervention.
4. Evaluate the behavioral intervention.

The heart of the behavioral approach is the intervention, during which you administer various behavior modification methods (see figure 3.3). In general, behavioral interventions are quite simple to design, but it is an art to develop, administer, and maintain a behavioral plan that will effectively change the behavior or performance of the student or class long-term. Use checklist 7 to get started. Next, we'll examine a variety of methods to increase desirable student behaviors using the behavioral approach.

# REVIEW

1. In sequence, describe the steps necessary to design a behavioral approach.

2. What is the difference between baseline data and intervention data?

3. Discuss various methods for observing and recording behaviors, such as event, duration, interval, and group time sampling recording. For each method, justify why and when you would use that particular method over another method.

4. Describe the difference between interobserver reliability and intraobserver reliability. Calculate intraobserver reliability by observing a skill or behavior of one of your students.

5. Consider a student you are teaching who is displaying a behavior you would like to change. Outline a behavioral plan to change that student's behavior. Collect baseline and intervention data. Use figure 3.1 as a model for collecting the information, worksheet 1 in appendix 2 to record data, and then construct a graph similar to figure 3.2 to show your information.

## CHAPTER 4

# Behavioral Methods for Maintaining and Increasing Student Behaviors

It was the end of the seventh week of school, and Mr. Rozenek was sitting in his office thinking about his ninth grade physical education class. During the past two weeks, he had observed an escalating pattern of poor sportsmanship incidents. On Monday, he had reviewed the class rules and had spent time briefly discussing the importance of demonstrating proper sportsmanship with the entire class. He had also provided the class with clear examples of both good and poor sportsmanship. Throughout the week, he had taken a few students to the side who were displaying poor sportsmanship and had spoken to them about how they could do better. Yet the poor sportsmanship among students had seemed to get worse. Specifically, he had observed the more-skilled boys verbally putting down the less-skilled students, including swearing at them and refusing to pass them the ball during the soccer drills and games.

As you know, such behavior does not promote a positive atmosphere in which all students feel comfortable performing and learning. Based on past experience, Mr. Rozenek knew the behavior would not go away without action on his part. He

*continued*

wondered what he could do. He wanted to be positive in his approach as he felt this promoted better sportsmanship among the students in class. He thought about an article he recently read that explained how to design a point system to promote proper sportsmanship (Davis and French 1986). Using the ideas in the article as a springboard, he began to think of ways he could have his class earn points for showing proper sportsmanship.

First, Mr. Rozenek thought about the characteristics of the students in his class. He knew that typically, ninth graders seek the approval of their peers. So he thought that maybe having students work together in their squads to earn points for demonstrating good sportsmanship might work. He wondered what he should use for a reward, then remembered that the students were always asking him for more time to play soccer games. He decided that he would allow the squads who earned a certain number of points by demonstrating proper sportsmanship Monday through Thursday of each week the opportunity to play minisoccer games on Friday. Over the weekend, Mr. Rozenek outlined his plan on posterboard, defining and giving examples of good sportsmanship and how many points each squad must earn by the end of Thursday's class to earn the reward. At the beginning of class on Monday, he presented his plan. The idea of earning more time to play soccer appealed to the majority of the students. As the first week of the plan progressed, Mr. Rozenek observed more and more students demonstrating good sportsmanship, such as encouraging one another during drills and games. In class and in the locker room, he noticed students reminding each other about earning more time to play soccer. By Friday, all but one of the squads had earned the privilege of playing minisoccer games. Mr. Rozenek recognized he should have implemented this plan at the beginning of the school year!

## ACCENTUATING THE POSITIVE

In this chapter, we'll discuss various behavioral methods you can use to increase desirable behavior. The positive methods we'll introduce have not only been successful in physical education settings in controlling inappropriate student behavior (French and Henderson 1993; Hellison 1995) but also in enhancing student performance (French and Lavay 1990). We'll focus on different types of reinforcement, various methods, and examples of how to give positive reinforcement to maintain and increase positive student behavior.

We can define positive reinforcement as the offering of something valued after the desired behavior has been exhibited, resulting in an increase in the frequency of the behavior. Naturally, to be motivating, the reinforcer must be something the individual wants. For example, a younger student will continue to answer questions in physical education class if you reinforce his efforts with positive statements. The behavior of answering questions is strengthened by the reinforcement of praise and will likely occur again.

Unfortunately, many people confuse positive reinforcement with bribery, but bribery is the illegitimate use of gifts to corrupt or manipulate a student's conduct before the student acts, while reinforcement is given only after the appropriate behavior has been maintained or increased (Rhodes, Jenson, and Reavis 1993).

But it is all too easy to forget to be positive and unintentionally reinforce behaviors you don't wish to increase! For example, each time Nicki makes noises during warm-up exercises, Ms. Sayers tells her to stop. Nicki may enjoy the attention she is receiving from Ms. Sayers and find it reinforcing because attention is what she wants. Consequently, her noisemaking increases. Ms. Sayers is better off praising the students who are quiet, thereby positively reinforcing the desired behavior.

Successfully identifying potential reinforcers for each student is not always easy, especially since what one student finds reinforcing may not be reinforcing to another. To determine who prefers what type of reinforcer, consider using preference scales or lists; surveys; student, parent, or homeroom teacher interviews; or direct observation. Simply asking the class or individual the reinforcers they enjoy is a good idea, because when the class or student is involved in the decision-making process, the strength of the reinforcer increases (Walker and Shea 1995). It also helps to observe students during the physical education class or recess time to see what type of activities and equipment they select.

Keeping up with changing preferences is an ongoing process. Simply because students respond favorably to specific reinforcers one week does not necessarily mean the same reinforcers will be effective the following week! Thus, it is important to have a variety of highly motivating reinforcers available to help maintain changing student interest. To help you get started, worksheet 2 in appendix 2, "Physical Education Reinforcer Preference List," provides a sample survey appropriate for middle school students.

# TYPES OF POSITIVE REINFORCEMENT

Many types of positive reinforcers exist. Primary reinforcers are those that satisfy a biological need in a person, such as food when hungry or water when thirsty. They are innate needs that do not have to be learned. Secondary reinforcers are those that people have learned to like, such as shooting a basketball successfully, receiving stickers, or feeling good about themselves.

Reinforcement can be extrinsic or intrinsic. Extrinsic positive reinforcement comes from an outside source, usually in the form of a reward, such as a trophy or sticker. Intrinsic positive reinforcement is the most sophisticated type of positive reinforcement and is an internal, intangible feeling of accomplishment (Jansma and French 1994). For example, the student may be motivated to perform an aerobic routine because she feels a sense of accomplishment within, not because she receives an award. You should strive to move your students from extrinsic to intrinsic reinforcement.

Keeping in mind that the most important property of an effective reinforcer is that it is desired by the student or group you are targeting, we'll take a closer look at the three types of positive extrinsic reinforcers in the following sections: social, tangible, and physical activity. You can develop the information in table 4.1 into reinforcer preference lists such as the one presented in worksheet 2 (appendix 2).

## Social Reinforcement

A smile, an approving nod, a high-five, an arm around a student's shoulder, or an approving verbal statement regarding the student's behavior or actual performance are all examples of social reinforcement. Positive verbal reinforcement is most effective when it includes a comment about the desired behavior, for example, "Good running with your knees high!" or "You all lined up quickly in your squads, ready for the warm-up! Excellent!" When reinforcing students with praise, especially younger students, it is important to consider their level of language comprehension. Use simple, single-action words or limit sentences to a few words. For example, "Wow, nice jumping using your arms!"

It's easy to fall into the habit of noticing only the negative and ignoring the positive. So remember to catch students being good. Otherwise, corrective or negative comments might become the only statements you make during a lesson.

## Tangible Reinforcement

Tangible reinforcers are material objects the student desires, such as toys, stickers, or medals, used to increase the desired behavior (see table 4.1). When possible, pair social reinforcers with tangible reinforcers. This way, the student associates the social reinforcers with the tangible reinforcers, and eventually you can phase out the tangible reinforcers. If you cannot immediately give tangible reinforcement, you may wish to use a token economy system (see page 51). Tangible reinforcers can be expensive, so when possible, use less costly reinforcers, such as physical activity reinforcement.

## Physical Activity Reinforcement

Many physical education activities are potentially reinforcing. In addition, you can reinforce appropriate behavior by giving students privileges, such as using certain equipment, being a squad or exercise leader, distributing equipment, or being a peer tutor (see table 4.1). Physical activity reinforcers not only serve as an effective form of reinforcement but also may improve physical performance. For example, if

TABLE 4.1

## Examples of Social, Tangible, and Physical Activity Reinforcers

### SOCIAL REINFORCERS

*Nonverbal*

Smiling, grinning, giving an approving nod or wink

Giving a high-five or pumping the arm in the air

Placing an arm around the shoulder, giving a pat on the back, or a hug.

*Verbal*

"Wow, nice running!"

"Terrific swimming, you are kicking your feet more!"

"Excellent, your group is the first to be lined up and on the pool deck!"

"Thank you for listening to and following directions!"

"Way to go—you made 9 out of 10 free throws!"

"I appreciate your helping me arrange the exercise stations for class!"

"Thank you for helping James with his forward roll!"

### PHYSICAL ACTIVITY REINFORCERS

*Equipment*

Hula hoops

Parachutes

Scooterboards

*Low-organization games and activities*

Jumping rope

Juggling scarves

Volleying a tennis ball

Sports

Pickle ball

Tennis

Basketball

Soccer

Flag football

### TANGIBLE REINFORCERS

Stickers, decals, or stamps

Trading cards, pictures, or posters (sport stars or action heroes)

Models or puzzles

Simple, inexpensive games or toys

Trophies, certificates, or medals

Reading or coloring books

Money

*Privileges*

Being a squad or exercise leader or team captain

Distributing, setting up, or collecting equipment

Being a peer tutor to another student

Demonstrating a skill, activity, game, or sport

Choosing an activity or a partner

Assisting teacher with grading, attendance, an activity, or locker room procedures

Performing an errand for the teacher

Participating in an after-school physical education demonstration or sports field trip

the student or class chooses to participate in aerobic dance as a reinforcer, not only is their good behavior reinforced, they also receive cardiorespiratory benefits from the activity.

Physical activity reinforcers are usually free, saving your physical education budget for other needs. When you consider that certain students may not respond to social reinforcers and that

tangible reinforcers can be quite expensive, this form of reinforcement is an attractive alternative.

Focusing on physical activity reinforcers will make it easier for you to teach students to develop a greater appreciation for intrinsic, rather than extrinsic, rewards. After all, achievement itself can be an intrinsic reward! And the more time students spend physically active, the more

## CATCH THE PERSON BEING GOOD: WHY IT IS IMPORTANT TO BE POSITIVE

White (1975) recorded the natural rates of teacher approval and disapproval in the classroom. The rates of teacher verbal approval dropped markedly after the second grade; in every grade thereafter, the rate of teacher verbal disapproval exceeded the rate of teacher verbal approval. Thomas, Presland, Grant, and Glynn (1978) examined the natural rates of teacher verbal approval and disapproval in 10 seventh grade classrooms. The majority of the teachers in this study displayed individual approval rates. Jones and Jones (1981) reported a study of first grade teachers in which it was found that only 9 of 17 teachers displayed reinforcement rates over 50 percent. Of the 9 positive teachers, 7 displayed reinforcement rates above 70 percent. These data were correlated with how well the children liked school. Baseline data indicated that more than 90 percent of the first graders liked school during the first two weeks of the school year. Returning in February and surveying the same children, the experimenters found that 90 percent of the children whose teachers achieved 70 percent verbal approval still liked school. Children in classrooms where verbal disapproval exceeded verbal approval generally disliked school; in fact, 100 percent of them disliked school in those classrooms where verbal disapproval was 60 percent or higher (adapted from Dunn and Fredericks 1985, pp. 342-343).

they'll grow and develop physically, socially, and emotionally. This growth, in turn, will lead to greater achievements to be proud of. So design activities to allow learners to progress to more challenging tasks in a sequential manner. To make the activities even more reinforcing, have each student keep track of his progress on an index card that shows his weekly skill and fitness progress to be read only by him. This concrete evidence of progress can be intrinsically rewarding as well.

## REINFORCEMENT MENUS

Display a menu of reinforcers where all your students can see it. For some students, simply looking at the reinforcement menu items on a bulletin board in the gym, outdoor facility, or locker room can be quite reinforcing (figure 4.1). You can post pictures on a menu for students who are unable to read. To maintain student motivation, change reinforcement menu items as needed. Whenever possible, allow students to choose which reinforcers to place on the menu (Walker and Shea 1995). Looking for more ideas? You can use some of the examples from worksheet 2 (appendix 2) and table 4.1 to create a reinforcement menu.

## REINFORCEMENT SCHEDULES

You can use different schedules to administer reinforcement, depending on your students' needs. Continuous reinforcement means you must immediately follow every occurrence of the desired behavior with a reinforcer. This approach is most appropriate when a student is in the initial stages of learning a behavior. Once the student has acquired or established the behavior, however, you must work to systematically eliminate the reinforcer before its effectiveness fades. Follow a schedule by which you gradually and systematically delay the reward for demonstrating the behavior. The specific type of schedule to follow will depend on the type of behavior targeted. See the section "Different Types of Reinforcement Schedules" on page 50 for a list of definitions and examples of when to use some of the most common types of reinforcement schedules.

## POSITIVE REINFORCEMENT METHODS

In this section, we'll examine various proven, positive methods widely used in physical

**Figure 4.1** Posting a list of rewards that students can earn helps to reinforce desired behaviors.

## DIFFERENT TYPES OF REINFORCEMENT SCHEDULES

**Continuous reinforcement:** The reinforcement is provided each time the appropriate behavior occurs.

**Intermittent reinforcement:** The reinforcement is provided at specific times when the appropriate behavior occurs. Some type of schedule is used.

**Ratio reinforcement:** The reinforcement depends on the number of times the behavior is demonstrated.

*Fixed ratio reinforcement:* The behavior is reinforced after a specific or predetermined (fixed) number of times the behavior occurs, for example, rewarding a student with five minutes of physical activity reinforcement time for every five volleyball serves successfully completed.

*Variable ratio reinforcement:* The behavior is reinforced after a variable number of times the behavior occurs with the schedule of reinforcement constantly changing, for example, reinforcing the student the third time she correctly performs a volleyball serve, but the next time rewarding her on the fifth correct serve.

*continued*

**Interval reinforcement:** The reinforcement depends on the period of time in which the behavior occurs.

*Fixed interval reinforcement:* The behavior is reinforced after a specific, predetermined period of time the behavior occurs. For example, the student earns one point or a check mark toward a desired reinforcement for every five minutes he is on task correctly swimming two laps in the pool.

*Variable interval reinforcement:* The behavior is reinforced after a variable period of time the behavior occurs with the schedule of reinforcement constantly changing. For example, the student is reinforced for remaining on-task correctly swimming laps in the pool after one minute, then three minutes, and then six minutes.

education settings to develop, maintain, or increase positive behavior. We'll start by looking at the less sophisticated interventions you should try first, then we'll discuss the more sophisticated ones you should reserve for the most difficult behavior problems. Which intervention will work best? The answer depends on the particular situation, but as a rule of thumb, choose the intervention that requires the least reinforcement to change the targeted behavior. When possible, pair the behavioral intervention with a social reinforcer to help you when it comes time to phase out the behavioral intervention. For example, pair a tangible reinforcer with a smile and brief statement, explaining to the student why she earned the reinforcer so that, ultimately, you can wean the student off the tangible reinforcer and onto the social reinforcer.

There is no such thing as a quick fix or cookbook approach that will work with all students in all situations. Simply put, not all students will respond the same to these methods. Thus, you must develop a wide repertoire of reinforcement methods, then tailor your behavior management program to the particular student or class, thereby maintaining interest and increasing desirable behavior. So feel free to use the positive methods that follow individually or in combination.

## Prompt

A prompt is giving a cue to get a student to perform a desired behavior. Use a variety of prompts to successfully meet the various needs of the students in class and correctly teach the skills. Examples of a continuum of prompts from minimum to maximum are verbal, modeling, physical cues, and physical assistance. For example, when teaching a student to properly set a volleyball, use a simple verbal prompt: "Make a triangle by meeting the first finger and thumb of each hand." If the student still has difficulty, model the proper way to place the fingers and thumbs. If modeling is not effective, physically move the student's fingers and thumbs into the triangle position. When selecting a prompt, consider the least amount of intervention or prompting that you believe will be effective (see figure 4.2). But what does prompting skill development have to do with behavior management issues? Students who get the help they need to develop skills develop confidence; confident students are more likely to be on-task and out of trouble.

It is also important to gradually fade and eventually eliminate a prompt. Depending on the student and her age, you should reduce the number and intensity of the prompt gradually. You could, for example, reduce the amount of physical guidance you use to prompt a student to step with opposition when throwing a ball from moving the student's entire leg to only gently touching the thigh. Remember, the goal is for each student to eventually perform the skill independently.

## Token Economy System

When holding class in a gym, swimming pool, field, or playground, it will not always be

**Figure 4.2** If prompts such as verbal cues and modeling aren't enough, you may need to give a student physical assistance.

convenient for you to immediately give tangible reinforcers to a student or class. A token economy system—even though it is a delayed method of administering reinforcement—can solve this problem. In such a system, the student receives a token immediately following successful performance of the targeted desired behavior, later exchanging the token for the desired reinforcer (McKenzie 1990). You can use the various reinforcement schedules (page 50) to schedule such exchanges.

Whatever you choose to use as tokens, you need to be able both to easily dispense them and to quickly record their use. Consider using check marks, points, stamps, poker chips, tickets, stickers, smiley faces, or marbles. Canter (1992) developed a variety of seasonal and monthly tickets to exchange for reinforcers with young elementary students. For example, in October you could use a ticket with a picture of a ghost, pumpkin, or witch. To keep track of each student's tokens, you can use a class reinforcer pocket chart with each student's name dis-

played on a pocket. It is wise to write the student's name on his ticket in ink to keep students from "borrowing" others' tickets. For older students, record check marks on a point card. Responsible students can keep track of their own points with minimal monitoring (Jansma and French 1994). If you have a problem with students adding check marks they have not earned, have trustworthy individuals, perhaps squad leaders, add check marks, or periodically oversee this procedure yourself. Worksheet 3 in appendix 2, "Example of a Point Exchange Card," shows a photocopy-ready example of a weekly physical education point card used by middle or high school students who can earn one point for properly following each of the class rules, which they check off in the appropriate blank on the card.

## Premack Principle

The Premack principle states that you can use highly reinforcing activities to promote less popular behaviors (Premack 1959). The Premack principle can also be expressed as "Grandma's rule," that is, "If you eat all your vegetables, you will get your dessert!" An example of the Premack principle is allowing students who successfully complete the five fitness self-testing stations (less popular behavior) during the first 25 minutes of class to spend the remainder of the period playing a volleyball game (more popular behavior), an activity chosen by the students. Those who do not finish during the first 25 minutes do not earn the volleyball game reward and must continue to participate in the fitness station activities.

The Premack principle is effective because you can use activities desired by the student as physical activity reinforcers. Refer to worksheet 2 (appendix 2) and table 4.1 when designing reinforcers.

## Public Posting

This method involves publicly posting the names of students who successfully perform the desired behavior. Remember, however, to choose a desired behavior that is one that all the students are capable of successfully performing. For example, everyone can be successful at improving a behavior such as transitioning from one activity area to the next, but some may fail to measure up when it comes to a particular motor skill, causing them to become discouraged and unmotivated.

For example, public posting combined with physical activity reinforcement greatly reduced the physical education transition time of students at one middle school (Rodriques 1996). Students who transitioned from the locker room to their squad lines for the warm-up and from their squad lines to the first teaching site in the allotted amount of time were reinforced by having their names publicly posted on the physical education bulletin board in the gym. In addition, each student earned physical activity, based on the number of times his name was posted. The teacher provided a list of possible activities and had each student circle three of his or her favorite activities. Activities selected by the class included flag football, volleyball, floor hockey, basketball, water games, and a sport option with a variety of equipment and sport activities available. The results showed a class decrease of 40 seconds transitioning from the locker room to the warm-

up area from baseline to the intervention and a decrease of 18 seconds from the warm-up squad lines to the first teaching site. Concurrently, student behavior improved as students focused on teacher expectations more.

## Contract

A contract can be either a verbal or a written agreement between you and a student regarding behavior or performance improvement over a specific period of time in exchange for a reinforcer. Written contracts are usually more effective because the terms are clearly recorded for all parties to see. You should design the contract to meet the needs of a particular student, but you can develop one or two forms for the entire class. You can write simple contracts to include only the behavior to be worked on and the reward to be earned (see figure 4.3) or you can write more complex contracts (see figure 4.4). The range of responsibility for contracts will vary from your developing the contract and monitoring its effectiveness to your allowing students to plan their contracts with you and monitor themselves. In general, relate the amount of influence you allow students to have on the development and implementation of a contract to the level of personal responsibility and maturity they display.

Here are some guidelines for developing and implementing contracts (French and Henderson 1993): When developing a contract, be sure it is fair and suitable. Ask yourself, "Realistically, are the terms attainable by the student or class?" Have the contract signed by all parties involved, including the student, parent, yourself, and any other teachers. It is a good idea to have at least a third person read and sign the contract. Give each signing person a copy of the contract. Stress accomplishments or behaviors the student or class will perform, not what will not be performed. Design the initial contract with small incremental accomplishments in order to help the student or class successfully meet the target behavior. Initially this allows for frequent rewards. Then as behavior improves, you can gradually delay rewards. Be sure that the reward is highly prized by the student or class and not easily obtained outside the conditions of the contract. Including a bonus clause to reinforce outstanding and persistently appropriate behavior or performance will help motivate the student(s) to

I _____ (name of student) will put equipment away in the equipment cart each day for one week and then will be able to select an activity partner.

Signed (Nicole) _____ March 24, 1998

Signed (Ms. Danielle) _____ March 24, 1998

**Figure 4.3**  A simple contract includes the behavior to be modified and the reward to be earned.

I _____ (name of student) understand and agree with the following Grading Point System in Physical Education Class.  I understand I can earn points toward my grade each day of class by following these rules.  I also understand that when I earn 100 points I can choose the Friday Sport Option Day from the list of sports and activities provided by Mr. McNeil.

2 points for dressing properly for physical education class

2 points for following and participating in all directions given by the teacher

2 points for performing all the required exercises during the 10-minute warm-up period

2 points for completing the performance skill worksheet during the 40-minute lesson

2 points for cooperating with classmates by sharing equipment, taking turns, and giving a high-five to another student

You can earn a total of 10 points each class meeting.  The following is the grading system:

**GRADING SYSTEM - 5 DAYS**

| Grade | Points |
| --- | --- |
| A | 50-45 |
| B | 44-40 |
| C | 39-35 |
| D | 34-30 |
| F | 30- below |

Student's signature _____ October 5, 1998

Physical Educator's signature _____ October 5, 1998

Parent's signature _____ October 5, 1998

**Figure 4.4**  An example of a complex contract.

behave positively. Be sure that you enforce the contract consistently and systematically, giving reinforcers immediately following adequate compliance with the contract. If the initial contract is ineffective and if you can see that the student or class is going to be unable to meet the terms, renegotiate it. Use checklist 8 in appendix 1 when developing and implementing contracts.

A goal of Mr. Lacourse is for every student to help with equipment distribution and collection. Sally, a seventh grader, constantly forgets when it is her turn to perform these duties. Mr. Lacourse recognizes Sally has a learning disability, and he has been patiently reminding her when it is her turn. Sally tries hard and wants to please, but she is beginning to get frustrated because Mr. Lacourse has had to remind her each time it has been her turn throughout the school year. So Mr. Lacourse decides he needs to try a different approach with Sally. At the beginning of the school year, Mr. Lacourse had spoken with Sally's special education teacher, Ms. Stein, who was very helpful in explaining Sally's learning disability and the medication she is taking for her attention deficit disorder. Mr. Lacourse decides to meet with Ms. Stein to discuss Sally's problem of forgetting to help distribute and collect equipment. Ms. Stein suggests that Mr. Lacourse try using a contract approach with Sally. Sally is familiar with contracts because Ms. Stein has successfully used them to get Sally to complete reading assignments. Ms. Stein also mentions to Mr. Lacourse that because of Sally's information processing difficulty and short attention span, he will need to keep the contract simple and read it to her. Sally, Mr. Lacourse, and Ms. Stein all meet to discuss the problem. During the meeting, they ascertain that Sally would really like to have Clayre, a classmate and friend who lives in her neighborhood, as an activity partner. When designing the contract, Ms. Stein and Mr. Lacourse are not sure that Sally can distribute and collect equipment for five consecutive days in order to receive her reward, so they decide that if she successfully completes the task four out of five days without Mr. Lacourse reminding her, she will be rewarded. They also explain to Sally about a special bonus clause through which she can receive an additional reward for successfully distributing and collecting equipment for five consecutive days. The teachers explain the contract to Sally and type it, then everyone agrees to it and signs it (see figure 4.5). Sally keeps a copy of the contract in her desk. During the next week, each day before going to Mr. Lacourse's physical education class, Ms. Stein has Sally read the contract out loud to her. The contract is effective as Sally remembers to distribute the equipment to classmates all five days and only forgets to collect equipment on one day. Having Clayre as an activity partner not only motivates Sally to remember her responsibilities but also helps her to stay on-task during lessons. Mr. Lacourse decides to have Sally continue the contract for another week.

## Group Contingencies and Good Behavior Games

A group contingency is the presentation of a highly desired reinforcer to a group of students based on the behavior of one person or on the behavior of the group as a whole (Vogler and French 1983). A group contingency is usually effective with students who want peer approval more than teacher approval. It is a fairly sophisticated type of reinforcement so you may need to reserve it for use with students who have developed more personal responsibility and goal-setting abilities than the average class (see chapter 6).

You can choose from several kinds of group contingencies. The most commonly used involves having the group earn a desired reinforcer that depends on the behavior of the entire group of students. A similar group contingency method involves only one student who is responsible for earning the desired reinforcer for the entire group of students. When using these two types of group contingencies, first consider whether or not every student in the class is capable of earning the reinforcement. This helps to ensure that students do not place undue peer pressure on any one student or group of students. In addition, designing a separate contingency program may be necessary for a problem student or group who is consistently ruining the chances of the entire group being reinforced. In another type of group contingency, you and the class develop a group goal, and students work individually to earn the desired reinforcer. This alternative method helps eliminate the competitiveness of the first two types of group contingencies. See page 57 for specific examples of good behavior games using group contingency methods.

I _____ (name of student) will distribute equipment to my squad members and put equipment away in the equipment cart each day for one week. If I can successfully do this for 4 out of 5 days I will be able to select an activity partner during the following Monday and Tuesday of class.

## Bonus Clause

If I am able to distribute and collect equipment all five days of the week I will receive an additional day on Wednesday to select an activity partner and be able to select one physical education activity to participate in from the class list.

Signed (Sally) _____ March 24, 1998

Signed (Mr. Lacourse) _____ March 24, 1998

Signed (Ms. Stein) _____ March 24, 1998

**Figure 4.5** Sally's contract.

When teachers used a group contingency good behavior game with elementary students with behavior disorders to improve the frequency of on-task behavior in a physical education class, it proved quite effective (Vogler and French 1983). Students were told they could earn 10 minutes of free time as a squad to participate in physical education activities they enjoyed by following class rules, such as staying on-task during the lesson. Each day each squad began with 10 points and was awarded 10 minutes of free time if they still had at least 8 points by the end of the class period. The teachers subtracted points for not following class rules. All groups were capable of earning the reward and were not necessarily competing against one another. After the good behavior game was introduced, the percentage of on-task behavior for all groups as well as for individual students increased dramatically from baseline.

## Negative Reinforcement

We can define negative reinforcement as a reinforcer used to increase a desired behavior by encouraging students to perform that particular behavior in order to avoid, escape, or eliminate something they dislike (Rhodes, Jenson, and Reavis 1993). Notice that both negative and positive reinforcements produce similar results: an increase in a desired behavior. The methods you use, however, are quite different. Positive reinforcement results in an increase in a desired behavior by presenting the student with something valued, called a pleasant stimulus, after the student has exhibited the behavior. In contrast, negative reinforcement results in an increase in a desired behavior because you have removed something the student perceives as unpleasant and wishes to avoid, called an aversive stimulus, as the "reward" (Loovis 1995). For example, a student in physical education class avoids losing points off her class

## EXAMPLES OF GOOD BEHAVIOR GAMES

### The Flip Chart Good Behavior Game

This is played using a flip chart or a scoreboard that students can easily see. Have the class vote on possible physical activity reinforcers. Explain to the class that while playing this game they have the opportunity to earn 10 minutes participating in the physical education activities they voted for. Say, "Today 10 times during class I will scan the class, and each time everyone in class is on-task and participating in the lesson, I will reward the class by giving you one point on the flip chart (or scoreboard). For each point you earn, you'll get 1 minute of free-choice physical activity time, which we'll have toward the end of class. If any of you are not on-task participating in the lesson when I check, I will not give the class a point that particular time. But each time you are all participating, the class can earn a minute at the end of class for a possible total of 10 minutes. At the end of the lesson, I will add up all the points and see how much time you earned as a class." If there is a problem student in the class who is consistently ruining the group's ability to be rewarded, she can work individually to earn the desired reinforcer.

### Run the State Good Behavior Game

Form groups who race each other on a map of your state or from New York City to Los Angeles or have the class develop their own route, which you display on a bulletin board in the gymnasium. Allow students to exchange each completed fitness item, such as running a lap or performing so many push-ups or crunches, for a certain number of miles on the map, depending on how long the route is and how quickly you feel the desired behavior needs to be reinforced. Represent each group on the map with a picture of a running shoe. If desired, award miles for good behavior, such as following class rules or getting to class on time, instead of or in addition to miles earned for fitness efforts. When a group reaches their destination, give them a reward (Rhode, Jenson, and Reavis 1993). If necessary or desired, have each student work individually to earn the desired reinforcer. Make this a cooperative activity by having the entire class accumulate miles as one group. You can even extend this activity to having the entire school earn mileage cooperatively.

grade (aversive stimuli) by performing all her warm-up exercises (increase in behavior). The student recognizes that this is the only way to avoid receiving a lower grade. A student who doesn't want to sit in the bleachers and write a report (aversive stimuli) will dress for physical education class (increase in behavior).

Negative reinforcement is often confused with punishment. Punishment, however, decreases a behavior by either presenting an aversive stimulus or removing a positive stimulus. For example, if you make a student sit in time-out (presenting aversive stimuli) in order to get the student to stop talking out of turn in class (decreasing a behavior), you are punishing the student. Or if you take away a student's already-earned tokens (removing a positive stimuli) in order to get the student to stop misusing equipment (decreasing a behavior), you are punishing. Simply put, use punishment methods to decrease an undesirable behavior and negative reinforcement methods to increase a desired behavior. We'll investigate the issue of punishment further in chapter 5.

## PRINCIPLES OF ADMINISTERING POSITIVE REINFORCEMENT

❑ Make reinforcement contingent on the student or group demonstrating the appropriate behavior.

❑ Individualize the reinforcer to meet the unique needs of each student. For the reinforcer to have meaning, it must be perceived as valuable to the student! Choose age-appropriate reinforcers.

❑ Be patient with the plan. The positive behavior or performance you wish to increase may not happen immediately.

❑ Once you see the desired behavior, reinforce the student immediately. This is especially important when the student is first learning the behavior.

❑ Pair social reinforcers with tangible reinforcers. This helps the student associate the social reinforcers with the tangible reinforcers, making it easier for you to eventually phase out tangible reinforcers. When possible, use physical education activities as reinforcers (see table 4.1 and worksheet 2, appendix 2).

❑ On the continuum of reinforcement methods, choose one that requires the least amount of intervention or reinforcement to change a behavior. In other words, reinforce as little as possible to achieve the results you're looking for.

❑ Once the target behavior or performance reaches a satisfactory level, reinforce less. Design a schedule along which you gradually reduce the frequency of reinforcement (see section entitled "Different Types of Reinforcement Schedules" on page 50).

❑ Understand that using reinforcers is not the same as bribery. Bribery is the illegitimate use of gifts to corrupt or manipulate a student's conduct before the student acts, while reinforcement is given only after the appropriate behavior has been maintained or increased (Rhodes, Jenson, and Reavis 1993).

See also checklist 9 in appendix 1 titled "Administering Positive Reinforcement."

## SUMMARY

Administer the behavioral approach positively, consistently, and directly, being sure that both you and your students understand and agree on what is expected of all parties involved. A variety of behavioral methods may maintain and increase desirable behavior, and you should choose along the continuum the one that requires the least intervention but is still effective in achieving the desired behavior. Reinforcement methods include various positive reinforcements, such as social, tangible, and physical activities; prompts; token economy systems; the Premack principle; public posting; contracts; group contingencies; and negative reinforcement. Use these methods singly or in combination as you see fit.

There is no quick fix or cookbook approach to administering various positive behavioral interventions. Therefore use a variety of methods, adapting them when necessary in order to maintain students' interest, thereby effectively increasing desirable behavior. Refer often to checklist 9 in appendix 1 as you experiment with what works for you. But don't get so caught up in using these methods that they become ends in themselves; instead, always think of them as ways to help you meet your educational goals.

# REVIEW: VIGNETTE APPLICATION EXERCISES

For each of the three vignettes on page x, select behavior management methods described in this chapter and discuss in detail how you would implement each of the methods to manage the behavior. After you have developed your own methods, see the suggestions that follow, which we intend as only some of the many creative ways you might apply the information we've covered in this chapter. See also sample plans that integrate the approaches to these behavior problems from all of the chapters in "One Last Look at the Vignettes."

1. Hector, the overactive third grader, has many problems. Where should you start? Concentrate on his four main behavior problems to ultimately help him with his poor gross motor coordination: inability to stand or sit on his assigned spot in the gym for any length of time, running when he should walk, difficulty following a series of directions, and becoming easily upset. Meet with Hector and his classroom teacher to develop a point system through which he may earn points for performing the following behaviors: staying on his assigned spot during attendance and the warm-up, walking from one activity area to the next when requested to do so, listening to and following all teacher directions, and remaining calm. Depending on the severity of Hector's problems, the teacher may need to work on one behavior each week, then combine them. Determine the types of activities or privileges Hector likes. Allow him to trade points for the activities or privileges agreed on. Write the behaviors to follow and how many points he needs to earn to receive various reinforcers in simple terms on a chart or index card for Hector to keep in his physical education locker or classroom desk. Include a bonus clause that allows Hector to earn additional points to trade in for time to work with you one-on-one on various motor skills after class or school. This privilege not only serves as an effective reinforcer but may also improve Hector's motor skill deficits. Each day during warm-ups, review the point system with Hector until he clearly understands and remembers it. In conjunction with the reward system, use a very structured teaching approach with Hector. For example, establish clear signals he can easily understand, such as when to start and stop activities, and provide tangible boundaries such as a poly spot where he is to stand. Be sure to use poly spots for everyone so as not to single out Hector. Give Hector one direction at a time, then ask him to repeat the direction before proceeding. Assign a classmate as a buddy or peer tutor to model appropriate behavior and remind him of the directions he needs to follow. Praise him whenever he remains calm, especially when he's frustrated.

2. Ashante and Jim are fighting over Shannon in the locker room after class. Any form of fighting is a serious problem behavior that you must handle immediately, making sure that the students recognize that this type of aggressive behavior is unacceptable. First, separate the students. Most schools require an automatic detention or suspension for fighting, and you should support your school's policy. This will give the boys time to cool off, perhaps making it easier for them to problem solve with you. When Ashante and Jim are ready to return to class, meet with them privately. At this time, consider implementing positive behavioral methods such as contracts and group contingencies. You can design individual contracts to help Ashante and Jim refrain from fighting. For example, if Ashante and Jim do not fight with each other or anybody else for a certain number of days, agreed on between you and them, they can earn privileges they help choose, such as being a squad leader or choosing an activity they enjoy. A group contingency may be more effective in reducing the aggressive behavior of fighting with students who desire peer approval. For example, if Ashante and Jim do not get into a fight for so many days then the class or squad

*continued*

can earn certain privileges. The group contingencies, however, will be effective if the group encourages Ashante and Jim to act positively and only if they are capable of earning the privileges. If Ashante or Jim cannot earn the privileges, the group may turn against them. If group pressure encourages conflict, this method will not work either. So use this method carefully. You can also pair Ashante and Jim with mature students in class who will model appropriate behavior.

3. Jill and Molly do not bring their gym clothes and consequently do not dress for class. To make things worse, they convey the attitude that they do not care about physical activity, and at times, they are a behavior problem because they are bored sitting out of class. Adopt the philosophy that all students should be as actively involved in physical education as much as possible in order to enjoy the lifetime benefits physical activity can bring. This cannot occur, however, if students are not participating. So discuss with both girls the importance of physical activity and why dressing for class is important.

More importantly, however, ascertain the reasons behind their not dressing for class. Perhaps they do not care for the activities you are offering. In this case, determine what activities they enjoy and explain that you will include some of these activities as part of the curriculum later in the school year. Since Jill and Molly are friends, have them work together to encourage each other to dress and participate.

In addition, during this meeting, review your expectations, including the rules for dressing and participating. Be positive but firm, explaining that not participating in class will result in not earning points for class, which, in turn, will result in a failing grade.

To this end, show each student her current grade point average. Then, on the days they do not dress, require each of them to write a report by the end of the period on the topic or unit the class is participating in. Do not allow them to work together. This strategy is a constructive way to keep Molly and Jill on-task, preventing behavior problems stemming from boredom. They may want to avoid writing the report (negative reinforcement) and consequently dress for class. End the meeting on a positive note by explaining to both students that you are confident they can dress and participate each day. Privately plan to try another strategy if the negative reinforcer doesn't work as overuse of report writing may give the girls a negative attitude toward academic work.

Another strategy is to use a simple behavioral contract. For example, you could say that if Jill and Molly dress and participate in class for so many days, they will earn a reinforcer or a privilege you and they agree on. For example, they could choose one of the activities they told you that they enjoyed and have the entire class participate with them. Remember that for a reinforcer to have meaning, it must be one the individual really desires and is willing to work toward.

## CHAPTER 5

# Behavioral Methods for Decreasing Inappropriate Student Behaviors

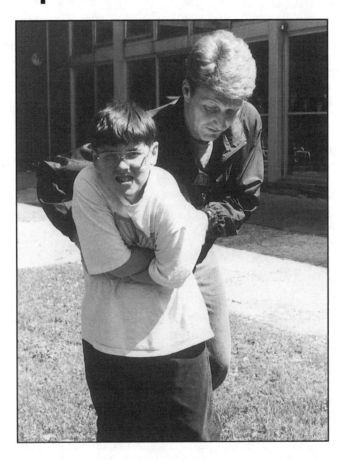

Ms. Jackson had just completed her first week of teaching physical education to elementary students at Nottingham School. She was frustrated because some of the students in the larger classes tended to goof off and not follow game rules. She remembered that in the behavior management class in her physical education training program her professor had said time-out could be very effective in decreasing inappropriate behaviors. To help her think through the situation, Ms. Jackson wrote a description of the behaviors she wanted to eliminate. She decided to have any student who exhibited any of those behaviors sit in a specific area of the gym for one minute for an observational time-out. She explained her plan to the students on Monday morning, telling them which behaviors would result in time-out. As is typical, the students thought of this plan as a game and at first behaved inappropriately simply to see what time-out was like. They soon realized, however, that they did not like sitting in time-out, watching the other students having fun playing the game. Soon the undesirable behaviors disappeared almost entirely.

## APPLYING PUNISHMENT WISELY

In this chapter, we'll continue discussing the behavioral approach by elaborating on punishment methods designed to decrease inappropriate student behaviors. Specifically, we'll examine three methods: the withdrawal of a reinforcer, the presentation of an aversive stimulus, and the requirement of an aversive behavior. To help you see how to tailor these methods to your own situation, we'll give you specific steps and examples to follow. Then, we'll discuss the possible side effects of punishment and guidelines for using punishment methods cautiously yet effectively.

"Punitive methods of social control no doubt work. They would not have been so widely practiced throughout human history if they did not. But they have unfortunate by-products: The student who is studying to avoid punishment will find other ways of avoiding it such as being truant or dropping out. Punitive control may lead him to vandalize school property, to attack teachers, and when he becomes a voter, to refuse to support education. All these by-products can be avoided by turning to non-punitive ways."
—B.F. Skinner, 1973

In order to create an environment that is conducive to learning, we must use reinforcement methods to increase the frequency of positive behavior. Indeed, you should always first attempt to correct the undesirable behavior with positive methods such as the ones we have discussed thus far before using punishment. There are times, however, when students ignore positive efforts and continue to exhibit inappropriate behaviors, interfering with their own and others' learning. When students misbehave in ways that are so extremely undesirable, such as fighting, you may feel that they must be dealt with more strongly than other forms of misbehavior. You may then find it necessary to use a punishment method to decrease the likelihood of future misbehavior.

Before choosing a response to misbehavior, however, determine how severe it is. Mildly inappropriate behaviors include talking when you are giving directions, not wearing clean gym clothes, chewing gum, and tardiness. Severely inappropriate behaviors include fighting, throwing equipment at another student, and stealing. You must know how to use a variety of appropriate management methods to decrease these behaviors. Remember, in the behavioral approach, you use punishment as a consequence for an inappropriate behavior in order to decrease the probability that the behavior will occur in the future. Specifically, the question to ask yourself is "What punishment is, appropriate for the severity of the misbehavior?"

## PUNISHMENT METHODS

You can administer punishment in three forms:

1. Taking away something that the student likes, known as the withdrawal of a reinforcer
2. Presenting something that the student does not like, known as presenting an aversive stimulus
3. Requiring students to do something they dislike, known as requiring an aversive behavior

### Withdrawal of a Reinforcer

There are three basic methods of withdrawing a reinforcer to decrease behavior: extinction or planned ignoring, response cost, and time-out. These are considered mild behavioral methods of punishment. Let's examine each method in detail (see also checklist 10, appendix 1, "Withdrawing a Reinforcer").

#### Extinction or Planned Ignoring

Extinction, also called planned ignoring, is the withholding of the reinforcement when an inappropriate behavior is exhibited in order to encourage that behavior to decrease in the future. In other words, the reinforcement for a previously reinforced behavior is discontinued. To extinguish an inappropriate behavior, however, you must first identify the behavior, determine what is reinforcing it, then determine how to take the reinforcer away. For example, Joe was making duck noises (inappropriate behavior) and Stella was laughing at him (reinforcement) while Mrs. Ivanov gave instructions. Mrs. Ivanov took Stella aside and asked her not to laugh at Joe (withdrawal of the reinforcement). She did the same when anyone else laughed at Joe. Eventually, Joe stopped making the noises because he was not being reinforced.

Note that Mrs. Ivanov approached the other students privately, because public attention to the problem would have simply given Joe's misbehavior more reinforcement.

Consider the following when using extinction:

1. The greater the magnitude of the reinforcer, the greater the resistance to extinction. That is, if the student really likes the reinforcer, he will continue the behavior for a longer time after the reinforcement has been discontinued.

2. The longer the behavior has been reinforced, the more resistant it will be to extinction. In other words, an entrenched behavior is usually harder to extinguish than a new behavior.

3. The more frequently the behavior has been extinguished, the more quickly extinction will occur.

Consider these variables when using extinction so that you will not be surprised by how the student responds.

Although extinction may appear easy to administer, a number of concerns are associated with this method:

- Sometimes it is difficult to identify what is reinforcing the student's behavior.

- It is not always possible to control the student's environment, for example, the other students, the parents, or siblings involved.

- Extinction is gradual. Moreover, undesirable behavior will increase before it decreases.

- Do not use the extinction method to eliminate behaviors that are harmful to the student or other students. In other words, you cannot simply ignore dangerous behavior.

While using extinction, look for appropriate behaviors the student exhibits and reinforce those behaviors. You can also reinforce the appropriate behaviors of other students. For example, compliment Anup for listening to directions quietly, while you ignore Joe's duck noises: "I like the way Anup is listening, sitting quietly." Leaving off the "Why can't you do that too, Joe?" can be difficult, but such a comment can reinforce inappropriate behavior by giving Joe attention and is not part of a warm and supportive classroom climate. So simply let peers serve as models of good behavior. Meanwhile, be patient: Extinction can be very effective when used appropriately.

### Response Cost

For this method, you must take away a reinforcer from the student who has misbehaved. This method is commonly used in everyday life. A parent may take away a child's allowance if he did not clean his room, an employee may have her pay docked if she comes in late, or a driver may get a speeding ticket and have to pay a fine for going over the speed limit. Rules of games use the concept of response cost, too. For example, in football when a player commits a foul, his team loses yardage.

This method is very effective, and you can easily apply it in the physical education setting (see figure 5.1). For example, if a student behaves inappropriately, you can take away points toward her grade. Or you can take away privileges or activities that are reinforcing to the student; free time, by requiring the student to stay in for detention; the privilege of attending basketball games, soccer matches, swimming meets, football games, or field trips; or maybe something as simple as taking away the student's next turn in a game.

### Time-Out

To use this method, you remove the student from a reinforcing environment for a certain period of time when she exhibits an inappropriate behavior in order to get the behavior to decrease in frequency. The three basic types of time-out are observational, exclusion, and seclusion.

1. **Observational time-out:** Remove the student from the activity for a certain period of time but allow him to watch the other students participating and behaving appropriately. This method is very effective if the student enjoys participating in physical education.

2. **Exclusion time-out:** Make the student sit in a corner or other isolated part of the physical education setting where she cannot see the activities of the other students. When the class is outside on the playground, the exclusion time-out area can be any area away from where the rest of the students are playing, such as a bench or bleacher, where the teacher can still see her.

**Figure 5.1** The free throw in basketball is an example of the response cost method of extinguishing undesirable behavior.

## GUIDELINES FOR USING RESPONSE COST

1. Reinforcers must be available for good behavior. When a student performs a desirable behavior, such as serving as a peer tutor for another student who is having trouble on an assignment, you must notice the behavior and reinforce it with social praise and perhaps extra credit points.

2. A student must have earned the reinforcer before you can withdraw it. If the student already has a low grade, taking more points away will not mean very much. Likewise, if the student could not attend the soccer match anyway because of parental restrictions, then taking away that privilege is meaningless.

3. The reinforcer must be important to the student. If the student does not like basketball, taking away the privilege of attending a basketball game is meaningless.

4. You must keep the withdrawal of reinforcers to a minimum. If you take reinforcers away from a student too frequently, he will feel defeated and stop caring about the reinforcers.

5. You must make sure the student understands beforehand which behavior is causing you to take the reinforcement away. If, for example, you are

*continued*

going to take points toward a grade away from a student for turning in a paper late, you must ensure that you tell the student of this possibility before the assignment is due.

6. You should refrain from warning, nagging, or threatening the student. It is far more effective to simply administer the response when the misbehavior occurs than to warn or threaten the student with the punishment. Warnings often prolong the misbehavior as the student will expect a number of warnings before being punished and will use all he can get, often making a game out of it and seeing how many times he can go without being punished.

7. Be careful not to debate the administration of the response cost once the punishable behaviors occur, trying to justify your response. Never give in when a student tries to debate with you about the misbehavior with such pleas as "I'm sorry, I didn't mean to do it" or "I won't do it again" or "Please, just give me one more chance." This too becomes a game and he will try your patience as he continues to misbehave. Calmly state the punishment and resume teaching.

8. Be careful not to become emotionally involved. For example, students often try to make you feel guilty for punishing them. Do not buy into this ploy. Detach yourself enough from the situation and say, for example, "You chose to throw your bat when you struck out, so you will miss a turn at bat." Then refocus on the entire class.

9. When possible allow natural or logical consequences to take place. For example, when one student is showing off during an activity or game, she is likely to miss a turn which is probably more of a punishment than if you make her sit down and miss a turn.

3. **Seclusion time-out:** Make the student leave the physical education setting completely. This method works best when the time-out area has very little visual and auditory stimulation and has no other students around. Yet, you must ensure that this area is supervised, safe, and properly lit and ventilated. For example, some options for this type of time-out area are the physical educator's office or the principal's office.

Often the rules of games give the time-out for you. For example, in basketball, if a player commits five fouls, she must sit out the rest of the game; in soccer, if a player exhibits unsportsmanlike behavior, the referee can give her a red card, banning her from playing the rest of the game.

## GUIDELINES FOR USING TIME-OUT

1. Inform the student specifically which behavior elicited the time-out, for example, say, "Felix, you threw your bat; sit in time-out for one minute."

2. Administer time-out in a consistent and matter-of-fact manner. Do not discuss or negotiate the behavior or the time-out with the student. When undesirable behavior occurs, state the rule violated, for example, "No hitting" and take or send the student to time-out. Say nothing else; give no explanation.

3. Make sure that the time-out is not reinforcing. For example, some students like to be alone or like to sit in the hall and interact with students who pass by. So being alone or being in the hall may actually be more reinforcing than cooperating in the physical education class.

4. Make sure the student is not getting out of a situation that she does not like. Time-out may be negatively reinforcing, that is, the student gets out of doing an activity that she does not like to do, such as running sprints or doing warm-up exercises. So you are actually reinforcing the misbehavior, and the next time you run wind sprints, it is likely that Katerina will talk with Irena so they can go to time-out instead of running sprints.

5. Specify the period of time to be in time-out in advance. It should not be too long or it will lose its effectiveness. One to five minutes is sufficient.

6. Wait until disruptive behavior stops before starting to time the time-out. If, for example, the student is having a temper tantrum and screaming obscenities, wait until he calms down and stops screaming to start timing the time-out.

7. When the time-out is over, have the student state the rule that he broke, then tell what he plans to do to keep from breaking that rule again. Then return the student to the task he was engaged in when the inappropriate behavior occurred so that he cannot use time-out to avoid doing tasks that he does not like.

8. When the student is not in time-out and is engaged in appropriate behavior, be sure to reinforce the appropriate behavior he is exhibiting. Say, for example, "Gee, I sure like the way you put the bat down by the dugout." Be sure to use a genuinely enthusiastic and sincere tone of voice.

Remember, use checklist 10 in appendix 1 to make sure you withdraw reinforcers appropriately.

## Presentation of an Aversive Stimulus

An aversive stimulus is one that is unpleasant to whom it is presented. Two of the most common methods of presenting aversive stimuli to decrease misbehavior are direct discussion with the student and giving the student a verbal reprimand. These are considered mild methods of punishment. The third method, corporal punishment, is the most severe form of present-

ing an aversive stimulus. Refer to checklist 11 in appendix 1, "Presenting Aversive Stimuli," to review your use of aversive stimuli.

## Direct Discussion

To effectively manage the misbehavior, you must determine its cause. Perhaps the best way to do this is to have a nonthreatening discussion with the student. Show concern for the student and be sincere. It is important to discuss the behavior with the student to try to determine what caused the behavior to occur. If still necessary, you must set and enforce a consequence for the behavior (see also chapter 6).

### Verbal Reprimand

A verbal reprimand involves telling the student that the behavior she exhibited is unacceptable and why it is unacceptable. Then tell or ask what she should do instead. For example, if she is interrupting you when you are giving instructions, you might say, "Joy, interrupting is impolite. It makes it difficult for others to follow my instructions. Please wait until I am finished to ask your question."

## PRINCIPLES OF ADMINISTERING VERBAL REPRIMANDS

1. Be specific. Tell the student exactly what inappropriate behavior you are reprimanding. Then encourage the student to behave appropriately and include a statement of the appropriate behavior in the reprimand. For example, "Other students cannot hear my instructions when you are bouncing the ball. Please hold the ball."

2. Reprimand the behavior; do not degrade the student. Say, for example, "Interrupting is impolite," rather than "You are impolite."

3. Avoid sarcasm. Some teachers use sarcasm to chastise or cut down a student in an attempt to control behavior. Using words as a weapon of control, however, can alienate the misbehaving student as well as the other students in the class. Many times a physical educator unconsciously slips into using this method or considers it a form of joking to get the point across. Sarcasm is generally not considered funny by the student and could negatively affect both her self-image and her status with her peers. In short, it is not a behavior builder. Indeed, sarcasm is detrimental to both the target of the sarcasm and, ultimately, to the overall class climate.

4. Always praise the desired behavior when the student performs it. For example, say, "I like how you held the ball and paid attention while I was giving instructions." Leave off the "for once" and you reinforce the positive behavior.

5. Reprimand immediately after the behavior occurs. A delayed reprimand loses its effectiveness.

6. Be firm. Make sure the student understands that you disapprove of the behavior.

7. If the student or others may be harmed by the behavior, remove the student by giving her a time-out.

8. If necessary, back up the reprimand with a loss of privileges (response cost). For example, say, "Throwing a bat is unacceptable behavior. You will miss your next turn at bat."

9. Be calm. Getting upset along with the student only compounds the problem and shows the student a poor role model.

10. Avoid embarrassing the student in the presence of peers and others. Take the student aside to reprimand whenever possible. Before reprimanding, try using nonverbal reprimands such as the time-out signal, a finger to the lips, a stern look, holding up the number of fingers matching the number of the rule being broken, or the like.

*continued*

11. Do not use guilt! For example, do not say, "I am disappointed in you, I never thought you would get into a fight."

12. Observe the student's reaction to the reprimand to determine if it is aversive. If the student's behavior does not decrease with the use of this method, try some other method.

13. Always follow through. If you tell a student he will have to sit out a turn for using inappropriate language, make sure he sits out.

14 When it's over, it's over. Do not keep reminding the student of the misbehavior.

## Corporal Punishment

Corporal punishment is the hitting of a student as consequence of a misbehavior. Some districts define corporal as any touching of students for the purpose of discipline, starting with putting your arm around a student's shoulders to discuss a problem and including dragging a child into time-out. Whatever your district's policy, it is *never* appropriate to hit a student. When a student is exhibiting aggressive, dangerous, and destructive behaviors, the best solution is to get away and get others away from the violent student. The second option is to use physical restraint to protect yourself and others.

## Physical Restraint

You must avoid touching a student when you are angry. With aggressive, self-destructive, or dangerous behaviors, however, physical restraint may be appropriate when you are unable to get away from a violent student or when you need to stop a violent student from hurting himself or others.

It is important that you know how to properly physically restrain a student. The preferred method is to stand behind the student and hold the student's wrists with the arms crossed over the chest (see figure 5.2). When using physical restraint, hold the student firmly, but not roughly, giving the feeling of protection but not punishment. Hold the student until he calms down and you feel he is in control.

School districts may vary in their recommended use of physical restraint. Some districts may not allow teachers to touch the students at all. Find out what your school district's policy is regarding this before your first day of teaching. Check out your school district's policies regarding other methods of discipline as well. Finally, we recommended that you attend any available inservice training on behavior management.

### Corporal Punishment in the United States

Corporal punishment in schools is prohibited in all the developed countries of the world except the United States, South Africa, and parts of Canada and Australia. In the United States as of 1994, 27 state legislatures had passed laws prohibiting physical punishment of students. Since these rulings, the number of students struck each year in the public schools has decreased from 1,415,540 in 1982 to 555,531 in 1992 (National Coalition to Abolish Corporal Punishment in Schools 1992). See figure 5.3 for a list of all states that have banned corporal punishment. Make sure you know your district's policy regarding corporal punishment (see example in figure 5.4).

**Figure 5.2** The preferred method to physically restrain a student is to stand behind her and hold the wrists with the arms crossed over the chest.

| | | |
|---|---|---|
| Alaska | Michigan | Oregon |
| California | Minnesota | Rhode Island |
| Connecticut | Montana | South Dakota |
| Hawaii | Nebraska | Utah |
| Illinois | Nevada | Vermont |
| Iowa | New Hampshire | Virginia |
| Maine | New Jersey | Washington |
| Maryland | New York | West Virginia |
| Massachusetts | North Dakota | Wisconsin |

**Figure 5.3** A list of states that have banned corporal punishment.
1992, National Coalition to Abolish Corporal Punishment in Schools

# GRANITE SCHOOL DISTRICT

340 EAST 3545 SOUTH • SALT LAKE CITY, UTAH 84115-4697 • PHONE: (801) 263-6100
FAX: (801) 263-6128

## ADMINISTRATIVE MEMORANDUM NUMBER SIX

### CORPORAL PUNISHMENT

It is the practice of the district that incidents which involve corporal punishment or the use of physical force by school authorities to correct unacceptable behavior should be avoided. While the law is clear that the schools do act in loco parentis, and while the courts have upheld teachers who have, under certain circumstances, used corporal punishment, the complications which arise out of such incidents suggest extreme care should be used before using any physical force.

If school staff find themselves in a situation where they think that circumstances may result in physical action against a student, they should refer the student, situation permitting, to the administrative offices. Hopefully this action will result in a satisfactory resolution of the student behavior involved without using corporal punishment.

The above is not meant to rigidly prohibit physical action if provoked and/or warranted, such as actions taken in defense against physical attack by a student or to protect the life or safety of another student or staff member. These examples are more descriptive of self defense than of corporal punishment. Clearly our district position is not to engage in acts of physical aggression toward students which could be defined as corporal punishment.

Loren G. Burton
Superintendent

**Figure 5.4** An example of a school district policy on corporal punishment.

## THE USE OF CORPORAL PUNISHMENT IN THE SCHOOLS

"I believe that there is no longer any use for corporal punishment in schools and much to be gained by suppressing it."
—B.F. Skinner

"In this era of reform, is it too much to expect educators to think of more civilized ways to correct students?"
—Akron Beacon Journal, 8/28/87

"The fundamental need of American education is to find ways of engaging today's children in the thrill of learning. Fear of pain has no place in that process."
—The Christian Science Monitor, 3/21/89

"The use of corporal punishment in schools is intrinsically related to child maltreatment. It contributes to a climate of violence, it implies that society approves of the physical violation of children, it establishes an unhealthy norm . . . its outright abolition throughout the nation must occur immediately."
—U.S. Advisory Board on Child Abuse & Neglect, 9/15/91

"As millions of children across the USA prepare to go back to school, teachers are laying down their weapons—the paddles they use to dole out corporal punishment. A teacher does best armed only with knowledge. Corporal punishment is a cruel and obsolete weapon."
—USA Today, 8/22/90

"The worst thing seems to be for a school to work with methods of fear, force, and artificial authority.  Such treatment destroys the healthy feelings, the integrity, and the self-confidence of the pupils.  All that it produces is a servile helot."
—Albert Einstein

Note: All these quotes are cited in National Coalition to Abolish Corporal Punishment in Schools (1992).

## Requiring an Aversive Behavior

There are several ways to punish a misbehavior by requiring the student to do something aversive. These include requiring a physical activity, reparation, and overcorrection. These methods are considered moderate methods of punishment. Use checklist 12 in appendix 1, "Requiring Aversive Behaviors," to check your own use of these methods.

### Requiring a Physical Activity or Extra Academic Work

If a student misbehaves, you could require the student to perform a physical activity, such as running a lap or sprints, or doing sit-ups or push-ups, however, using physical activity as a punishment can give students a negative attitude toward physical activity. The result may be that the student perceives physical activity as something to avoid. We do not condone this method because it defeats our goal as physical educators to promote the desire to lead healthy, physically active lifestyles.

### Reparation

In this method the student is made to pay for a misbehavior with money or time worked. If after missing a goal in hockey, the student breaks the hockey stick, she must either pay for the hockey stick or work, for example, around the school grounds picking up trash for a specified number of hours to pay for it. If work around the school grounds is the punishment you choose, it is advisable to have a conference with the parents and students to explain the philosophy behind the punishment and to ask for alternative punishments. School district policy should be reviewed to assure that the technique is acceptable. We have found that often parents want to pay for the equipment for the student. This is only acceptable if the parents then make the student work to earn the money to repay them. Otherwise, the student has only learned that her parents will bail her out when she misbehaves.

### Overcorrection

This method requires the student to assume responsibility for her behavior by making her recognize the impact of her inappropriate behavior. The two basic types of overcorrection are restitutional overcorrection and positive practice overcorrection.

- **Restitutional overcorrection** is a method by which a student is made to rectify the situation by returning the environment to an improved state. For example, if the student throws trash on the playing field, require her to pick up all of the trash on the entire playing field. If a student steals something, make her return the stolen object. This is very effective, especially when the student has to face the person they stole from and apologize. This method works best if the punishment is immediate and if it relates to the inappropriate act.

- **Positive practice overcorrection** is a method that forces a student or a group of students to repeatedly perform a behavior appropriately as a consequence of performing the behavior inappropriately. For example, if students come into the gym and are noisy and playing around, you might have the class practice several times going out of the gym and walking in quietly and sitting in their assigned places properly.

# NEGATIVE SIDE EFFECTS OF USING SEVERE FORMS OF PUNISHMENT

Punishment is the most familiar and frequently administered behavior change method in the school setting (Walker and Shea 1995). It is used frequently because of its immediate results. If a severe enough punishment method is used, the probability is high that the undesirable behavior will stop immediately. So if stopping the undesirable behavior was our only goal, we would conclude that we should use the most severe forms of punishment every time a student exhibits an undesirable behavior.

Unfortunately, the solution to misbehavior is not that simple. When severe forms of punishment are used to the exclusion of milder forms of punishment or more positive methods to manage behavior, we run the risk of damaging students physically, emotionally, psychologically, and spiritually. But because our primary goal as physical educators is to create an environment conducive to learning in which students feel safe, are willing to take risks, and are motivated to learn, we must not make students feel threatened by extreme forms of punishment, nor should we subject them to the negative side effects. In other words, if our goal is to create a learning environment in which students feel safe, secure, and nurtured so that they are more likely to enjoy physical activity and adopt it as a lifestyle choice as adults, we must as a profession avoid severe forms of punishment.

A number of researchers have examined the effects of more severe forms of punishment on students. In the following sections, we'll look more closely at some of these effects.

## Decreased Motivation to Learn

Punishment can cause emotional harm to a student and, in addition, may impair the student's desire to think, learn, and function. The desire to cooperate with you or classmates may decrease and her sense of personal responsibility may diminish as you take more responsibility for controlling her. It may also affect the student's ability to enter into relationships with others.

If you punish a student often, he will come to fear you. This fear may cause the student to withdraw emotionally and therefore stop performing and learning in class. Skipping class and even skipping school may result. The student who has been punished often learns how to escape punishment by lying. A second grade student one time was asked by her physical educator where her homework assignment on her favorite sport hero was. Fearing punishment for not doing her assignment, she lied and said, "I did it, but I erased it."

## Increased Emotional Disturbance

Punishment can cause emotional damage to a student. Some common aversive side effects of punishment are social deviancy, rigidity, regression, and other forms of poor adjustment. Students who are victims of emotional assault frequently feel attacked, vulnerable, and highly defensive. Other potential emotional effects of punishment include pessimism, depression, constriction of thinking, and psychosomatic diseases, such as speech disorders, lags in physical development, and failure to thrive syndrome.

When a student is punished, he senses the lack of empathy and love from the punisher. Over time, punishment seems to have a cumulative effect. The results may be low self-esteem, self-destructive behaviors, apathy, withdrawal, and depression. The student who is frequently punished typically has low self-esteem because of the feeling of not being able to "do anything right." The lower the self-esteem, the more likely it is that the student will misbehave and a vicious cycle begins.

A student who is punished may receive the message, "I am a bad person because I misbehaved." So whenever you reprimand a student, ensure that the reprimand is specific to the behavior and not to the person who committed the misbehavior. For example if a student displayed poor sportsmanship, you might say, "Throwing the bat is unacceptable. I'm afraid someone will get hurt," instead of asking, "Why are you being such a poor sport?"

Sometimes teachers and parents use guilt, either knowingly or unknowingly, to try to make the student behave the way they want him to. Guilt is a very strong emotion, and often it will control a student's behavior. For example, when Bobby misbehaves and you say, "Bobby, how could you have done such a thing?" the goodness of the student is in question, and the student feels ashamed of himself. This has a detrimental effect on Bobby's self-esteem and in the long run may lead to more misbehavior.

## Increased Aggression and Misbehavior

Violence begets violence. Children learn what they are taught, copying adult behavior. Students who are punished harshly, frequently, and seemingly unnecessarily may become angry and revengeful against the punisher (Bavolek 1990). Some students may even resort to violence and aggression and may vandalize the school or be involved in fights in and out of school. Every pain inflicted on a student, whether emotional or physical, may be passed on sooner or later to someone else younger or more helpless (see figure 5.5).

## Failure to Solve the Behavior Problem

Students who are punished in one situation for a particular behavior will refrain from that behavior in that situation only and will often display those same behaviors in another environment. For example, if a student is punished for aggression at school, she will not be aggressive at school but may become more aggressive at home.

The effects of punishment for one behavior may generalize to other related behaviors that we do not want to suppress. If, for example, you reprimand a student harshly for talking while you are giving instructions, the student may not talk during group discussion or when asked a question.

Students often identify punishment with the punisher instead of with the inappropriate behavior. They will misbehave again when the punisher is gone. Ironically, often the misbehavior will reoccur at a higher rate than before.

Severe forms of punishment affect different people in different ways. A number of factors determine the extent of the effect extreme forms of punishment may have on a student:

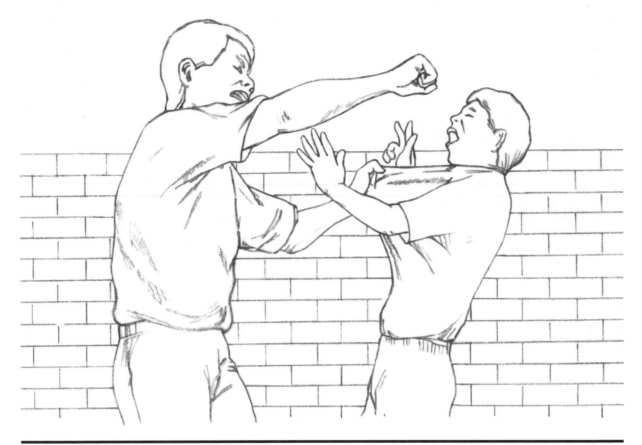

**Figure 5.5** Unnecessarily severe punishment often prompts students to prey on someone weaker.

- Student's self-esteem: Punishment will have a greater negative effect on a student who already has a low self-esteem. The message that punishment sends to a student is "Your behavior was bad." The student often translates this to mean "I am bad," which is harmful to the student's self-concept.

- Student's perception of the physical educator: Punishment has a much stronger effect on a student if the student views the physical educator as an important person.

- Method used: The more severe the punishment method used on the student, the stronger the effect on the student. In examining the continuum of punishment methods (see figure 5.6), the methods toward the end of the continuum tend to have a more negative effect on the student.

- Frequency of punishment: When a student is punished frequently, often the punishment becomes less effective and eventually fails to suppress the misbehavior. It is as if the student becomes immune to being punished. He may become callused or withdrawn and less responsive to the punisher.

- Nature of behavior punished: If a student is punished for what is considered a mild infraction of the classroom rules, the feeling of being watched over too closely may cause the student not to care and to quit trying to obey the rules or become personally responsible in class.

All too often we want the student who is displaying an inappropriate behavior to stop the behavior and stop it immediately. Therefore, we may be tempted to use severe punishment to

**Figure 5.6** It is important to choose a punishment method that is an appropriate consequence to the inappropriate behavior of the student.

## GUIDELINES FOR USING PUNISHMENT

Whenever possible, use positive methods to manage behavior, because severe forms of punishment, even when used with the best intentions, may affect students negatively. In order to minimize the negative effects of punishment if you do use it, follow these guidelines.

1. Establish classroom rules. Don't punish students if you haven't told them what the punishable behaviors are and what the consequences will be. Send a list of rules, unacceptable behaviors, and consequences home so parents know what is expected of students (see chapter 2).

2. Maintain self-control. Do not lose control over your own emotions. The problem will only become worse if both the student and you lose control. When emotions are high, the likelihood of a rational solution to the problem being presented is not very high. Instead, you should model appropriate behavior.

3. Avoid confrontations. Do not confront a student, especially in front of the student's peers. Secondary level students, in particular, tend to function as members of a group and are quite protective of each other. By confronting one student, you may lose the respect of the other students as well as of the student you are confronting.

*continued*

4. Punish immediately. Do not allow a student to exhibit an inappropriate behavior for too long, giving it a chance to increase in intensity before you attempt to intervene. Punishment must occur immediately after you observe the behavior.

5. Specify the behavior that warranted the punishment. When a student behaves inappropriately, make sure that you specify which behavior brought about the punishment. For example, you might say, "Hitting is an inappropriate behavior, so you must sit out for five minutes."

6. Ensure that your use of punishment is fair. If you punish one student for a behavior and then another student exhibits the same behavior, you must punish that student as well. It is easy to overlook misbehavior from a student who is generally well-behaved and to punish a student who is always in trouble for the same misbehavior. You must avoid this. Students must see that you are consistent and fair.

7. Make sure the punishment fits the intention of the crime. It is important to distinguish between unintentional and intentional disruptions. You must not treat students who accidentally make a mistake and those who misbehave on purpose in the same manner. For instance, you should treat a student who accidentally throws a ball that hits you differently from a student who intentionally hits you with a ball. Sometimes intentions are obvious, sometimes not, so you must be careful to be perceptive and accurate or you may be accused of being unfair.

8. Be consistent. As with all forms of behavior management, you must be consistent in your use of punishment. What is wrong today must be wrong tomorrow, and the consequences must be the same. If you are not feeling well or are having a bad day, you may be tempted to punish students for a behavior that you may not punish them for tomorrow when you are feeling better or are in a better mood. Students need to know that the consequences of a behavior will be consistent from day to day.

9. Return to positive methods. If punishment for a misbehavior is necessary, return to a positive behavioral method as soon as possible. Reserve punishment to gain immediate control over serious misbehavior but never use it as a primary method of managing behavior.

10. Never hit! Hitting is completely inappropriate. There are too many negative side effects of hitting a student for it to ever be an approved method. In addition to all the negative repercussions for the student, you must consider the issue of legal liability; remember, corporal punishment is against the law in 27 states.

stop a mildly inappropriate behavior. But this causes the student to feel that the punishment was unfair. The student will likely exhibit her disapproval by acting out in some other inappropriate way. It is important, then, that you make sure that the punishment method is a fair consequence for the severity of the inappropriate behavior you observed. Refer to "Guidelines for Using Punishment" often. See also checklist 13 in appendix 1, "General Use of Punishment."

## SUMMARY

If we as physical educators are concerned about the well-being of our students, we should examine how we manage behavior in our classes. To begin with, we need to structure our classes so that behavior problems are prevented or decreased. Then, we must use positive methods to increase appropriate behavior. And finally, if punishment methods are necessary, we must use mild methods and follow appropriate guidelines. Through this process, we will help create an environment that is conducive to learning and that enhances the emotional well-beings of our students.

Recognize that there is no easy answer to various behavioral problems. Therefore, develop a cadre of methods from which you may choose to maintain student interest and effectively change undesirable behavior. When managing behavior, be sure to use the least amount of intervention. It is helpful to develop a continuum of behavioral methods from mild to severe for decreasing inappropriate behaviors. This will help you match the intervention to the severity of the behavior problem. In general, behavioral interventions are quite simple to design, but it is an art to administer and develop a behavior change that is maintained over time and can effectively change the behavior or performance of the student and/or class. Refer often to checklists 10, 11, 12, and 13 in appendix 1 to assess how you are doing.

## REVIEW: VIGNETTE APPLICATION EXERCISES

For each of the vignettes on page x, select two behavior management methods described in this chapter and discuss in detail how you would implement each of the methods to manage the inappropriate behavior. Do not use the same method more than once. The following are possible applications of the material in this chapter. Of course, there are many other creative ways to apply this information. See also "One Last Look at the Vignettes," in which we consider all the methods discussed in this book for the same vignettes.

1. Remember Hector? He is the overactive third grader who is so disruptive his physical education teacher has asked his regular classroom teacher not to send him to physical education class.

Discuss the situation privately with Hector and tell him that you are concerned about specific behaviors and why. Encourage Hector to set a goal for each behavior, such as, listen quietly 60 percent of the time, follow verbal directions 80 percent of the time, and wait his turn calmly 90 percent of the time. Be sure he understands that 60 percent means 6 out of 10 times or 3 out of 5 times and so on. Choose numbers that can be achieved in one week's time. Set up a self-evaluation chart for Hector, listing each of the target behaviors and clearly marking the number of times he must perform the behavior to earn a reinforcer so he can grasp what you are requiring. Establish a weekly reinforcer that he wants to earn for achieving his goal and a punishment for when he does not. Possible reinforcers might include getting to choose the game to play during activity time on Friday, getting to be captain of his team, getting to set up equipment the next week, getting 15 minutes of free time on Mondays, or the like. Possible punishments might include not being allowed to play during activity time at the end of class (response cost) or having to sit immediately in time-out for 1 minute. To put the plan into action, each day at the beginning of class review it until you are sure he remembers and understands what you expect of him. Each day at the end of class, have him put a "+" each time he has stayed in his assigned space while listening quietly when others were talking, has followed verbal directions, or has waited his turn calmly and a "−" each time he has not performed a behavior.

Every Friday, meet with Hector and evaluate his progress together. If he has reached his goal for each of the behaviors, he gets the reinforcer; if he does not, he gets the punishment. Be sure to award reinforcers and enforce punishments consistently.

*continued*

2. Let's look again at Ashante and Jim's fighting in the locker room after class in light of what we've discussed in this chapter. First, tell the boys to stop fighting. If they do not stop, use physical restraint on the one who is the aggressor at the time. Hold him securely, talking to him gently until he calms down. At this point, support your school's policy regarding suspension or detention for fighting. Then, when the boys are ready to return to your class, meet with them privately to discuss the fight. Remember, this will give them time to cool off, perhaps making it easier for them to problem solve with you.

First, ask them to tell you what caused the fight. After you have discussed the cause of the fight, giving each student a chance to talk without interruptions, ask them each to tell you a better way of dealing with this situation. Then have them sit in time-out during "game time" in physical education class the next day. Tell them that if they get into a fight again in physical education class, you will have a conference with their parents, then remind them of your school's policy regarding detention for fighting.

3. How can you guide Jill and Molly in light of the information we have discussed in this chapter? Find out why they were not participating in physical education class. Then provide activities in the curriculum to make it more fun and challenging for them. Develop a behavior chart, listing the two behaviors in a positive way: bringing clean gym clothes and participating in class activities. Have each girl establish a goal, such as, "Bring in clean clothes and participate four out of five days." Reinforce each girl each day for these behaviors. If they do not bring clean clothes, require them to write a report by the end of the period on the topic or unit the class is participating in. Another method is to have a direct discussion and ask them why they did not bring their clean clothes. The reason(s) why would lead the discussion to determine an appropriate consequence. Ask them to tell you the benefits of physical exercise. At the end of the week, refer to the chart to see if the goal has been met. If they meet the goal, give them the agreed-on reinforcer. If it was not met, subtract points earned toward the end-of-the-quarter grade or field trip.

## CHAPTER 6

# The Psychodynamic Approach

Ms. Collier has been a physical educator in Arlington County for 15 years. Because of her communication and behavior management skills as well as her successful track record working with children of diverse cultural backgrounds, she was asked to transfer to the district's new elementary school, which will serve students of diverse backgrounds from the inner city. In this position, she will be responsible for developing the physical education program for kindergarten through sixth grade.

At her previous school, Ms. Collier had successfully implemented some of the strategies of Hellison's Teaching Personal and Social Responsibility Model. After accepting the new teaching position, Ms. Collier read Hellison's book *Teaching Responsibility Through Physical Activity* (Hellison 1995) and busily planned ways to integrate this model into the new school's physical education program. She designed a bulletin board to depict the levels of responsibility and developed some creative ways to implement appropriate strategies throughout her curriculum.

During the faculty retreat in August, Ms. Collier gave an inservice workshop for the other teachers in the school to discuss the model so that the teachers would better understand her physical education program. She also suggested ways that they could implement some of the strategies in their own classrooms.

*continued*

Ms. Collier felt well-prepared for her new and challenging teaching position, and the new year started smoothly. The students responded positively to this new approach. At parent-teacher conferences just before winter break, a father told her that it is the first time his son has actually looked forward to going to physical education class. He had even requested that his dad take him to the library to write a report on his favorite sports figure. He asked Ms. Collier what her secret was.

The psychodynamic approach to behavior management focuses on three aspects of behavior management: understanding the psychological causes of behavior, developing a trusting relationship between the physical educator and students, and teaching students self-control. In this approach students must

- recognize that their own behavior is a problem,
- recognize why it is a problem,
- understand what motivated the behavior, and
- determine through discussion with the teacher alternative ways to behave in similar situations.

If you use the psychodynamic approach, your responsibilities will include

- developing a safe, nurturing environment in which all students feel a sense of belonging (see chapters 1 and 2),
- understanding student behavior and feelings,
- being willing to listen to, then help students understand both their behavior and their feelings,
- teaching the students personal responsibility,
- encouraging the students to learn, and
- helping the students recognize that behavior limits are to protect them, not punish them.

Many physical educators shy away from using the psychodynamic approach for a variety of reasons. To begin with, most have not been taught how to use the methods properly, so they do not feel qualified to use them. They think that only psychologists, therapists, counselors, or social workers should use them because they require more time, energy, and expertise to apply than the behavioral approach. But the models using the psychodynamic approach we'll discuss in this chapter have been used effectively in physical education settings and are well worth the time and energy they require (Hellison 1985, 1995; Hellison and Templin 1991; Stiehl 1993). The psychodynamic approach will help you and your students analyze behavior, plan strategies to change, and evaluate a behavior change program. In effect, this approach teaches students to take responsibility for their own behavior—a skill that will help them throughout life!

Specifically, in this chapter, we'll examine the following methods that have been successfully applied in physical education settings: responsibility models, reality therapy, and counseling methods such as the talking bench and self evaluation.

## RESPONSIBILITY MODELS

Responsiblility models are designed to provide students with experiences and interactions that allow them the opportunity to develop personal, social, and environmental responsibility. "This includes fulfilling our obligations, keeping our commitments, striving to do and be our personal and moral best, and nurturing and supporting one another" (Stiehl 1993, p. 39). An assumption of these models is that students are capable of accepting responsibility for their own actions as well as for the consequences of their own behaviors. Responsibility is a choice that is motivated internally. In addition, students who learn how to make more choices for themselves learn that they are able to create their own opportunities for change and can design their own futures (Stiehl 1993). When used in an educational setting, these models can help students feel empowered, this, in turn, helps them learn to act with a purpose and make responsible commitments to themselves, others, and their environments.

Note that the responsibility models we'll discuss in this chapter are alternative curriculum approaches that use physical activity settings as a medium for teaching responsibility. Although behaviors will change as a result of using these models, the intent is to change perceptions and feelings and to create responsibility, not merely to manage behavior.

## Becoming Responsible

Don Morris and Jim Stiehl have developed a program used in schools to teach responsibility to students. This program is called "Becoming Responsible." In their program, the authors define responsibility as "taking care of ourselves, others, and our surroundings" (Morris 1993).

### Types of Responsibilities

You can use this program to develop three types of responsibility: personal, social, and environmental.

Personal responsibility involves being able to

- make and keep agreements,
- set goals and create ways to achieve them,
- accept consequences of personal choices, and
- acknowledge personal accomplishments.

Social responsibility involves being able to

- communicate with others in a way that empowers them, not demeans them,
- honor others' rights, dignity, and worth,
- work together toward common goals,
- negotiate problems and conflicts successfully, and
- create opportunities for others.

Environmental responsibility involves being able to

- become conscious of the various contexts in which we function,
- respect property and take care of equipment, the classroom, the school, and the larger community, and
- recognize the importance of the individual taking care of the environment as well as influencing others to take care of the environment.

### Steps of the Model

The strategy used in the Becoming Responsible Model includes three basic steps.

1. Make students aware of language and behaviors that are irresponsible or that do not support the well-being of self, others, or the environment.
2. Offer alternative language and behaviors that are appropriate.
3. Give students a choice between irresponsible and responsible behavior.

### Helping Students Become More Responsible

Some teaching suggestions to help students become more responsible include modifying teacher talk, student talk, teacher actions, and student actions.

#### Teacher talk.

You must become more aware of how your language affects students. You send messages to them both through your words and your actions. The positive messages you send to students enhance their senses of self, helping them feel valuable, worthwhile, and capable. For example, when a student is listening to instructions, you might say, "Marcelo, thank you for standing quietly and listening to instructions."

#### Student talk.

When a student blames other people or things for her behavior, she excuses herself from personal responsibility. Then she feels she does not have to do anything about her behavior. A common phrase that points blame is "makes me." For example, "Jessica makes me mad" or "Mike made me miss that goal." Phrases such as these take control away from the student. But she can learn to change the way she phrases her talk so that she takes more responsibility for her feelings and her behavior, thereby taking power and responsibility back. Instead, teach such a student to say "I choose to be mad at Jessica" or "I missed that goal."

#### Teacher actions.

You can provide opportunities for responsible behavior by designing activities that nurture responsibility. The first step in this process is to determine what responsibility means. The second step is to determine why responsible behavior is important. Third, specify what responsible behaviors are. Then give students a list of responsible behaviors, such as having clean gym clothes, doing all the activities at each station, and caring about the feelings of other students. Next, ask students to make a checklist listing the behaviors for which they are willing to be responsible. This allows students to not only take responsibility for their behavior but also for evaluating their own behaviors. Then you and each student establish consequences for behaving responsibly and irresponsibly. After putting the plan into action, you reinforce students for behaving responsibly and punish them for behaving irresponsibly.

In addition to improving behavior, when using the Becoming Responsible Model, you are also encouraging the student to become more responsible for his feelings and thoughts. When you perceive feelings are playing a part in the performance of a student, you might ask him how he feels. For example, if he is only watching when the rest of the students are walking on a balance beam, you might say, "How do you feel when you walk on the balance beam?" If the student voices fear, you might ask what the consequences of those feelings are. He may say that he does not like to play on the ropes course or to climb on playground equipment that is high off the ground. When he understands the connection between his feelings and his behavior, however, he can learn how to become responsible for his feelings. You could give the student his power back by talking with him and letting him know that he can overcome the fear. Then you can create ways to help him overcome the fear, such as walking on a board on the floor first, then raising the board up several inches until he works up to the height of the balance beam. When the student does walk on the balance beam, provide a spotter who walks with him, holding his hand. Reinforce the student frequently throughout this process.

You can design your curriculum to include opportunities to teach responsible behaviors. One way to do this is to plan activities that challenge a wide spectrum of abilities. Then you give students a choice of activities and levels of difficulty within each activity. These activities can create "teachable moments" through which students may learn valuable lessons, such as accepting the outcomes of their decisions, accepting the support of others, accepting the contributions of other members of the class, respecting the choices of others, and so on. For example, Kim may decide to play basketball on the A team, which has higher-skilled players. In choosing to do this, she must be willing to accept the fact that she may not be as successful because the players on the A team will pass the ball harder and faster and expect her to play with more skill than she would have to on the "B" team. In this situation, Kim may learn to accept the outcome of her decision and accept the support of others who will try to encourage her to play on the A team. Likewise, teammates on the A team can learn to accept Kim's choice to play with them.

### Student actions.

You should provide students with opportunities to demonstrate responsible behavior through their actions. One effective technique is to encourage students to participate in social responsibility activities that encourage mutual support within a group, such as cooperative games. Other effective techniques include creating opportunities requiring students to use conflict resolution skills and to deal with peer pressure (Fluegelman 1976, 1981; Grineski 1996; Orlick 1978, 1982).

### Projects

As students become more responsible for their behaviors and feelings, ask them to develop a personal responsibility project. Require students to follow these steps:

1. Each student thinks of an idea for a project.
2. Each student makes commitments and promises, similar to setting goals and objectives. A commitment is a goal that the student has for herself, for example, to improve her physical fitness. A promise (objective) is the action she will take to fulfill the commitment, for example, jog for 20 minutes a day, three days a week.
3. Each student develops strategies for implementing her project.
4. Each student establishes timelines for achieving the goals and objectives.
5. If a student needs help to achieve the goals and objectives, the student identifies individuals who can provide that help.
6. Each student implements her project.

See figure 6.1 for an example of a personal responsibility project (Stiehl 1993).

Some examples of student projects include "resolving personal conflicts with words instead of fists, ensuring that the playground is safe,

## Personal Responsibility Project

Date: Nov. 1, 1997

**GOAL #1:**

My goal is: to improve my physical fitness

Activities I can do to achieve this goal are:

jog 20 minutes a day 3 days a week

Ways I can measure my progress toward this goal are:

keep a journal and write down the number of minutes I jog each day.

**GOAL #2:**

My goal is: to resolve personal conflicts with words instead of fists.

Activities I can do to achieve this goal are:

whenever I get angry at someone I will talk to them and explain how I feel and try to reach a solution by discussion.

Ways I can measure my progress toward this goal are:

keep a journal. For every time I get angry and talk about it, put a "smiley face." For every time I get angry and get into a fight, put a "frowny face."

**Figure 6.1** A personal responsibility project.

friendly, and inviting, and forming a partnership with local corporations to help sponsor a 'healthy kids, healthy neighborhood project'" (Stiehl 1993).

In the process of completing the project, students will inevitably experience breakdowns in the process. For example, during the project in which the students are teaching their peers to talk about their conflicts, two boys get into a fistfight. When a breakdown occurs, students will frequently blame themselves or try to find someone or something else to blame. Remind students that blaming others takes away the power to change. Help students see that breakdowns are merely opportunities to find another way to do a project. Encourage students to admit when a breakdown has occurred. Then have them restate the vision of the project, establish new goals and timelines, and implement the revised project.

The Becoming Responsible Model has been used in a variety of physical education settings with marked success in helping students take responsibility for themselves, others, and their surroundings. It helps students understand that they play an important part in creating their future by the choices they make. With careful planning, you can facilitate this process. For more information on the Becoming Responsible Model see articles by Morris (1993) and Stiehl (1993) and others in the Additional Reading List for chapter 6.

# Personal and Social Responsibility

The Teaching Personal and Social Responsibility Model was developed by Don Hellison to help students

- develop themselves despite external forces,
- live by their values,
- understand their connections with others, and
- respect the rights, feelings, and needs of others (Hellison 1995).

This model is not a behavior management plan. Instead it provides you with a conceptual framework though which to teach personally and socially responsible behaviors. Through the Teaching Personal and Social Responsibility Model, Hellison gives you a conceptual framework to present to kids through various media,

including posters, class discussions, personal discussions, written assignments, and any other means you can think of throughout the year. But you will need to integrate behavior management techniques that we describe in this book to manage student behavior within the context of this model. Even so, you can expect that increasing responsible behaviors in students will decrease irresponsible behaviors and therefore will decrease the need to use punishment techniques.

## Challenges to Teachers

Although students face more challenges today than ever before, they are receiving less guidance in making decisions. Moreover, many students lack motivation and discipline. Furthermore, increasing violence, irresponsible sex, and easy access to illegal drugs have created an unstable society. Students must learn to cope with and provide leadership for our changing world. The challenges students face create challenges for us as physical educators as well. Hellison (1985, 1995) challenges us to do the following:

- Improve class control through modeling and teaching self-control (see figure 6.2). Students need to learn self-control to avoid interfering with the rights of others.

- Help students develop personal responsibility. Expect students to take responsibility for their own learning, for making wise choices, and for developing a meaningful and personally satisfying lifestyle, including areas of personal health and recreational activities.

- Help students lead more stable lives. Personal stability requires both a long-term commitment to individually satisfying activities and a sense of identity. Social stability requires cooperation, caring, helping, and a sense of community. Teach students to make commitments to others and to recognize their needs for support and interdependence.

- Find ways to make school more effective by finding better ways to help students succeed. Make your school more personal to combat the tendency of large schools to have an impersonal atmosphere.

- Find ways to meet these needs and still maximize the time students spend participating in physical activity.

**Figure 6.2** Unless you learn to control yourself, you cannot expect to control your students.

Hellison (1995) believes that physical education is an excellent place to develop personal and social responsibility because the environment is emotional and interactive as well as attractive to students. Physical education activities provide many opportunities for students to demonstrate personal and social qualities in activities, games, group discussion, and dialogue. But to develop responsibility in students, you must be willing to shift a significant portion of decision-making responsibilities to them (Hellison 1995). He cautions, however, that changes in students' feelings, attitudes, values, and behaviors are more likely to occur if you think about, plan for, and model them.

### Values Necessary for Personal and Social Responsibility

Because applying Hellison's model is intended to help students take more responsibility for their own well-being while becoming more sensitive and responsive to the well-being of others, you must teach specific values. The two values Hellison (1995) relates to personal well-being are effort and self-direction. The two re-

lated to social well-being are respecting others' rights and feelings and caring about others. He places these values in a loose progression of developmental levels, or goals. The levels represent values and behaviors in a hierarchy so that you can build each value on the one before it. Hellison points out, though, that you may teach these values out of sequence with less emphasis on the progression.

### The Responsibility Levels

The six levels as defined by Hellison (1995) are as follows:

- Level 0: Irresponsibility
- Level 1: Respect
- Level 2: Participation
- Level 3: Self-direction
- Level 4: Caring
- Level 5: Outside the gym

### Using the Levels

The intention of the level system is to help students become aware of experiences, make

## THE RESPONSIBILITY LEVELS (HELLISON 1995)

## Level 0: Irresponsibility

Students at this level are not motivated to participate in sport and exercise activities, are undisciplined, make excuses and blame others for their behavior, and usually feel powerless to change their lives. Their behavior includes discrediting or making fun of other students' involvement as well as interrupting, intimidating, manipulating, and verbally or physically abusing other students and perhaps even the physical educator.

## Level 1: Respect

Respect involves self-control, the right to peaceful conflict resolution, and the right to be included. Self-control means the students, not you, control their own behavior so as to show respect for the rights and feelings of others without constant supervision or prompting from you. To encourage students to respect the right to peaceful conflict resolution, teach them to recognize and accept differences of opinion, to negotiate, and to resolve conflicts peacefully. In short, teach that everyone has a right to participate.

## Level 2: Participation

Here, focus on helping students participate in physical activities that can become a regular part of their lives. Under your supervision, encourage students to willingly play, accept challenges, practice motor skills, and participate in fitness activities by having them explore the issue of effort, by encouraging them to experience new activities and approaches, and by showing them how to explore their personal definitions of success. Specifically, teach students to make their best efforts to improve not only in physical endeavors but also in life skills. Finally, teach students how to determine what success means to them in a task by asking themselves questions, such as, "Is my goal to merely participate? Is it to improve? Is it to achieve a set standard? Is it to be a leader?"

## Level 3: Self-Direction

This level emphasizes the need for students to learn to take more responsibility for their choices and shows how to link these choices to their own identities. Students at this level show self-control, are involved, are able to work without direct supervision, and eventually take responsibility for their intentions and actions. They are able to identify their own needs and interests, can set their own goals, and can plan and execute their own physical education programs. For them to do so, you must first teach them to work independently on a task, which involves developing self-discipline. Then show them how to develop and implement a personal physical activity plan by establishing personal goals or purposes and related tasks for achieving them. Then teach them to evaluate whether they have achieved their goals, perhaps through having them keep written records of goals, objectives, and related tasks to refer to in the evaluation process.

## Level 4: Caring

This level deals with the need for social stability in students' lives by encouraging students to reach out beyond themselves to others by cooperating, giving support, showing concern, and helping. First, help students develop interper-

*continued*

sonal skills. Then, encourage students to act out of compassion for others. Next, guide students to act out of compassion without the expectation of extrinsic rewards. Finally, encourage students to become contributing members of the community and beyond.

## Level 5: Outside the Gym

Here, help the students see how to apply the skills acquired at the other four levels to situations outside of the physical education program: on the playground, in the classroom, after school, on the street, and at home. It is one thing for students to be able to work on these issues in the safe environment of the physical education setting, but quite another to apply them to the real world. You can coach students as to how to handle real-life situations through holding awareness talks and group meetings and by providing individual counseling. For any of these approaches, you can have students role-play hypothetical situations to practice the skills they have learned.

decisions, and reflect on their thoughts, beliefs, and behavior in a progressive manner (Hellison and Templin 1991). Use these levels as a framework to help you plan, teach, and evaluate your use of the Teaching Personal and Social Responsibility Model more effectively. Obviously, in order for students to progress through these levels, they must be spending time in activities that expose them to opportunities to develop these goals. Hellison (1995) has suggested the following six general strategies to put the levels into practice.

### Awareness talks.

The purpose of this strategy is to increase awareness of the levels. You can explain the levels, post them on the wall, refer to them when students are exhibiting behaviors consistent (or inconsistent) with a level, develop one-liners to explain the levels for large group, small group, and one-on-one meetings, or hold up the correct number of fingers to signal a level. An example of a one-liner might be, "Juan, if you are influenced by what other people tell you to do, they are in control of you" (level 1). Another method is to conduct student sharing sessions to discuss the levels. This is often referred to as "incidental teaching" because students teach each other seemingly inadvertently.

### Levels in action.

Create chances for students to experience one or more of the levels while participating in physical activity. One way to do this is through inviting students to experience different levels through direct questioning: "Who can tell me a way we could modify the game so everyone can play successfully?" (level 1); "Show me another way to kick the soccer ball so that it goes through the two cones" (level 2); "What is one goal you have for your own personal physical activity program plan?" (level 3); "Will you teach Samuel how to shoot a foul shot?" (level 4); and "Tell me how you can encourage others to do their best when you play in your neighborhood this weekend" (level 5).

In addition, you can incorporate self-paced challenges and reciprocal teaching or coaching, which permit students to work at their own rates and levels, or you can implement service projects.

### Reflection time.

Give students time during the lesson to reflect on their behavior and to determine the level at which they think they are operating. This can be accomplished through writing in a journal, completing a goal-setting checklist (see worksheet 4, appendix 2), or facilitating student discussion. Have students state the levels on which they feel they are working, giving the reasons for their evaluations. You may need to help by asking students specific questions, such as, "Did you hurt anyone?" (levels 0-1); "Did you meet your goal?" (level 3); or "Did you help anyone?" (level 4).

### Individual decision making.

Allow students to negotiate and make choices in each of the levels. In level 1, for example, you might offer the choice either to stop calling another student names or to sit out of the game for a specified period of time—the student can make his own decision. In level 2, consider allowing students to grade or evaluate themselves in selected areas. In level 3, guide students as they determine personal goals, for example, when developing an individualized fitness program. In level 4, you might let students choose a helping role, such as peer teacher or coach.

### Group meetings.

Holding group meetings allows students to share opinions, feelings, and ideas about the physical education program. Consider allowing students to offer input on a variety of topics, including making rules, how things are going, the problems that have occurred, and possible solutions to the problems. You can schedule these meetings on a regular basis or hold them as needed. Facilitate by asking students specific questions, such as, "How can we protect the rights of everyone in the class?" (level 1); "What is your opinion about the game?" (level 3); or "How can we resolve this issue?" (level 4). Questions like these are essential because they help students feel empowered, giving them ownership in the program so that they want to work toward the goals.

### Counseling time.

Some teachers shy away from any counseling as they feel that it requires specialized training and takes too much time. Yet, on an informal basis you are probably already counseling students all day long. So build time into your program for one-on-one interactions with students. This way, you can check on how each student is doing and what she is feeling. In addition, you can evaluate her level of responsibility, then encourage her to develop a plan for change. Keep in mind that it is important that you make time to counsel all students, not just those in trouble. When might you counsel during your busy day? Counseling time may be a few minutes of discussion during the warm-up or for students who really need it, it may be necessary to find a larger block of time such as recess, lunch, or after school to talk with the student.

When students constantly practice interactions with the levels in mind, they are more likely to incorporate these values into their lives. Students feel empowered and purposeful, learn to make responsible commitments, strive to develop themselves, and understand how they are related to others (Hellison and Templin 1991). The choices, however, rest with them.

A number of curriculum options are available for implementing the Teaching Personal and Social Responsibility Model. Your selection will depend on the needs of your program, the characteristics and individual needs of your students, and your teaching style (Hellison 1995). Remember, however, to incorporate behavior management strategies within the model. For specific examples of ways other teachers have used this model in their programs, see the text *Teaching Responsibility Through Physical Activity* (Hellison 1995). Through experience with this model, you will learn what works for you.

## REALITY THERAPY

In the traditional psychoanalytic approach to behavior problems, the emphasis is on determining what in the child's past contributed to the misbehavior. But in reality therapy, Glasser (1975) looks at the present (the "reality" of the situation), claiming that it is what a person does to work out problems in the present that matters. This technique is another effective way to deal with discipline problems in a nonpunitive way while teaching students to be responsible for their own behavior. It allows students to maintain their own integrity and enhance their senses of self-worth by evaluating their own behavior and developing their own plans to improve.

Although this theory was first used in clinical settings, Glasser later extended it to the classroom. He believed that by using his framework, teachers, including physical educators, could help students make better decisions about their behavior in school. Indeed, you can integrate Glasser's ideas into your physical education program.

### Basis of Misbehavior

According to Glasser, misbehavior is a student's attempt to fulfill unmet needs. If the needs are fulfilled, the behavior problems disappear. When the needs are not successfully fulfilled, the person misbehaves and "denies the reality of the world around [him]" (Glasser 1975). Reality therapy is an attempt to help someone accept the real world and to fulfill his needs in ways that work in the real world.

## SAMPLE CLASS FORMAT

The following is an example of a class format using Hellison's strategies:

At the beginning of the class or during the warm-up, you can use awareness talks with the class or individual students to introduce the basic concepts of the levels, discussing their relevance to the upcoming lesson.

During the day's lesson, you can have the students experience the levels in action by allowing them to practice individual decision making in the warm-up, drills, games, and cool-down. For example, you might have them play inclusion games, such as following the all-touch rule for a six-person soccer game, or you might allow students to decide what drills they want to participate in to improve their soccer skills. Another way to provide experiences through which students may work toward personal goals is to encourage students to develop their own fitness routines and perform them at their own paces. In addition, consider allowing students to serve as peer tutors to give them experience evaluating themselves and others. When appropriate, you can hold group meetings so that students have an appropriate forum through which they may respond to issues that may arise. For example, if students are disgruntled about an umpire's call in a softball game, a group meeting may allow students to discuss their feelings about the call instead of acting unsportsmanlike.

During the last five minutes of the class, give students time to reflect on and share their feelings and thoughts in a group meeting. Finally, you can have older students write their experiences in a journal, relating the levels to the day's activities.

In summary, the Teaching Personal and Social Responsibility Model "requires physical educators to be confident enough in their abilities to be open to incorporating parts of the model in their programs if it makes sense to do so, vulnerable enough to share problems with students, reflective enough to analyze their own style, setting, and students, and creative enough to modify and change the model as needed" (Hellison 1985, 1995, p. 163). Checklists 14 and 15 in appendix 1, "Promoting Personal Responsibility" and "Strategies for Putting Hellison's Levels Into Practice," provide helpful forums for assessing your teaching of personal responsibility.

## Physiological and Psychological Needs

All humans have the same physiological and psychological needs. The physiological needs, or survival needs, are food, warmth, and rest. The two basic psychological needs are the need to love and be loved and the need to feel worthwhile to self and others. The basis of reality therapy is helping the person fulfill these psychological needs.

The need to love and be loved is incredibly strong in humans. It is the forming of human connections that motivates most of our behavior. It is the desire for the approval of the teacher or their peers that makes students behave the way they do. As an educator, you can capitalize on these needs and channel student behaviors into socially appropriate ones.

Standards, values, and right and wrong behaviors are all intimately related to the fulfillment of our need for self-worth. To feel worthwhile, we must maintain a satisfactory standard of behavior. We must learn to evaluate our own behavior, to credit ourselves for good behavior, and to improve our behavior when it is below standard. Drawing from these two basic psychological needs, Glasser (1977) has developed a 10-step approach, based on his Reality Therapy Model. This approach deals with discipline problems in a nonpunitive way, maintaining the integrity of the students and making them responsible for developing strategies for improving their own behavior.

Through this approach, you can teach students to own their behavior, plan a way to change it, and evaluate it. Allowing students to take control of a situation and create a positive learning experience from it can enhance the sense of self-worth, but more punitive approaches can decrease the sense of self-worth.

## Glasser's 10-Step Approach

1. Select a student who is an ongoing discipline problem with whom you are willing to work. Then try to determine what behavior management methods you are currently using when the student is disruptive. Write these down.

2. Analyze these methods to decide if they are working. Chances are they are not if the student is still a discipline problem. Commit to not using these methods anymore.

3. Build a better personal relationship with the student. Become involved with the student so she can begin to face reality and see how her behavior is unrealistic. Strive for an honest relationship in which the student—perhaps for the first time in her life—realizes that someone cares enough about her not only to accept her but also to help her fulfill her needs in the real world. You can do this by giving special attention to the student: providing extra encouragement, showing concern, talking with the student about her interests, and so on. For example, when the student comes into the gym, ask her how her day is going. Then ask if she would like to help you set up equipment for the soccer drills you are going to do today. Then talk to her while you are setting up the equipment together.

4. When the student disrupts the class, have a conference with her. Emphasize behavior, not feelings; refer to present behavior, avoiding references to the past. Keep in mind that nothing that happened in the past, no matter how it may have affected the person then or now, will make any difference once she learns to fulfill her needs in the present. Focus the student's attention on the disruptive behavior by having her describe it. This gets her to think about the behavior and helps her own up to what she's done. Reject the unacceptable behavior but accept the student and stay involved with her. When the student describes the behavior accurately, say to her, "Disrupting the class is unacceptable, please stop."

5. If the disruptive behavior persists, have another conference with her. During the conference, do not discuss excuses. Ask the student what she was doing when the problem started. For example, if the student got into a fight after being fouled during a basketball game in class, ask her to describe her reaction to being fouled. Have the student evaluate her behavior, then have her state whether the behavior is against the rules or recognized expectations (see also chapter 2). Next, ask her to make her own decision to do something different if the situation comes up again in the future. Finally, have the student tell you what she should be doing instead of the problem behavior. For example, the student may make a plan to take three deep breaths when she feels frustrated or angry after getting fouled. You may need to offer your own input when first using this method with a student, but gradually the ideas will be more student-generated.

6. If the behavior still persists, have another conference. This time, ask the student to come up with a written plan to follow the rules. This plan must be a way for the student to fulfill her needs within the confines of reality and to move toward more responsible behavior. It should be short-term, specific, and simple. The more input the student has, the more likely the plan will work. At the end of the planning conference, tell the student that if the behavior persists, you will have to put her in time-out.

7. If the student continues to misbehave, place her in time-out during class. Time-out in this situation involves having the student sit on the bleachers and develop a new written plan of how she is going to follow the rules. Once she comes up with a plan you can approve, she must make a commitment to follow it by verbally committing and signing it.

8. If the student continues to disrupt, she must go to an in-school suspension with the principal or a counselor or, if one exists, go to a supervised in-school suspension room. Make sure that all adults communicate to the student that she is wanted in school and in the physical education class, but in order to return to class, she must follow the rules. As soon as the student can develop a workable plan to follow the rules, whether it takes her one hour or two months, she can return to class.

9. If the student still misbehaves, ask the parents to take her home. Explain that she is

welcome back when she can convince you and the principal that she can follow the rules. Please note that individual school or district policies may override your right to suspend a student. We encourage you to examine your school's policy before attempting this step.

10. Students who will not commit to and follow the rules should be expelled from school. They should be referred to community agencies for further help. Keep the door open for the student if she ever commits to following the rules and can convince you that she can do it. Of course, make sure that you are aware of your school's policy on expulsion before employing this step.

After trying Glasser's 10-step approach for awhile, refer to checklist 16 in appendix 1, "Applying Glasser's 10-Step Approach to Reality Therapy," to see how you're doing.

## Making the School Attractive

Glasser's 10-step approach will only work if the school is a place in which students want to be. According to Glasser (1992), a school that students feel is a "good place" is a warm, comfortable, noncoercive environment in which people communicate with each other without fear of criticism or punishment. Yelling, sarcasm, and denigration are not used. It is a place where people laugh because they are happy to be involved with caring people engaged in relevant work; one where positive communication is practiced. Refer often to chapter 1 when striving to develop a more positive learning environment.

In order to facilitate a counseling-teaching environment, Glasser (1992) suggests explaining to the students that you will not use threats, coercion, or severe forms of punishment. You will, however, confront all students who behave inappropriately. Of course, the ideal situation is for you and your students to talk maturely about your feelings and discuss solutions to problems whenever they occur. But it is unrealistic to think that by simply displaying a poster, you'll create this ideal situation. In reality in most classrooms today, at least some students would abuse the privilege of asking for class discussion, so you will probably have to modify the poster statement to prevent such abuses, taking into account the behaviors and maturity levels of the students in your classes. Yet, the poster as described by Glasser is a good model for which to strive.

## THE TALKING BENCH

An easy-to-use technique that helps to increase communication skills and resolve conflict is the "talking bench" (Horrocks 1978). This method is an attempt to provide opportunities for students to resolve their own conflicts in the physical education setting. To use this method, you tell the students who are in conflict that the causes of conflicts are misunderstandings and mistakes. Then you tell students to sit on the talking bench and discuss the situation with each other until they have both agreed on the reason for the conflict and have apologized to each other. This method increases interpersonal communication and understanding. Students are motivated to resolve the conflict because they want to return to the class activity. It is important, however, for you to determine whether the students are really understanding the causes of the conflict or whether they are merely saying that they have resolved the conflict because they want to return to the activity. One method is to have the students report to you before they resume the class activity. Ask the students questions such as the following:

## POSTER

One technique to help you implement Glasser's approach is to have the students make a poster that includes the following ideas:

"In our class, if anyone, including the physical educator, is upset or has any problem at all, we will talk it over and try to solve the problem. In solving the problem, we will never hurt or criticize anyone. We will always be willing to participate in a whole-class discussion, and anyone can ask for a class discussion at any time" (Glasser 1992, p. 273).

- Did you determine how the conflict started? How?
- Was the conflict started by a misunderstanding?
- Was the argument caused by a misjudgment or a mistake that one or both of you made?
- Ali, did you apologize to Pedro?
- Pedro, do you accept this apology?
- Pedro, did you apologize to Ali?
- Ali, do you accept this apology?
- Do both of you feel that the argument is finished?
- What could you do to prevent this conflict from happening in the future?

If you are not convinced that the students are sincere in their resolution of the conflict, send them back to the talking bench to resume discussing their differences of opinion. Horrocks (1978) believes that resolution of conflicts are more readily accepted when arrived at by students rather than by a teacher.

Now let's look at a specific situation. During a basketball game Brent and Daryl were arguing over whether Daryl fouled Brent when he was shooting a basket. Ms. Perez, their physical educator, told the two boys to sit on the bleachers (the talking bench) and discuss the misunderstanding (see figure 6.3). When a solution was agreed on by both parties, they reported to Ms. Perez. She approved of their solution and praised them for their conflict resolution skills. Then she sent them both back into the game.

## SELF-EVALUATION

Self-evaluation is a process through which the student compares his behavior to a set of criteria and then makes a judgment as to whether the behavior meets the criteria or not. You reinforce the student when the behavior meets the criteria. Self-evaluation systems have been successful in modifying a wide range of behaviors in a variety of settings from preschool through high school (Rhode, Morgan, and

**Figure 6.3** The "talking bench" technique encourages students to communicate to resolve conflict.

Young 1983; Sainato et al. 1990; Smith et al. 1988).

Self-evaluation systems rely on the concepts of modeling, self-regulation, and reflective thinking (Bos and Vaughn 1991). To use such systems with secondary level students, describe and even demonstrate the target behavior. For example, the target behavior may be "encouraging others to play cooperatively." When playing a game with the students, play on team A alongside the students. When Jessie on team B makes a soccer goal by kicking the ball through your legs and into the goal, give her a high-five and say, "Well done, nice goal!" Encourage students to model the target behavior and reinforce them for the appropriate behavior. Tommy, who is very competitive and gets into fights when someone scores on him, will see you model the appropriate behavior and will monitor his own performance of the target behavior. Moreover, he will become more aware that the other students are observing his behavior and evaluating his performance. This pressures him to perform the target behavior. At the end of a specified period of time, have Tommy and the rest of the class reflect on their behavior, evaluating their performances for that time period in regard to the target behavior.

Self-evaluation methods can be used with elementary students, too. Start by discussing behaviors that display good sportsmanship, such as clapping for others when they make a goal or saying "Good try" when another student puts forth effort. Then ask the students at the end of class to each name one behavior they did today that showed good sportsmanship. Reinforce each student for the appropriate behavior. If the students know that they might be asked to give an example at the end of class, they are more likely to try to perform an appropriate behavior so they can respond to your query. See checklist 17 in appendix 1, "Using the Self-Evaluation Approach," to help you monitor your use of the self-evaluation approach.

You can use this method individually, giving one student a target behavior to monitor and evaluate for herself. You can also use this method with a group of students, divided into teams. At the end of a specific time, each team negotiates among themselves to determine its own rating. Then offer your own rating of the team for comparison. Reinforce each team, based on the team's behavior and accuracy in

rating their behavior. (See chapter 4 for a discussion of group contingencies.)

According to Salend, Whittaker, and Reeder (1993), group evaluation methods give students opportunities to achieve a positive interdependence by creating a mutual goal relating to their behavior and fostering their dependence on each other to earn the reward, by helping them learn how their behavior can contribute to earning a reward for the group, and by teaching them how to negotiate with each other to reach agreement on the group rating.

Use group evaluation in physical education by dividing the class into small groups. Then guide each group in developing goals. One method of doing this is to challenge the students to "play the game without an unkind word being said to other students" or to "perform a practice soccer drill in which they encourage other students to kick the ball into the goal." When students are exhibiting the target behavior, reinforce them. When they look like they may want to say an unkind word to another student, you may give a physical cue such as a finger to the lips. At the end of the period, have each group evaluate their behavior to determine if they achieved the goal. If so, reinforce the behavior.

## SUMMARY

The psychodynamic approach is based on the understanding of the psychological causes of student behavior. To use this approach, work to develop a learning environment that is safe and nurturing, to understand students' feelings and behaviors, to teach personal responsibility, to encourage the students to learn independently, and to help students understand that behavioral limits are to protect them. There are a number of models that use the psychodynamic approach and are particularly effective in a physical education setting. These models include Morris and Stiehl's Becoming Responsible Model, Hellison's Teaching Personal and Social Responsibility Model, and Glasser's Reality Therapy Model. Refer often to our descriptions and practical examples of how to use these methods in physical education as you design your own approach. In addition, study the counseling methods and communication skills we have described to help you communicate more effectively with your students. Depending on the level of maturity of the students in your class, their age, and the class size, you may need to modify these techniques to meet your individual behavior management needs. Finally, use checklists 14, 15, 16, and 17 in appendix 1 to review the concepts we have covered.

## REVIEW: VIGNETTE APPLICATION EXERCISES

For each of the vignettes on page x, select two behavior management methods described in this chapter and discuss in detail how you would implement each of the methods to manage the inappropriate behavior. Do not use the same method more than once. Then review the sample answers below. Remember, these are merely samples; many creative ways exist to solve the problems using the methods we have described in this chapter.

1. Let's take another look at Hector, our overactive third grader, in light of the information we've discussed in this chapter.

Discuss the problems with Hector, telling him that you are concerned about his behavior. Focus on the behaviors one at a time, trying to get Hector to take responsibility for his behavior by asking questions pertaining to levels 1 through 3 of the Personal and Social Responsibility Model such as the following:

- Why do you think you have trouble listening quietly while others are talking?

- Why do you think your not listening quietly while others are talking might concern me?

- Why might it be important for you to learn how to listen quietly while others are talking?

Then give him specific examples of when he did not listen while others were talking and ask him what he could do in the future to change this. Then encourage him to set a goal to change this behavior, such as listen while others are talking 7 out of 10 times (70 percent). Set up a self-evaluation chart for him in which he puts a "+" each time he listened quietly when others were talking and a "−" each time he did not listen. Establish a reinforcer that he wants to earn when he achieves his goal and a punishment for if he does not. The punishment could be response cost in nature in which Hector might lose points toward being able to do an activity that he likes to do. On Fridays, meet with him and evaluate his progress together. If he listened quietly 70 percent of the time, give him the reinforcer; if he did not, give him the punishment.

Follow the same procedure for the other three behaviors: not following directions, not waiting his turn calmly, and running when he should walk. If necessary, focus on only one behavior a week until Hector understands what behaviors you expect from him.

2. Remember Ashante and Jim who are fighting over Shannon in the locker room after class? The following is one of the ways you could apply this chapter's ideas.

Tell the boys to stop fighting. If they do not stop, use physical restraint on the one who is the aggressor at the time. Hold him securely, talking to him gently until he calms down. Then enforce your school's policy regarding detention or suspension for fighting. When the boys are ready to return to your class, discuss the fight privately with them.

If one or both of the boys blames the other, for example, if Ashante says, "Jim makes me mad," explain to Ashante that he needs to take responsibility for his own feelings. Say, "You're choosing to be mad at Jim." Then have him restate his feelings with a sentence such as, "I choose to be mad at Jim."

*continued*

Using Hellison's Personal and Social Responsibility Model, discuss level 1 with the boys. Remind them that in level 1, students learn to control their own behavior to respect the rights and feelings of others. They also learn to recognize differences of opinion, to negotiate, and to resolve conflicts peacefully. Discuss ways that they respect each other's feelings about this issue. Then, ask the boys to openly and honestly communicate their feelings about the other's behaviors in an attempt to reach a mutual understanding. Finally, explore constructive ways to resolve the problem. Check with the boys every day or so to see how things are going in regard to this situation.

3. Let's look again at Jill and Molly's problem in light of Hellison's model. Begin once again by discussing the situation with Jill and Molly, asking them why they have not been participating in physical education class. If they say that physical education is not fun, ask them to tell you what it is that they do not like about the class and why. Then ask them what types of activities they would like to do in class. Try to include some of those activities in the curriculum. Ask them to be class leaders and teach activities to the class. Make sure that you reinforce them when they do participate and when they do a good job teaching other students. Set up weekly meetings with Jill and Molly to discuss their feelings about the class and any other ways to continually make it a challenging and enjoyable experience for them.

## CHAPTER 7

# Nontraditional Behavior Management Methods

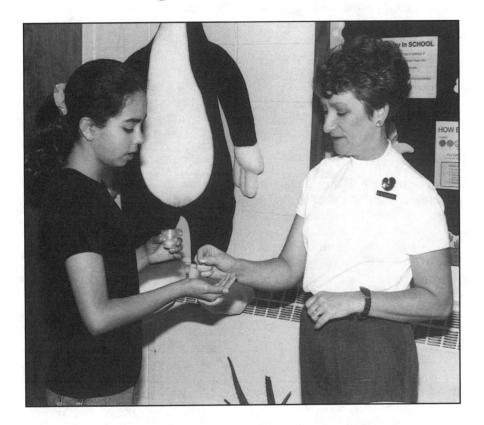

Frank's middle school teachers, the school counselor, and parents are frustrated with his behavior in class. For at least the past three years and especially the past four months, he has been inattentive, impulsive, and even aggressive. Not only has his behavior made it difficult for him to learn, it has taken away from his classmates' learning. Frank's physical educator has created a highly structured learning environment and has tried various behavior management methods, such as contracts and token economies. In addition, Frank is in private family counseling with his parents and group counseling in school. Unfortunately, however, the counseling does not seem to be helping him behave and perform better.

Frank's parents want him to participate in classes with his friends but have accepted the fact that if his behavior does not improve, he will need to be placed in a special class. They are considering other approaches, such as relaxation training, medication, and even diet management.

# WHEN ALL ELSE FAILS

When traditional behavior management methods such as those we have already discussed in this book fail to remove or reduce a problem, consider adding nontraditional methods. The nontraditional approaches we'll discuss in this chapter are based on the premise that behavior is not merely environmental but is often related to biological variables—such as genetic abnormalities, neurological impairments, chemical imbalances, diet, and medication—and/or tension, anxiety, and overactivity. Many times these behaviors are related. We'll examine other approaches used successfully in physical education and sport settings that you can use to manage behavior, particularly behavior related to stress, to medical conditions or specific medications, or to nutritional deficiencies or sensitivities. But we can only give you an overview of these methods, so if you have not been trained to use these methods effectively, consider attending a workshop related to the specific method in order to learn more. Perhaps you can ask your district to provide such a workshop for the many teachers in all fields who will surely be interested. In addition, learn to recognize when a problem is too big for you to solve alone. Don't hesitate to reach out to other professionals, such as the school psychologist, a dietitian, a physician, or a special educator, to get the help you need to help especially needy or difficult students.

We are not recommending that you act as a physician. You need to discuss medications in depth with a physician and consult with school administrators regarding district policies concerning prescribed medication. In addition, keep in mind that medications should be considered as the last resort and are generally used in combination with other interventions, most notably behavior modification or the behavioral approach discussed in chapters 3, 4, and 5. Ultimately, the primary purpose of medication should be to make other interventions more effective.

# DEALING WITH STRESS-RELATED MISBEHAVIORS

We can define stress in children as an anxiety-inducing inability to effectively respond to environmental demands. In other words, when the equation between what is expected of the child and what the child feels she can produce is out of balance, the child feels stressed.

Stress can impact performance. Some factors that have been reported to cause stress and anxiety in students are death of a close family member, high parental or teacher demands, divorce or separation of parents, peer conflicts, personal injury or illness, health problems of a family member, injury to self, grades, being yelled at, being blamed unnecessarily, and changing schools (Gipson, Lowe, and McKenzie 1994).

Some approaches that may help reduce stress are relaxation training, medication, and nutrition. In the following sections, we'll look closely at each of these approaches.

## Relaxation Training

Today's intense living pace can lead to potentially stressful situations. This stress may be positive and improve performance or negative and disrupt performance. Very few students are aware of mounting tension or overstimulation within themselves and still fewer know how to calm down deliberately and relax at the appropriate times.

A certain amount of tension is necessary for action and productivity, but excess tension hinders successful living, obstructing peak performance. This tension is not just limited to the physical contraction of muscles, it also involves the mind. Indeed, most often, tension is mental in origin but manifests itself physically. For example, the cardiorespiratory, muscular, and neurological systems are affected by stress (Nichols 1994; Pangrazi and Dauer 1995). Moreover, for over 20 years, we have known that stressful life events can increase the risk of disorders ranging from common health complaints, such as hypertension, backaches, chest pain, indigestion, insomnia, dizziness, and headaches, to heart disease (Pangrazi and Dauer 1995).

### Benefits of Relaxation Training

Relaxation training can have a calming effect on children that may extend throughout the school day (Nichols 1994). Simply put, the training involves helping students to deal with stress in a socially acceptable manner. Specifically, relaxation training teaches students to interpret events, situations, and interpersonal relationships. Learning how to relax under stressful circumstances is a vital life skill as well.

Many people tend to think of relaxation training as applying only to the athletic realm. We know, for example, that it is essential for athletes to learn to relax to regulate responses to the pressure of competition, and in turn, avoid any detrimental effects on performance. "Some hold that relaxation is not something that athletes have the time or desire to engage in. Most sport psychologists and elite athletes, however, believe that learning how to hang loose allows athletes to take a giant step toward optimal enjoyment and performance" (McGill 1993, p. 25). The same is true for the students in your physical education classes.

Relaxation training allows both students and athletes to become more aware of their bodies, thereby gaining a sense of control over basic physiological functions, such as breathing and heart rate. Beyond the physical, relaxation training helps the individual control anxiety to decrease the following negative influences on performance:

- Muscular tension, causing decreased muscular coordination
- Narrowed and internal focus of attention when a broad visual scan is needed in most competitive environments
- Increased metabolic rate, which wastes energy resources

The use of relaxation training to reduce stress and anxiety has been shown to improve pain tolerance, reduces the likelihood of injury, and strengthens the immune system (Anshel 1991). Relaxation training may also improve an athlete's mental approach to competition indefinitely if used prudently and correctly, that is, if tailored to the individual's needs (Anshel 1991). For example, not all athletes have the same psychological needs. Moreover, some degree of stress is desirable since being too relaxed will negatively impact performances as much as being too tense. As a general rule, an athlete should not practice relaxation training within 30 minutes of most types of sporting events. Instead, once the athlete has learned the skills, she should use relaxation training as a rejuvenating 5- to 10-minute break during practice to help increase sensitivity to her body, reduce arousal, and facilitate both recovery and the clearing of the mind (Hardy and

Croce 1990). For example, Davis (1991) reported that a varsity football and a swim team who practiced relaxation training during team workouts experienced a 33 percent reduction of tension for football players and 52 percent for swimmers, based on number of injuries each session throughout the respective seasons. The next year, however, the new football coach chose not to include the psychological component in his team's practices. While a cause and effect relationship could not be determined, it is interesting to note that the number of severe injuries increased among the players on this team.

Applying relaxation training in the physical education setting may reduce both behavior management incidents and injuries. Indeed, physical education is the perfect curriculum area through which to address this topic not only to enhance student performance in physical education but also to help them cope with stress in society. At any rate, more relaxed students are more focused, calm, and cooperative. Next, we'll examine specific ways you can apply this method to physical education settings and significantly impact students' daily lives at the same time.

### Progressive Relaxation

Progressive relaxation is a stress-reducing technique you can teach as a short unit in the physical education curriculum. Then, you can revisit it periodically to ensure students remember how to relax. Specifically, progressive relaxation is a technique in which different muscle groups are first tensed and then relaxed while you concentrate on the sensations of muscular tension. During the lesson, give a signal for the students to tense a particular muscle group and then instantly relax it. Within five lessons, this approach generally helps students recognize the difference between tension and relaxation. The original progression muscular relaxation techniques (Jacobson 1974) take 30 to 45 minutes to complete, but you can use one of several 15-minute versions at the beginning or end of class. We recommend the end of class, as many classroom teachers appreciate students coming to their classes calmer after physical education class (Smith and Momack 1987). After introducing students to the 15-minute relaxation routine, you may wish to reduce it to a 5-minute routine to save class time. Encourage students to practice a relaxation routine at home as well.

## Exercises

In this section, we'll discuss various types of progressive relaxation exercises appropriate for students at the elementary through secondary school levels. First, however, consider the following general session-starting guidelines:

1. Say to students, "Loosen tight clothes, lie in a comfortable position, feet slightly apart (approximately six inches) and flat on the floor, knees apart, and head resting in a comfortable position." Make sure the temperature is comfortable and lights are lowered with adequate space for each student to do the relaxation exercises without distractions from others.

2. Encourage students to allow any distracting thoughts or sounds to flow into the brain and then tune them out.

3. Say, "Begin with your eyes open, but when I signal you (after 10 minutes), allow your eyes to slowly close to a count of five."

4. Continue, "Breathe through your nose, placing one hand on your chest and one hand on your stomach to feel the rise and fall of your breathing."

5. If necessary, use reinforcers to teach relaxation. Depending on the student, the reinforcers could range from tangible to social reinforcers. Generally praise is sufficient.

6. When students are having a problem tensing and relaxing various parts of the head and face because they cannot see what they are doing, have them practice in front of a mirror.

7. Get written physician consent for students with high blood pressure to participate in relaxation training exercises that involve tightening muscles, because isometric exercises such as these may increase blood pressure. You could have these students do only the more specific relaxation exercises that follow the session-starting activities.

8. Observe to see if your students are relaxing. Look for tension as evidenced by wrinkles on the forehead area, sweating, fast heartbeat, crossed legs, grinding teeth, and flushed face. If possible students can wear a heart rate monitor.

9. Have students monitor their progress in writing. See worksheet 5 in appendix 2, "Relaxation Training Log Sheet," for an example of a performance record sheet. If you are interested in how well your students feel they have performed, instead of using Xs, ask them to tell you how well they believed they relaxed by rating themselves on a scale of one to five: The higher the number, the more relaxed they believed they became.

## ELEMENTARY LEVEL EXERCISES

1. Knees to head: Say, "While lying on your back, gently pull both your knees to your chest. Now pull your head up, then gently rock back and forth from your shoulders to your buttocks, pretending to be a rocking chair."

2. Hands and arms: Say, "Pretend there is a wet sponge in your left hand and try to squeeze the water from it as hard as you can. Drop the arm and relax. Do this two or three times and then repeat with the right hand."

3. Arms and shoulders: Say, "While lying on your back, pretend you are a lazy cat and stretch your arms straight up to the ceiling. Next raise them high above your head along the floor. Stretch even higher. Then drop your arms back to your side. Then stretch again."

4. Shoulders and neck: Say, "Pretend you are a turtle sitting on a rock by a quiet pond, relaxing in the warm sun. An alligator passes by so you as a turtle pull your shoulders up to your ears and push your head into the shell house. The alligator passes, so you can come out and feel the sunshine again." Repeat two or three times.

5. Jaw: Say, "Pretend you are chewing a large bubble gum jawbreaker. It is very hard to chew. You must use your neck muscles because the gum is so hard. Now relax." Repeat.

6. Hips: Say, "Make large circles with yours hips as if using a hula hoop, then slowly make the circles smaller. Next slowly raise your arms overhead and then back to your sides."

7. Legs and feet: Say, "Pretend you are walking across a swamp in your bare feet with the mud squishing between your toes. Many times you will have to push hard with your legs. Now step out of the swamp and relax your feet and toes." Repeat.

8. Face and nose: Say, "Pretend a large insects lands on your nose. Try to get the insect off your nose without the use of hands. Try to wrinkle up your nose as many times as possible. Now relax." Repeat.

9. Stomach: Say, "Pretend a baby elephant is walking through the grass and stumbles right where you are resting on the ground. Get ready, make your stomach hard—tighten up! The elephant regains his balance and begins to move away. Oh no, he is coming back—get ready to tighten up!" Repeat.

## SECONDARY LEVEL EXERCISES

Offer the following 20-minute series of exercises in sequence to secondary level students. Have students lie on their backs in a quiet environment. Have students hold (tighten) each exercise for 5 to 10 seconds, then relax for a 15-second rest period before doing the next exercise.

Emphasize that students should keep their breathing slow and rhythmical, never held while performing the exercises (Pankau 1980).

Have students tighten and relax the muscles of the body in the following order:

1. Eyes, nose, and mouth
2. Neck
3. Chest and shoulders
4. Upper and middle back
5. Upper arms, lower arms, and hands
6. Stomach and lower back
7. Hips
8. Upper legs and knees
9. Feet and toes

### Use of Music in Relaxation Training

You may wish to introduce music into the relaxation training program after students can adequately perform the relaxation activities. Instrumental music with strong and simple melody lines, whether classical or contemporary, works well because students find it easier to relax when they are not distracted by the words. Specific pieces of music that have a calming effect have been identified by Reif (1993), including Debussy's "Clair de Lune" and Beethoven's "Fur Elise."

### Visual Imagery in Relaxation Training

If desired, you can incorporate visual imagery with progressive relaxation training or use it separately. As with relaxation training, have students lie down with their eyes closed in a comfortable position. When they are comfortable, suggest one visual image at a time, allowing students ample time to create their own mental pictures (see figure 7.1). Make sure that each image you choose is appropriate for your students' maturity and developmental levels. To help you get started, tell students to pretend to be one of the following:

1. A leaf floating down to the ground
2. An ice cube on the pavement, slowly melting as the sun comes up and gets hotter
3. A winged animal soaring above the Earth
4. Floating on a safe and comfortable cloud
5. Traveling on a caterpillar that changes into a butterfly that flies about
6. A rag doll, slowly falling to the floor
7. A slowly melting ice cream cone on a hot summer day

You can gain more knowledge and training regarding the use of the technique by requesting information and assistance from your local school counselors and psychologists.

**Figure 7.1** Visual imagery can be incorporated into progressive relaxation training.

## VISUAL IMAGERY EXAMPLES

Submarine on the go: Ask students to imagine they are in a miniature submarine that can trowel through the blood vessels in the heart. Have them explore, taking refreshing oxygen to each part of the body, thinking about how feelings are expressed by each body part, for example, the arms move gracefully, the eyes open widely with excitement, and the face smiles with happiness.

Clock freeze: Have your students watch a large clock with a second hand. Ask them to "freeze" the body until the second hand moves from _____ to _____. Then have them relax. Vary the lengths of tension and relaxation.

Activity freeze: Have your students perform a physical activity, such as bouncing a ball, doing jumping jacks, or walking. Tell them to freeze at random and stand like a statue for four to five seconds.

Feather float: Drop a feather and have students pretend they are also a feather. Encourage them to see how slowly they can float like a feather to the floor.

Simon says: Have students perform slow movements when Simon says.

Skunk walk: Have students crawl very slowly along the floor. Say, "If you want to be the skunk's friend, you cannot get to close to him, and you don't want to scare him. So move very, very slowly."

Mirror: Have students mirror each of your slow, deliberate movements. Vary the speed slightly.

## ALLAYING FEARS THROUGH VISUAL IMAGERY RELAXATION

Ask students to visualize a scene with stimuli that is unpleasant to them, such as heights or physical contact, while totally relaxed and close to something pleasing (e.g., ocean, mountain breeze). Incorporate steps from mild to severe anxiety-producing situations. For instance, if a student is afraid of climbing a rope, he could imagine himself doing the following tasks:

1. Standing next to the rope
2. Holding onto the rope
3. Hanging onto the rope, with his feet about 2 feet above mat, while you are standing next to him
4. Climbing 4 feet above the mat
5. Climbing 4 feet above the mat without assistance
6. Climbing 10 feet above the mat with your assistance
7. Climbing 10 feet above the mat without your assistance
8. Climbing 15 feet without assistance
9. Climbing 20 feet to the top with assistance
10. Climbing to the top without assistance

Don't expect to accomplish all the steps in a sequence in one session; gradually work up to the ultimate goal over time as the student feels ready. This empowers the student to grow emotionally and mentally at his own pace, making his accomplishments truly his, not yours.

# DISABILITIES, BEHAVIOR, AND MEDICATION

Numerous disabilities are associated with inappropriate behavior, including emotional disturbance, attention deficit disorder (ADD), attention deficit hyperactivity disorder (ADHD), traumatic brain injury, autism, and prenatal exposure to crack cocaine. In many cases, a student with such a disability may be on medication to help manage her behavior.

## Disabilities That May Affect Behavior

In the following sections, we'll briefly describe each of several disabilities, then offer information about common medications used to manage behavior associated with each disability. In addition to studying this information, we encourage you to study the student's file and talk to his other teachers as well as his parents to better understand his problems and needs. Most if not all such students will be on an Individualized Education Program (IEP), which should contain valuable information about each student's needs and state how the school must serve those special needs. Ask and expect to participate in periodic reviews of such students' IEPs: As a physical educator, you bring a unique perspective to the review process. If such a student is not already on an IEP, a referral can be made to have the student tested.

### Emotional Problems

Students with emotional problems represent the fourth largest group of children and youth receiving some type of special education services. These students exhibit one or more of the following characteristics over a long period of time, adversely affecting their school performance: "(a) An inability to learn that cannot be explained by intellectual, sensory, or health factors, (b) an inability to build or maintain satisfactory interpersonal relationships with peers and teachers, (c) inappropriate types of behavior or feelings under normal circumstances, (d) a general pervasive mood of unhappiness or depression, or (e) a tendency to develop physical symptoms or fears associated with personal or school problems" (Federal Register 1992, p. 44802).

While not all students with this disability exhibit all these characteristics, generally they are hyperactive, easily distracted, or impulsive—or all three. Some may steal, abuse alcohol or drugs, lie, or be withdrawn. Depending on the cause of the emotional problem, you can use numerous methods within the behavioral and psychodynamic approaches that we have discussed so far in this book (Loovis 1995). If the cause is considered to be a neurological dysfunction, however, a physician may prescribe medication. To help you become more familiar with the most commonly prescribed medications, see table 7.1, which lists medications and the behaviors they are used to alleviate. Then refer to this table when examining student records so that you can ask more specific questions when investigating student problems.

### Attention Deficit Disorder

Attention deficit disorder (ADD) and attention deficit hyperactivity disorder (ADHD) are other conditions that are associated with behavior disorders. A student with ADD is easily distracted by extraneous stimuli and has difficulty listening and following directions, completing a task, concentrating, and working alone (Craft 1995). A student with ADHD may display these characteristics as well as many others associated with hyperactivity, such as a high activity level, impulsivity, problems transitioning from one activity to the next, aggressiveness, social immaturity, low self-esteem, and low frustration level.

Worksheet 6 in appendix 2, "Behavioral Checklist for Students With ADD and ADHD" provides a checklist of possible characteristics of students with ADD as well as additional behaviors associated with hyperactivity (ADHD). Use this quick checklist to help identify a student who may either have one of these two conditions or who may have nutritional deficiencies or food allergies. Share blank copies of worksheet 6 with the child's other teachers and perhaps his parents to get their input as well. While you should be careful not to make a final "diagnosis," labeling a student, you can use the results of your investigation to suggest possible courses of action and school resources to tap into, such as the school counselor, psychologist, special educator, dietitian, or diagnostician.

It is estimated that from 3 to 10 percent of the school-aged population have one of these two conditions. ADHD is far more common in boys than girls, whereas, girls are more likely to have ADD. The same causes as of emotional disorders have been reported. Many experts believe that primarily general behavior modification techniques should be used to manage the behavior of such students (see chapters 3 through 5). In some cases, individual or group counseling and several other psychodynamic approaches have been applied (see chapter 6). Sometimes relaxation training is an effective approach to help children with learning disabilities and hyperactivity that may, in turn, facilitate performance of motor tasks by helping students focus their full attention on the task (Brandon, Eason, and Smith 1986). Relaxation training may also help students who struggle in school due to complications or trauma experienced in pregnancy, prenatal alcohol or drug exposure, or diet-related problems (Reif 1993). But if a student's problems have a neurological basis, she is generally given some form of drug therapy, based on the most obvious problems she displays.

### Traumatic Brain Injury

So far we have discussed how congenital or degenerative conditions affect behavior. These are conditions a student may be born with. In contrast, traumatic brain injury refers to a permanent injury caused by an external physical force leading to a concussion, contusion, or hemorrhage. Each year, 700,000 Americans are hospitalized for head injuries; 10 percent suffer severe injuries and are left with permanent, life-altering disabilities (Tucker and Colson 1992). Males are twice as likely as females to suffer a traumatic brain injury with the highest incidence rate among young men 15 to 23 years of age (Porretta 1995). Vehicle accidents, assaults, or falls are the most common causes of such injuries.

Many physical problems are associated with this injury, including sensory and motor impairments, seizure disorders, and poor gait coordination. In numerous instances, psychosocial and behavioral deficiencies are present right after injury but change in nature over time. The most prominent problems are anxiety, overestimation of abilities, depression, irritability, and psychomotor restlessness.

Most people with traumatic brain injuries recover without the aid of drugs. Others, however, must have drug therapy most often to manage depression, impulsive aggression, and moodiness. Counseling and behavior modification approaches such as token economies may also help rehabilitate the student with a traumatic brain disorder (Rose 1988).

### Autism

Autism is a developmental disability significantly affecting social interaction and verbal and nonverbal communication. Some other characteristics of a child with autism include incessantly engaging in repetitive activities, resistance to changes in routine, and inability to appropriately respond to perceptual stimuli (e.g., sounds, touch). It has been estimated that the incidence of autism is 5 to 15 per 10,000 live births and it is four times more common in males than females (Jansma and French 1994). While the cause of autism is unknown, structural deficiencies, which may be contributing factors, have been discovered in the brains of autistic individuals. Children with autism use behavior modification methods and in many cases medication to manage inappropriate behavior.

### Drug-Dependent Babies

It has been estimated that in the United States, 14 percent of pregnant women use alcohol or other drugs that can cause permanent physical damage to the fetus (Mullin 1992). Approximately 400,000 children are born each year who were exposed to crack or cocaine during gestation (Chasnoff, Landress, and Barrett 1990). It is well-known that the use of cocaine by a pregnant mother has devastating effects on the fetus, often worse than other illegal drugs. Children who were exposed to such drugs as cocaine and crack cocaine during gestation may exhibit inappropriate behavior. They may have a difficult time processing environment stimuli, have attention deficits, and exhibit excessive mood swings as well as display an inability to grasp cause and effect relationships, impulsivity, hyperactivity, and other behavioral disorders (Waller 1993). A combination of behavioral interventions, such as contingency contracts, daily report cards, and token economies, and medication is the therapeutic intervention used most widely with these children (Mullin 1992).

## Medication

It is important that you try to find out what medications your students are taking. This is because medications can negatively or

**TABLE 7.1**

## Medication, Behavior, Performance, and Learning

| TRADE NAMES | GENERIC NAME | COMMON USES | POTENTIAL ADVERSE EFFECTS |
|---|---|---|---|
| | | *ANTIDEPRESSANTS* | |
| Elavil, Triavil | Amitriptyline | Depression | Blurred vision, confusion, dizziness, fatigue, fainting, hallucinations, headaches, seizures |
| Norpramin | Desipramine | Depression | Blurred vision, fatigue, fainting, headaches, unsteady gait |
| Sinequan | Doxepin | Depression, associated anxiety | Blurred vision, dizziness, fainting, hallucinations, headaches, irregular heartbeat, seizures, tremors |
| Imavate, Presamine, Tofranil | Imipramine | Depression | Blurred vision, dizziness, fatigue, fainting, hallucinations, hypoactivity, incoordination, seizures tremors |
| Prozac | Fluoxetine hydrochloride | Short-term management of depression | Anxiety, headache, drowsiness, dizziness, muscle pain, weight loss |
| Zoloft | Serfraline hydrochloride | Depressive, obsessive disorders | Headache, tremor, dizziness, twitching, confusion, balance problems, postural hypotension, rash, increased sweating |
| Wellbutrin | Bupropion hydrochloride | Depression | Seizures, arrhythmias, headache, anxiety, confusion, tremor, rash |
| Luvox | Fluvoxamine, Maleate | Obsessive compulsive disorders | Seizures, impairs judgment, thinking and motor skills, headache |
| Paxil | Paroxetine | Obsessive compulsive disorders, panic disorders | Headache, sweating, nausea, dizziness |
| Effexor | Venlafaxine | Depression | Anxiety, nervousness, insomnia, headache, sweating, nausea, anorexia, dizziness, tremor, blurred vision |
| Serzone | Nefazone hydrochloride | Depression | Nausea, dizziness, blurred vision, confusion |
| Remeron | Mirtzapine | Depression | Headache, seizures, sweating, nausea, dizziness |
| | | *MAJOR TRANQUILIZERS* | |
| Thorazine | Chlorpromazine | Agitation, psychotic disorder, hyperactivity aggression | Confusion, fainting, hallucinations, mood changes, rapid heart beat, tremors, unsteady gait |
| Haldol | Haloperidol | Reduces anxiety, agitation | Blurred vision, drowsiness, fainting, hallucinations, tremors |
| Mellaril, Novoridazine, Thioril | Thioridazine | Reduces anxiety, agitation | Drowsiness, fainting, muscle spasms, tremors, unsteady gait |

| Brand Name | Generic Name | Use | Side Effects |
|---|---|---|---|
| Navane | Thiothixene | Reduces anxiety, agitation, psychotic disorder | Dizziness, drowsiness, fainting, less or unusual perspiration, muscle spasms, rapid heart beat, tremors |
| Buspar | Buspirone hydrochloride | Reduces anxiety, stress | Dizziness, nausea, headache, nervousness, light headedness, excitement |
| *MINOR TRANQUILIZERS, SEDATIVES, & HYPNOTICS* | | | |
| Novodipam, Rival, Valium, Vivol | Diazepam | Nervousness or tension | Confusion, dizziness, drowsiness, hallucinations, incoordination, tremors |
| Bamate, Equanil, Miltown | Meprobamate | Reduces anxiety, nervousness or tension | Confusion, dizziness, fatigue, fainting, headaches, joint and muscle pain, seizures, unsteady gait |
| Gardenal, Solfoton | Phenobarbital | Reduces anxiety, nervousness or tension | Confusion, dizziness, drowsiness, joint and muscle pain |
| *STIMULANTS* | | | |
| Benzedrine | Amphetamine | Controls hyperactivity in children | Blurred vision, chest pains, dizziness, headaches, irregular heartbeat, less or unusual perspiration, mood changes, rapid heart beat, weight loss |
| Dexampex, Dexedrine, Ferndex | Dextroamphetamine | Controls hyperactivity in children | Blurred vision, chest pains, dizziness, headaches, irregular heartbeat, less or unusual perspiration, mood changes, rapid heart beat, unsteady gait |
| Ritalin | Methylphenidate | Treatment for hyperactive children | Blurred vision, chest pains, dizziness, fatigue, headaches, mood changes, rapid heart beat, weight loss |
| Cylert | Demoline | Attention deficit disorder with hyperactivity | Seizures, hallucinations, abnormal oculomotor function, mild depression, dizziness, increased irritability, headaches, drowsiness |

Adapted from K.D. Daniel (1986). Pharmacological treatment of psychiatric and neurodevelopmental disorders in children and adolescents (Part 1). *Clinical Pediatrics, 25*, 65-71.

positively affect motor performance and behavior. Ways to collect information include sending home a short survey for parents to fill out and return and talking directly with parents as well as with the school nurse, special education and resource teachers, and physicians.

### Medical Survey

If time allows, it would be great if physical educators could review all their students' files to determine if there are any medical reasons indicating that a student should be provided some type of modified program or needs to be supervised a little more closely. To shorten the process, though, at the beginning of each school year or when a new student enters your class, send home a short survey regarding any medical conditions that the student may have that could negatively influence safe and successful participation in your physical education class. To streamline management, include the medical survey when you send home your class rules, grading policies, and other general information. On the same form, ask about any prescribed medication that the child may be taking that could also be detrimental to behavior, performance, or learning. Include space so that if the child is using a medication, the parents can give you information about reactions and side effects that you should look for. Some parents and guardians will provide this information because they know you want to protect their child. But a few may not respond to this request because they are worried that you may single out the child in class. Telephone such parents to reassure them that you will maintain the child's privacy and personally invite them to work with you to more effectively help the child grow and learn. If you still can't get the information you need, at least document for legal purposes that you asked.

### Other Sources of Medical Information

Many other professionals can help you obtain the medical information you need to effectively plan to meet each student's needs. Begin by asking the school nurse. The Council of Exceptional Children has designed a form specifically related to medication to help nurses provide such information to the teachers who need to know. But as with the medical survey, if the parents or guardians do not want this information released, document that you tried. If a student has been labeled as having a disability, contact the student's special education or resource teacher. As one of the child's teachers, you may review his file. Then refer to table 7.1 once you have been informed about medication use. If you have any questions, contact the parents or guardians for written permission to speak to the child's physician. This process will take a little time, but, like the old saying goes, "It's better to be safe than sorry." In fact, physicians want to collaborate more with physical educators regarding patients who have medical conditions for which physical activity may play a positive or negative role in treatment (Jansma and French 1994). It's up to us, however, to open the lines of communication with local physicians.

### Medication for Inappropriate Behavior

Many school-aged students with disabilities take prescribed medication to manage inappropriate behavior. Psychopharmacological medications are among the most efficient and widely available means to modify behavior caused by central nervous system deficiencies. This type of medication produces biochemical, physiological, or psychological changes. While these changes can help modify behavior, they can also cause many adverse side effects. The incidence and severity of these vary, however, depending on the medication, the dosage, and the individual.

You must know if a student is receiving psychopharmacological medications and how the medication could impact the student's social and motor performance. In table 7.1, we have offered brief explanations of the more traditional types of medications, subdividing each into four major types. As the name implies, antidepressants are the most commonly used medication for the treatment of depression. They affect the part of the brain that controls messages between nerve cells. Then we have listed the minor tranquilizers, sedatives, and hypnotics. These medications affect the limbic system of the brain, which controls emotions. Generally, their use results in decreased arousal and motor activity. The major tranquilizers produce easily arousable sedation and blunt or reduce emotional arousal. These medications suppress the brain centers that control abnormal emotions and behavior. Stimulants include amphetamines and related compounds such as cocaine and caffeine; these have great power to excite the central nervous system, both physiologically and behaviorally.

When a student is on medication, you may be asked to monitor the student's behavior, noting changes when the student begins to use a medication and reporting these changes to the parents or the family physician. As we have discussed, however, for reasons of health, safety, and planning, you need to know when a student is taking medication whether or not you are asked to monitor the response to it. For instance, many psychopharmacological medications may cause poor coordination, such as Tofranil. Others may cause disorientation or dizziness, such as Effexor, Triavil, Valium, or Equanil; blurred vision, such as Thorazine, Mellaril, or Ritalin; or fainting, such as Triavil, Benzedrine, Valium, or Mellaril.

Moreover, insist that you be informed of any "drug holidays." Drug holidays refer to times when the physician stops medication to determine whether she should continue to prescribe it or if she may adjust the dose. Carefully document any changes in behavior during these times so that the physician hears the whole story about the drug holiday and can therefore make a more informed decision regarding treatment. Remember, medication should be a last resort and should only be used in combination with proven behavior management techniques consistently applied. Drug holidays give everyone a chance to see if a student can "graduate" to a lower dose or to medication-free methods.

## NUTRITIONAL ISSUES

Poor diets and inadequate nutrition are important factors in behavior and learning. Many schools throughout the United States have initiated free breakfast and lunch programs not only to feed students but also to improve students' diets, to increase school performance, and to reduce behavior problems.

### Diet Management

Food choices and their quality affect the brain, which, in turn, impacts how a student feels, thinks, and behaves. For some people, diet may be associated with or may exacerbate such conditions as poor impulse control and tendencies toward violence and hyperactivity (Fishbein and Pease 1994). Whether or not they display hyperactive tendencies, some children have unusual reactions to certain foods, including sugar and caffeine; some nutritive elements, such as zinc, calcium, magnesium, selenium, chromium, iron, and potassium; and allergies to certain foods, such as milk, chocolate, cola, corn, eggs, peanuts, citrus fruits, tomatoes, wheat and small grains, and food dyes and other food additives.

While research results are limited and contradictory, on an individual basis, many parents have reported positive changes from modifying their children's diets. While few parents will strictly enforce a special diet, they will look for approaches that may work to reduce inappropriate behavior, for example, by reducing, rather than eliminating, certain types of foods, such as those high in sugar. Parents have told us that they know when their child has had a sugar product on the way home from school, based on their hyperactive or irritable behavior after arriving home. If you believe that this may be the case with a student, encourage both the parents and the student to monitor breakfasts and school lunches to avoid the negative impact the wrong foods can have on the child's behavior at school. If food does influence a child's behavior, it usually does so in the first 30 to 90 minutes after eating (Fontenelle 1992). While you may not be surprised that food allergies and sensitivities can cause or exacerbate hyperactivity, irritability, impulsivity, or aggression, food allergies can affect some children in ways you may not expect. For example, some children with ADD or ADHD who are allergic to certain foods (or who have asthma) may actually increase their inappropriate behavior as a result of the medication designed to control these conditions (Fontenelle 1992). What's more, some children are so sensitive to certain foods, that even one minor slip in the restricted diet can cause the undesirable behavior to resurface (Feingold 1975). As you can see, solving the mystery of nutritional problems can be very difficult. It certainly takes knowledge and persistence.

### Inadequate Nutrition

If you think inadequate nutrition, rather than food sensitivities, may be a possible reason for inappropriate behavior and poor performance, you can request that the parents and the student conduct a meal-behavior evaluation, using a special form, such as the sample presented in worksheet 7 in appendix 2, "Nutritional Evaluation Form." This could help everyone working with the child determine if a correlation between diet and behavior exists. If review of the data reveals a correlation, encourage the parents and student to adjust the student's diet. You may need to have a dietitian or an allergist help you analyze the data. Keep in mind, too, that some children may eat an adequate diet but their bodies may not absorb certain nutrients. Only a trained professional, such as a physician or dietitian, may be able to make this determination.

## Diet Modification and Medication

Not surprisingly, it's better to prevent a nutritional disorder than treat it after allowing it to develop; prevention holds the greatest promise for reducing behavioral problems (Lozoff 1989). Therefore, it's well worth the time and effort it takes to track down food allergies or nutritional deficits. In fact, in some cases, diet modification can reduce or eliminate the need to use medication (Feingold 1975). The fact that medication helps may suggest that the problem is biochemical and therefore that the nutritional approach may be helpful. It is better to at least try a diet, a more natural approach to dealing with the problem, to attempt to reduce or eliminate the use of drugs.

But a special diet is not easy to adhere to, especially for older, more independent students. The diet approach requires strict adherence; it is more effective when the whole family is on the diet along with the student so that there are fewer temptations to cheat. Insist on being a member of a team that includes the school counselor and nutritionist when the physical

activity component that usually accompanies the nutritional approach is determined. This could involve monitoring student behavior to determine if a behavioral change occurs in class over time or monitoring the type and quantity of food intake if responsible for lunch duty and providing appropriate physical activities to tailor your program to the student's special needs.

## SUMMARY

Numerous nontraditional behavior management methods exist to help you positively impact behavior. Decide what you can easily incorporate into your physical education or sport setting. If nothing else, use relaxation training not only to help students with behavior problems but also to help all students cope with our fast-paced, anxiety-driven society.

Parents usually initiate the medication and nutritional approaches when other more traditional school-initiated methods fail. In the medication approach, you may be asked to monitor the student's behavior to note and report motor and behavioral changes when the student begins to use or reduces the use of a medication so that parents or the family physician may consider your perspective. You may also be asked to help design the physical activity component that usually accompanies the nutritional approach, tailoring it to the individual's needs.

Please remember, however, that you and the other professionals working with difficult students should consider medications only as a last resort. Moreover, medications should always be used in combination with other interventions, most notably behavior modification or the behavioral approach we discussed in chapters 3, 4, and 5. Therefore, medication must be used as a tool to help make other interventions more effective.

# REVIEW: VIGNETTE APPLICATION EXERCISES

For each of the three vignettes presented on page x, determine if any of the behavior management approaches discussed in this chapter could safely and effectively augment the other approaches we have discussed in earlier chapters. Justify your answers. If you choose to use one or more of the nontraditional methods discussed in this chapter, write a paragraph describing your approach. Then review the possible plans we describe here.

1. Let's see how Hector, our overactive third grader, may benefit from nontraditional methods. First, use nonintrusive approaches, such as positive reinforcement, mild forms of punishment, a highly structured learning environment, and a peer buddy, to help him as much as possible.

If these approaches do not have a positive influence over time, try relaxation training. Teach the basic method to the entire class but have Hector practice it at home as well. Then, in physical education class when he feels upset or frustrated, allow him to leave the activity area and practice his relaxation exercises, then return. In addition, you may wish to encourage his parents to consider diet management to be monitored by the school staff during the school day.

Only if all else fails should you suggest that Hector's parents investigate the use of medication. Request that the parents inform you and other involved school staff if he is placed on medication and what type so you can monitor his behavior and provide him with a safe environment. Work with Hector's other teachers to complete a simple graph to chart his daily behavior.

2. As we have asserted throughout the book, support your school's policy regarding detention or suspension for fighting. Then, when the boys come back to your class, try to help them learn to deal with tense situations in more acceptable ways. For example, relaxation training might help Jim and Ashante deal with their aggressive behavior. This method may enable them to stop themselves when they begin to become overly tense. You could excuse them to go through a series of relaxation exercises.

If all the behavior modification and psychodynamic methods used singularly or in combination are not effective, of course medication could supplement relaxation methods to manage their behavior. But remember, medication should be the last resort to manage even this highly inappropriate behavior.

3. Clearly relaxation training, medication, and diet modification are not approaches that will help encourage Jill and Molly to dress for physical education. Proactive approaches accompanied by consistent and systematic behavior management or psychodynamic approaches are more appropriate.

# PART 3

# Putting It All Together

Are you feeling overwhelmed by all the information we've covered thus far? Are you wondering how you'll apply it to your unique situation to create your own behavior management plan? In part 3, we'll show you how. In chapter 8, we'll help you reexamine yourself in light of all you've learned in chapters 1 through 7. We'll show you how to lay a firm foundation for effective behavior management, then how to deal with specific problems. Along with our suggestions for how to complete these tasks, we will offer personal insights gleaned from our experiences. Think of this as a conversation in which we all discuss the problems we face as physical education professionals. As each situation arises think about how you would approach it based on what you have learned in this text. The goal is to design a behavior management program to fit your unique personality and teaching circumstances.

Then in "One Last Look at the Vignettes," we'll look one last time at our friends Hector, Ashante and Jim, and Jill and Molly as we apply all the methods we've covered, as appropriate. In "Increasing the Peace," we'll look at one more behavior management program that we hope will be a final inspiration to you to be creative in your own approach. In appendix 1, you'll find checklists to help you assess yourself. But remember: Simply being able to answer "Yes, I am consistent" to each statement will not make your program effective. View the checklists as a tool for reviewing and assimilating the information covered in this book as you strive to tailor the methods to meet your needs. Finally, in appendix 2, you'll find worksheets to help you assess your own style and individual student needs further.

## CHAPTER 8

# Developing Your Own Approach to Behavior Management

"The purpose of discipline in the classroom is to reduce the need for teacher intervention over time by encouraging students to develop self-control over their own behavior. When teachers understand and apply appropriate models of discipline, the hope is that students will internalize the need for self-discipline not only in the classroom but beyond its walls. The lessons learned will have long-range consequences for students, and ultimately for the world in which we all must live" (Charles 1992, p. vii).

Now that we've given you a broad overview of behavior management methods and applications, you may be thinking "How do I put it all together?" And we certainly don't believe that any one method or any one plan is *the* model to follow. In fact, you must consider so many factors particular to your situation in developing a behavior management plan that it's sure to be unique.

In this chapter, we'll discuss the steps to follow and the factors you should consider in developing your own behavior management plan to effectively meet your and your students' needs. These ideas are a compilation of a number of educational theorists (Charles 1992; Jones 1982; Martin and Sugarman 1993).

## REEXAMINE YOURSELF

Think about your own philosophies, values, and goals in education in light of what we've discussed in this book before you attempt to develop your personalized behavior management plan. Writing down your answers to the questions we will pose in this chapter may help you clarify your thoughts. This process will help you at any stage of your career—whether this is your 1st, 5th, or 17th year teaching. Indeed, writing may help you reflect on your experiences and assess your ideas and practices so that you may more clearly see what areas you might need to improve. But thinking about these issues while driving to and from school can be beneficial, too!

We have based the questions posed in this chapter on our own philosophies and experiences to guide you as you develop your own personalized behavior management plan. Because she felt that following a teacher through a year in the classroom/gymnasium would be the clearest way of illustrating the 10-step plan explained in this chapter, Hester has blended her own experiences and those of others into the middle school "year" which you are about to examine. While the incidents related did not, in fact, occur in one year of teaching in middle school, all the narratives are based on actual events in real classrooms. Remember that the sample answers are just that, samples, one way to look at an issue, based on her experience—not *the* definitive answers.

## Step 1: Examine Your Philosophy of Teaching and Behavior Management

What are your values and beliefs? What do you believe your role as a physical educator is? What is the student's role in the learning process? Does your role go beyond the established physical education curriculum? If so, in what other areas do you play a role?

I value education and believe that all children have a right to learn. My role as a physical educator is to create an environment conducive to learning in which students want to learn and are willing to put forth the effort to increase their knowledge and skills in physical education. I believe students need to take an active role in the learning process to benefit from their educational experience. My role goes beyond the established physical education curriculum, because I feel that education is a holistic system in which students learn to be responsible citizens who want to contribute positively to society. As their teacher, I can be a good role model, provide opportunities for them to learn responsible behaviors, and, through teachable moments, I can provide them with knowledge and guidance.

## Step 2: Based on Your Philosophy, Establish Your Teaching and Behavior Management Goals

What do you want your students to learn? In other words, what affective, physical, and cognitive goals do you have?

One goal I have for the students in my class is for them to be motivated to be physically active all their lives. So encouraging students to take personal responsibility is an integral part of my behavior management plan. Another goal I have is for the students to enjoy learning about the human body. Finally, I want students to enjoy learning how to improve their motor skills so I tend to focus on the cognitive process of learning as well as on the product.

What is your goal for your students in terms of their behavior? What is your role in the management of their behavior? What is the students' role?

My goal is for students to take responsibility for their own behavior. My role in the management of their behavior is to (a) help establish rules, (b) evaluate students' efforts to follow the rules, (c) facilitate the students' development of their own behavioral management plan, (d) apply sanctions, and (e) counsel and encourage students in their attempts to take responsibility for their own behavior. The student's role is to (a) provide input to the classroom rules; (b) develop his own behavior management plan; (c) evaluate his own adherence to the plan; and (d) take responsibility for his own behavior.

# LAY YOUR FOUNDATION

You can prevent many behavior problems by using effective teaching methods. Therefore, you must examine your own practices. Start by listing the methods you used in your classes last week. Rate each method on a scale from one to five in terms of how effective you think that method was in helping students learn.

## Step 3: Evaluate the Effectiveness of Your Current Teaching Practices

If you use some methods you feel are not as effective as they could be, modify them, then implement these changes. Specifically, examine your teaching methods, your unique teaching situation, the interpersonal relationships in your classes, your attitude toward your students, and your current behavior management methods.

Student learning increases and misbehavior decreases with well-planned lessons and effective instructional strategies. Lessons and support activities should be stimulating and appropriately paced to maximize student engagement in productive tasks. Learning that is interesting and provides a sense of growing power and accomplishment is the best means of classroom management. In planning lessons, incorporate students' interests, teach more than facts, involve students in the learning process, and take into consideration the individual learning styles of your students (see figure 8.1). Individualizing instruction allows students to work at their own paces on tasks that are appropriate for their skill levels. Peer tutoring and instructional grouping can help you match instruction to ability when large student-

teacher ratios limit the time available for individualizing instruction.

In analyzing teaching methods, I recognized that students did not seem interested in some of my lessons. For example, when I taught how to find target heart rate, by the end of the period about half of the class was not paying attention. Perhaps the way I presented the information was not exciting. I think I covered too much information in our short lesson time, and some students did not have the prerequisite math skills to figure their target heart rates. I recognized that I needed to create more exciting ways to present the material. So I decided to make four changes. First, I planned to take at least two class periods to present it. Second, I planned to develop some fun application exercises to get the students more involved in the learning process, such as finding the resting heart rate of a friend in the class and then figuring out what each other's target heart rate is. Third, I planned to take time to teach the prerequisite math skills or coordinate this with the math teacher so the students can do the problems presented in my class. Fourth, I pledged to try to make the lesson more exciting and lively for the students in any other way I could think of.

In analyzing my instructional techniques, I recognized that I was not individualizing instruction as much as I could have, and some students were not challenged at all; others were struggling to understand concepts and complete assignments. So I planned to use more peer tutors, learning stations, and small group instruction.

### Have You Considered the Uniqueness of Your Situation?

As you design your behavior management program, think about the students in your classes. Consider the ages, the grade level, and the socioeconomic statuses. Consider the value placed on education in the homes as well as the behavior management methods employed by the parents. Pay particular attention to the students' learning styles, skills, interests, abilities, and personalities. Remember that each student is unique with many individual characteristics you must consider. Each student comes to you with a different set of thoughts, feelings, attitudes, and experiences warranting your individual attention. It is important to match these characteristics with the behavior management plan. After looking at the students as individuals, then look at the group as a

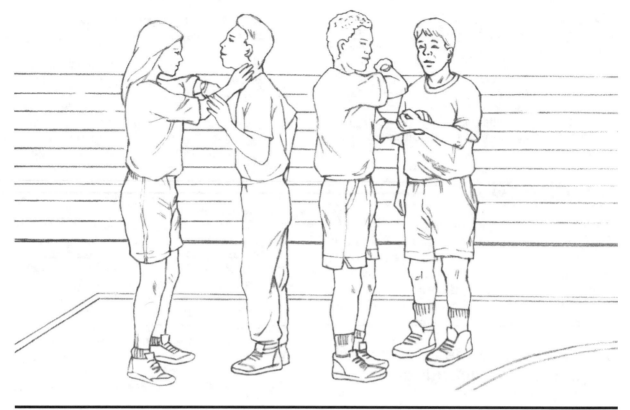

**Figure 8.1** To keep your students' interest, develop application exercises that keep the students involved in the learning process.

whole. When the class is relatively homogenous, the task is much easier than when you have a wide range of abilities, interests, and values. For the more heterogeneous group, you may need to develop different behavior management methods for individuals or subgroups within one class. This is, indeed, a very challenging aspect of teaching! Use the "Student Information Worksheet" in appendix 2 to guide you.

The students in my classes are 11 to 14 years old in the sixth, seventh, and eighth grades. Their socioeconomic statuses range from upper lower class to lower middle class. In some of their homes, education is valued highly; in others, it is not valued at all. They come from homes in which parents employ behavior management techniques that may or may not be effective. And my students have a wide range of abilities, interests, and talents. Because of the heterogeneous nature of the students in my classes, I do not use the same behavior management methods with all of my students. For example, Jamie cries when I even give him a stern look; he needs me to show him I care about him. So when I need to discuss a problem behavior with him I do so very gently. In contrast, Luke does not listen to me when I tell him to be quiet, to stop bouncing the ball, or to

participate in the class activity. He is belligerent when I reprimand him, and he often refuses to go to time-out when I tell him to. With Jamie, I will talk with him and tell him what behavior is inappropriate and why. I'll ask him to stop the inappropriate behavior and tell him what behavior I would like him to perform. For example, I might say, "Jamie, when you bounce the ball the other students cannot hear my instructions. Please hold the ball." With Luke, I would take the ball and hold it myself while standing next to him.

Examine your teaching style and describe the characteristics of your style. Are you democratic or authoritarian? Are you student-centered or teacher-centered? Are you extroverted or introverted? Are you enthusiastic or more subdued? Are you warm and caring or do you like to keep your distance? Do you require plenty of structure or only a little?

Thinking back on my first five years of teaching, I would classify my teaching style as mostly autocratic. The last couple years, though, I would say that I am leaning more toward a democratic style. I feel I am at least more student-centered now. I am extroverted and very enthusiastic. I care about my students as individuals.

Consider the community and socioeconomic factors in your school, such as the availability of resources and funds, the school's organizational structure, and the politics of the local school board. All these factors have a bearing on the types of problems you might encounter in your physical education setting as well as the resources available for both teaching and managing behavior. Some districts or schools have a district- or school-wide behavior management plan that you must consider when developing your personal plan to ensure consistency in managing student behavior. Teachers must communicate with each other on a regular basis, discussing the problems that occur with the established plan and revising the plan as needed.

The community in which my school is located is interested in education, but no one really takes a leading role in trying to increase community involvement in the schools. The resources and funds available are minimal. We do have a school-wide behavior management plan that was developed about eight years ago, but teachers have never been trained in this plan, although a description of it is in the policy manual. Teachers at my school develop their own plans and not much communication goes on among teachers unless we encounter a particularly disruptive student who misbehaves in several classes. In such a case, we confer, trying to determine a common behavior management plan to use with the student in question.

### Do You Establish Positive Teacher-Student Relationships?

It has been shown that positive teacher-student relationships are associated with positive student attitudes toward school, increased academic achievement, and more positive behavior (Jones 1982). Students want to know that you care about them as individual people. You can show you care in many ways, such as greeting students by name when they come into class, asking them a personal question like what they did over the weekend, or how their visit was with Uncle George, and reinforcing them for good behavior, participation, or skill performance.

In reflecting on my relationship with my students, I recognized that I had not taken time to establish positive teacher-student relationships with my students. I decided to set goals for myself each week to try to increase my positive interactions with my students. So week one, I made it my goal to learn each student's name and speak to each one of them at least once during class either by asking them a question about themselves, recognizing something they did in class or in school, or simply by saying, "Hello, Lindsey, you were great as a peer tutor today."

### Do You Facilitate the Development of Positive Peer Relationships?

Many behavior problems involve peer conflict. You can implement physical activities that

**Figure 8.2** Cooperative games are an excellent way to promote positive relationships among students.

enhance positive, supportive, peer relationships. Acquaintance activities can help break the ice and reduce anxiety and inhibitions. Many instructional activities reinforce cooperation and reduce competition (see figure 8.2). Cooperative or new games (Fluegelman 1976, 1981; Grineski 1996) are fun and help develop a sense of camaraderie and cooperation among students. You can reinforce cooperative behaviors of the students while they are participating in activities. Cliques can be dissolved by splitting up the students and having them be leaders in other groups that are performing a cooperative group activity. Sometimes open dialogue is necessary to combat peer pressure and cliques.

In analyzing my methods for developing positive peer relationships, I recognized that I had not used acquaintance activities and had not incorporated games that were designed to enhance cooperation into my curriculum. I had not been attentive to any cooperative behaviors the students may have exhibited in my class. So I found some acquaintance activities and some fun, cooperative games to play with my students and included them in my standard curriculum. I am working to be more attentive to the cooperative behaviors students exhibit during class activities and am making an earnest attempt to reinforce those students who cooperate and demonstrate caring for others.

### Do You Implement Methods That Seem to Improve Students' Self-Concepts?

It is important that students perceive the school as a positive, nurturing environment in which they feel safe and secure and have their needs met. You can help create this environment by establishing safety rules, by giving students proper instructions, and by encouraging students to try difficult skills with your support. Instructional activities that are challenging but programmed so that the students can be successful will enhance self-concept. Providing opportunities for students to develop positive relationships with their peers will increase motivation to learn and will enhance positive attitudes toward school. Showing that you care about the students and respect them will also enhance their self-concepts.

I feel I have been conscientious about establishing and enforcing safety rules, but I think I could be more emphatic about making sure all students understand my instructions. Once I gave instructions that students were to wait in the dugout until their turn at bat. But Tami, Tracy, Ryan, and Jacob were all standing by the first base line, and Tracy got hit by a foul ball. I pledged to make sure all students are following instructions or to stop the game to remind them. I think that I have provided challenging activities for the students in my classes, but I recognized that I had not been as supportive as I could have been of those students who were having trouble. I just gave them a lower grade and thought that would motivate them to do better next time. So I began working to find more creative ways to teach these students, such as giving them more individualized instruction personally or through a peer tutor. Once a student learns the skill, I make sure to notice and reinforce the effort. I have begun using students as peer tutors to teach others how to do the skill. I created opportunities for students to develop positive relationships with their peers by assigning group projects in which they work together, such as developing a school-wide fun day to raise money for the American Lung Association for children with respiratory problems.

### Have You Developed a Workable Set of Proactive Management Procedures Including Rules and Routines?

It is important that students have direct input in the development of the rules and routines as well as the consequences for inappropriate behaviors. It is also important that rules are stated in a positive way. Review chapter 2 for methods of developing rules.

In analyzing my method for establishing classroom rules, I realized that I had established the rules with no input from the students. I also had stated the rules in a negative way (i.e., "Do not interrupt when others are talking.").

I had a class discussion and asked the students what rules they thought we needed in our class and why these rules were needed. With my guidance, we stated the rules in a positive way (i.e., "We wait until others have finished talking to say what we want to say."). We discussed why it was important to have rules. We then wrote the rules on a poster and put the poster on the wall. We only made rules that were needed. We revised the rules periodically, discarding those not needed anymore. When a new rule was needed we followed the same procedure and added the new rule to the list.

### Have You Determined Methods for Developing and Increasing Desired Behavior?

Refer to chapter 3 for methods of designing a behavioral approach. Chapter 4 includes such methods for developing and increasing desired behaviors as social, tangible, and physical activity reinforcement; prompts; token economy systems; the Premack principle; public posting; contracts; and group contingencies.

I will look over the methods to develop and increase desired behaviors discussed in chapter 4 and determine which ones are most appropriate for me to use in my classes. For example, I may choose to use the Premack principle with my students because I know they are highly motivated when they can earn the privilege to play their favorite game. With secondary level students, group contingencies work well so I would probably determine ways to use this method in my classes.

### Have You Determined Methods for Resolving Conflict and Dealing With Students' Personal Adjustment Problems?

Refer to Chapter 6 for methods of teaching responsible behavior. Students feel more secure when you respond to inappropriate behavior with sensitivity, competence, and fairness. You must recognize individual differences and be willing to accept them. Students need to feel a sense of power. It is important to listen to students and consider their concerns when attempting to resolve problem behaviors. Give them choices that are acceptable to you so that they take responsibility for their own behavior by choosing what to do. If they fail to fulfill their responsibilities, insist that they accept the consequences. You must ensure that you apply consequences consistently and fairly, attempting to increase the student awareness of their responsibility for behaving properly. Then monitor the use of consequences carefully to be sure that they are having the desired effect on the behavior.

My methods for resolving conflict have been more autocratic. I determined what the classroom rules were to be and announced them the first day of class and gave the students a list of the rules to keep. When students did not follow the rules, I applied the established consequence without giving the student a choice of acceptable behaviors. I also was inconsistent with the application of the consequences. Some days I would apply consequences and on other days I would ignore the same behavior.

So I planned the following changes in my approach: I would allow the students to have input in the classroom rules. I would either allow them to develop their own plan to manage their behavior or give them a choice of acceptable behaviors so that they felt empowered to take responsibility for their behavior. I pledged to become more consistent in applying consequences for student misbehaviors.

## Step 4: Implement the Changes You Have Determined Need to Be Made and Analyze the Results

You can't simply talk about changes, you must make them. Then analyze the results as objectively as possible.

When I learned all of the students' names and made a point to talk personally with each one at least once a week, I noticed a positive change in their attitudes toward me. They were friendlier to me when they came into the class and would actually go out of the way to come and talk with me in the lunchroom. In addition, they were more interested in the things we were learning in class and did better on the tests.

I made it a point to let them play the fun acquaintance games at the beginning of the class period every Monday morning. I found that these games got the students more involved with each other, and so they participated more in the class activities.

I also incorporated a fun, cooperative game into the curriculum every Friday. The students seemed to laugh a lot more and try harder in these games. Even Maria, who had seemed bored with physical education since the beginning of the year, began to participate and make new friends.

I began reinforcing students for exhibiting cooperative behaviors during class activities and they began working together more and stopped being so competitive. They fought less in class; instead, they interacted more positively with their peers.

I am more thorough about giving class instructions before they begin an activity. I even orally quiz them about what they are supposed to be doing. Whenever someone is not following instructions, I make sure I go over and explain why it is important to follow the instructions.

I have established a peer tutor system in which the students who know how to do the skill I'm teaching are the tutors for those who are still learning. This technique has been beneficial for both the student being tutored as he is getting more individual attention and the student who is doing the tutoring as it is good for his self-esteem. This approach also reviews and reinforces the skill in a more interesting way for the tutor.

Our school-wide fun day was a big success in getting the students to work together on group projects. I could see many friendships developing as the students planned their projects, and we even raised quite a bit of money for the American Lung Association.

In developing classroom rules, I have asked the students to give their own rationale for why rules are important and have allowed them to decide what rules we need. I do still give my input, however.

When a student misbehaves I talk with him, then help him develop his own plan to manage his own behavior. As a result, the student takes more responsibility for his own behavior; indeed, very rarely has a student failed to carry out a behavior management plan he developed.

## ADDRESS SPECIFIC PROBLEMS

By this point, you have seen how to analyze and modify your teaching methods so that they form a fairly solid foundation. You should, however, address some specific problems more closely.

### Step 5: Decide What Remaining Problems You Need to Deal With

List all the behaviors that occur in your class that you would like to change. Rank these in order of importance. Consider the following criteria when ranking:

- Is the behavior physically harmful to the student or others?
- Is the behavior interfering with the student's ability to stay in the home? In school? To function appropriately with his peers?
- Is the behavior affecting the student's ability to learn in the class?
- Is the behavior affecting the ability of other students to learn?

- Is the behavior irritating to you as a teacher?
- Can you change this behavior without help from other personnel or do you need help?

For those problem behaviors that will require the cooperation of other staff, seek the appropriate help. Special educators, psychologists, counselors, principals, and vice principals are often good resources.

I listed five behaviors that I felt were problems in my physical education classes. Then I ranked them in order of most to least problematic. I considered the criteria and made my rankings based on my personality, philosophy, values, and beliefs. The five behaviors I chose to change were the following, beginning with the most problematic behavior:

1. Jeffrey getting into fights
2. Jennifer talking back and being rude to me
3. Tommy exhibiting unsportsmanlike behavior, such as throwing the bat when he strikes out, using foul language when someone beats him to the ball, and quitting when the other team scores a goal
4. Paul telling lies
5. Carol and Sharon talking while I am giving instructions

Next, go through the following steps with each of the behaviors you have ranked. Start with the behavior you ranked first.

### Step 6: Examine the Problem Behavior, Then Make an Earnest Attempt to Determine Its Cause

Why did Jeffrey pick a fight with Tim? Is it because he struck out and is so competitive that he cannot handle his personal defeats? Is it because the models he has observed on television or in the home are people who express their anger by fighting? Is it because his mom and dad are getting a divorce, and he does not have anyone with whom to discuss his angry feelings? Is it the first time Jeffrey has ever displayed aggressive behaviors or is this a recurring behavior?

Even though you have already examined your teaching style and made improvements, be willing to ask if any problem remains in your teaching practices that may be contributing to the problem behavior. Pay attention to the way you interact with the student. Are you warm, sincere, and concerned? Do you respect the student? Do you interact often with the student? Does the student know you care about him? Is it obvious to the student that you want him to be a contributing member of the class? Observe the student in other classes, or, if this is not possible, speak with other teachers who have the student in class (see figure 8.3). Does he behave the same way in other classes?

I thought about it and decided that, given the improvements I had made in the last month, I did not think my basic teaching style was contributing to the problem. I then looked at my relationship with Jeffrey and the way I interacted with him. I had not talked personally with Jeffrey for over two weeks to ask him how his classes were going when I saw him in the hall. I was preoccupied with trying to get to the cafeteria for lunch duty. I planned to make a conscious effort to talk with Jeffrey on a daily basis to let him know I care about him. I also planned to reinforce him for participating in class activities and for interacting positively with others.

Once I had made an honest effort to make sure I was providing the right sort of class and personal atmosphere for Jeffrey, I tried to find out what else might be contributing to his fighting behavior. I sat down with him after class and asked him to tell me what happened and why the fight occurred. He told me that Tim had sarcastically said, "Way to go!" when Jeffrey struck out. So Jeffrey hit him. I asked him what he thought the fight would do to solve the problem and he said that he thought it would teach Tim not to make comments to him when he struck out. I asked him if something was bothering him. He said, "No." I asked if he wanted to talk about anything and he said, "No." I then decided to see if other teachers were observing Jeffrey fighting. The math teacher told me that she had noticed Jeffrey being more irritable lately and that he was not doing his school work. She noticed him arguing with other students during group projects. She said that she overheard him telling Tyler that his dad had hit him when he came home late last weekend. She also said that he was going to go live with his mom when his parents split up. The English teacher said he had noticed that Jeffrey had seemed more withdrawn lately, but that he had not seen him display any aggressive behaviors. After talking

**Figure 8.3** Talk with other teachers about their experiences with the problem student.

with other teachers and realizing that Jeffrey's fighting behavior was more than his having a bad day, I decided to consult with the school psychologist and get her advice as to how best deal with Jeffrey. She was very helpful and offered to schedule time to talk with Jeffrey. She gave me some good ideas for talking with Jeffrey and showing him that I care about him. I included these ideas in my intervention plan.

## Step 7: Design an Intervention to Change the Problem Behavior

The first step in this process is to collect baseline data on the behavior. Define a target behavior based on the baseline data. For a detailed description of the steps to follow in this process, see chapter 3. Review the models we have discussed in this book, such as the responsibility models and reality therapy, then select the intervention you think you can adapt to your situation. Consider a number of other factors, including your teaching style, characteristics of the students in your class, and community and socioeconomic factors influencing your school.

Determine methods for developing and increasing desired behavior. Methods include social, tangible, and physical activity reinforcement; prompts; token economy systems; the Premack principle; public posting; contracts; and individual and group contingencies (see chapter 4). Select methods for decreasing undesirable behaviors. Methods include withdrawal of a reinforcer (extinction, response cost, and time-out), presentation of an aversive stimulus (direct discussion and verbal reprimand), and requiring an aversive behavior (requiring a physical activity or extra academic work, reparation, and overcorrection).

Select methods to meet your individual teaching style and situation. Through experience, you will determine which methods work best with which type of problem, situation, and students. When administering a method, however, be sure to use the least amount of intervention. Carefully consider the continuum along which behavior management methods occur, beginning with those methods used to manage minor infractions such as your giving the student a stern look for talking when she should have been listening to instructions, and continuing with those used for more severe

behaviors, such as having a student suspended from class for two days for getting into a fight. Ensure that you match the behavior management method to the severity of the behavior.

Based on my personality, Jeffrey's personality, background, family life, and experiences, and my successful experience teaching responsible behavior to students, I decided to use a modified version of a responsibility model as my intervention with Jeffrey. I made it my goal to have Jeffrey take responsibility for his behavior. When he got into a fight, I planned to ask him to tell me why the fight occurred, what level the fighting behavior is on, why the fighting behavior was inappropriate, and how he would develop a plan to change the fighting behavior.

## Step 8: Implement the Intervention, Then Evaluate Its Effectiveness

When applying an intervention, collect data on the frequency of the behavior on a regular basis (daily or weekly). Compare these data to the defined target behavior in order to determine if the target behavior was achieved. If the target behavior was achieved, decide whether to terminate the intervention for this specific behavior. Consider the following questions when making this decision: Will the student begin to exhibit the behavior again if you terminate the intervention? Is it necessary to continue with the intervention in order to make sure the behavior remains changed? Was the intervention responsible for the change in the behavior or some other intervening factor? Should you modify the definition of the target behavior to change the behavior even more? If the target behavior was not achieved, how can you change the intervention to make it more effective in this situation?

After getting the advice of the school psychologist, the intervention I implemented with Jeffrey was to discuss his fighting behavior with him. I scheduled a conference with Jeffrey and told him I was concerned about his fighting behavior and that I wanted to help him control his anger. I asked him if he knew how I could help him, but he did not offer any suggestions. I suggested that we develop a management plan to help him stop fighting. I asked him if he thought he could tune in to his feelings, and whenever he felt angry, stop and count to 10 and ask himself what was making him angry. He thought that he could do this and was willing to try. We then defined the target behavior as "Jeffrey will go 5 days without getting into a fight." He said that he would keep a journal, and we could meet at the end of each day to see how the technique was working. I kept my own data on his fighting behavior.

The intervention produced the target behavior. Jeffrey went 5 days without getting into a fight. Next, we modified the target behavior to be "Jeffrey will go 10 days without getting into a fight." I then continued with the intervention until Jeffrey achieved the new target behavior.

## Step 9: Repeat Steps 6 Through 8 for the Other Behaviors You Ranked

Now select other behaviors you feel need to be changed in order to establish and maintain control of your classes. Start over with steps 6 through 8.

My success decreasing Jeffrey's fighting behavior gave me renewed hope to approach the second-ranked behavior: Jennifer's talking back and other rudeness to me. This behavior is very distasteful to me and one that I, personally, have trouble tolerating. One of the most difficult challenges I face as a teacher is to separate a student's behavior from the student as a person. If the student's behavior is defiant and rude, it is not pleasant to be in the presence of that student. I had trouble separating the behavior from the person, so I often felt guilty when I had a student in my class that I did not like to be around. I had to realize that I liked the person; it was the behavior that I disapproved. Behavior is changeable. I respected the student enough as a person to want to put the time and energy into developing a plan to change her defiant and rude behavior. So I was motivated to act instead of being paralyzed by my feelings of guilt. Consequently, after recognizing my problem, I was much more effective changing these behaviors. After three months of intervention, Jennifer decreased her rudeness by 60 percent, and I have even started to like being around her.

I went through a similar process with Tommy's unsportsmanlike behaviors. All but his foul language have reached target behavior.

After trying unsuccessfully to change Paul's problem of telling lies, I recognized that his problem required professional help, so I sought the school psychologist's advice. He is working with Paul in group therapy, and Paul is beginning to lie less often.

I have used time-out and reinforcement of good behavior with Carol and Sharon, and they have stopped talking during class instructions altogether. They now socialize only at the established appropriate times. They have become model students.

## Step 10: Repeat the Entire Process at Least Annually

After systematically following these steps to develop a behavior management plan, you will have a first draft. This plan, however, will need continuous and ongoing monitoring, evaluation, and revision. Take into account changes in yourself, your students, your school, and your community. Remember to be patient: Behavioral changes take time.

My school population is a transient one with students moving in and out at a high rate. In December, I recognized that I was having more trouble with attendance and participation than I had at the beginning of the school year. No wonder! Since September, I had been given 23 new students and had lost 15. The new students definitely seemed less interested in physical education than the ones I had lost. They were often late for class or absent altogether. They forgot their gym clothes, refused to participate fully, and failed to turn in assignments. Some of the students that I thought I had trained began to follow suit. I knew I had to reexamine my behavior management plan—and fast! I looked at my class outline to make sure that I had clearly spelled out class rules, routines, and procedures. Sure enough, I had clearly stated these as well as the number of points lost off the final grade for not complying. I recognized that this consequence was not effective with the new students, so I knew I had to try another approach.

I decided to hold discussions with each of my classes to examine the issue. I asked probing questions to determine what the students did and did not like about the physical education program. I asked them to suggest changes I could make in order to make class more interesting. They offered some good suggestions and along with some of my ideas, we jointly decided to modify class content to include the following: (a) a weight training program, (b) line file sprints with a soccer ball instead of wind sprints, (c) more time to play games and less practice time spent on drills, (d) fitness tests to help each student develop an individualized fitness program, and (e) teams and contests to see which team could perform the most fitness activities.

I agreed to spend some time over Christmas vacation revising the curriculum to reflect their input. With the new curriculum the students felt they had a vested interest in the program, and tardiness decreased by 50 percent, attendance increased by 30 percent, bringing clean gym clothes increased by 40 percent, participation in all class activities increased by 50 percent, and completion of assignments increased by 60 percent. The students even asked me if they could plan a "Fitness Day" for the students at the local elementary school!

After one year of following the first nine steps of the plan, I knew that I had really grown as a teacher. I could see this in the way my students responded to me in and outside of the gym. By the end of May, many of the students who had given me so much grief last November and December when they transferred into my classes came in to visit with me after school because they knew I cared about them. This rapport had made behavior management considerably easier by the end of the school year. The students knew that I said what I meant, meant what I said, and did what I said I was going to do—all in a very matter-of-fact, but warm and friendly manner. They knew I was there for them as a mentor if they needed it, and they knew I would work with them instead of against them to solve any problems we had.

Still, I have many ideas for how to get off to a stronger start this coming Fall. For example, I am going to assign a peer buddy to each new student as he arrives to smooth the transition for everyone. Because I saw the power of positive reinforcement work so effectively last year, I am going to find more ways to accentuate the positive like creating a "Super Stars" bulletin board, featuring a student from each class who has improved performance or behavior the most each month. Furthermore, one of the main goals I have is to stay more alert to potential problems and intervene either before trouble starts or more quickly if it has already started, instead of waiting until something bothers me so much I can't stand it. Finally, in order to give my students more one-on-one attention, I am going to involve community volunteers more in my classes. Hopefully, this will prevent attention-seeking misbehavior.

I must remember that change is a continual process—I plan to reflect and assess on an ongoing basis. I'm sure I'll keep modifying my approach as I learn and grow. After all, teaching is the only profession I know of in which I'll get a fresh start every year!

## CONCLUSION: YOU CAN DO IT!

Managing the behavior of the students in your classes takes time and energy, but it is possible! You will feel more productive as a teacher. Keep in mind that students want you to care enough to help them take responsibility for their behavior. Certainly, the benefits you and your students will reap are well worth the effort. You will spend more time teaching and less time managing behavior. Your students will be more successful academically and socially. Their self-concepts will be enhanced and they will like school more.

To be an effective behavior manager, you must be flexible, prepared, organized, interested, confident of your instructional role, and aware of your own strengths and weaknesses. You must analyze situations, study the variables involved, and determine which methods will work best in different situations with different students. Most importantly, you must be able to objectively analyze your teaching style and be willing to change. Use the checklists in appendix 1 and worksheet 8 in appendix 2, "Student Information Worksheet," to guide you.

This is an ongoing process filled with many ups and downs. There will be times when you will want to throw in the towel and apply for a desk job. Even when you are demoralized—even when you think no one appreciates all that you are trying to do—don't give up! If you apply the information in this book, you will become a more effective teacher, and the "ups" of teaching will far outnumber the "downs." More and more, you will see the positive influence you are having on your students' lives and will feel fulfilled. When a student comes up to you and says, "Thanks for caring about me. I am glad you are my teacher," you'll know that all the time and energy you put into behavior management have been worthwhile.

# REVIEW: VIGNETTE APPLICATION EXERCISES AND ONGOING GROWTH

For each of the three vignettes on page x, first write or think about how you would approach the situation in light of all we've discussed in this book, then read the suggestions in "One Last Look at the Vignettes" on page 129. Tap into the various methods we've discussed in this book, then tailor them to fit the behavior as well as the policies and procedures of your school district and your state, considering your own personality and the students' personalities.

For an example of a complete behavior management program that has been used successfully in physical education, see "Increase the Peace," page 134. In the years ahead, refer often to the checklists in appendix 1 and use the worksheets in appendix 2 to make sure you remain on the right track.

# One Last Look at the Vignettes

Following are comprehensive treatments of how we would approach each vignette situation in light of all we've discussed in this book. Use these examples to help review your understanding of how to handle behavior management problems, and to jog your own thinking about the difficulties you encounter in your own classroom/gym.

## VIGNETTE 1: OVERACTIVE THIRD GRADER

Let's consider Hector, the overactive third grader. First and foremost, adopt the teaching philosophy that all students should be actively involved in physical education. In fact, physical education class is an excellent place to allow overactive students to expend their excess energy, if done in a controlled and appropriate manner. So set a long-range goal for Hector to listen to instructions without interrupting, to participate in the day's activities, to wait his turn as needed, and to stay at the assigned station without wandering around the gym. With these goals in mind, you might approach this situation in the following manner.

Students who are overactive need an individualized physical education program prescribed for them so that they can use their excess energy in appropriate ways. First, assess Hector's physical fitness level. Then have a conference with him to share the assessment data with him and ask for his input in developing an individualized physical fitness program. Next prescribe a warm-up for him, along with the rest of the class, that will keep him very active, for example, jogging for five minutes, doing 50 crunches, doing 10 pushups, then jogging in place as a warm-up while waiting for you to give the class instructions. Then, with the parent's help using the assessment results and Hector's input, develop a very active and challenging individualized physical fitness program that he could perform at home or at school with a trained teacher's aide. Discuss the benefits of his sticking to this program as well as his responsibility for doing the activities prescribed on a daily basis. Develop a self-evaluation method (see chapter 6) so that he will be able to complete the checklist of activities for each day. Hector may need a peer tutor to help him fill out the self-evaluation checklist. Evaluate Hector's program weekly to ensure that he is completing the activities and that they are challenging to him. Increase the frequency, intensity, and duration of activities as warranted. Add new activities on a regular basis.

At the first conference (or a second conference if Hector's attention span requires it) discuss with Hector how his interrupting the instruction time and then asking you questions afterward are frustrating to you. Ask him what he thinks he could do to stop these behaviors. If he says he is willing to listen during instruction time and not interrupt, suggest that you work together to establish a behavior contract (see chapter 4) in which you state that if he does not interrupt your instructions for a week (or the number of classes you think he can handle successfully), he may choose the game the class will play on Friday, or a similar reward that

*continued*

Hector likes. Put the better listening behavior on his daily self-evaluation chart so that he can keep track of it. If Hector does interrupt your instructions, do not allow him to mark "good listening" on his self-evaluation chart that day.

Plan the physical education class so that students are active at least 90 percent of the time, minimizing the time they may have to wait in line. This is, however, an important social skill for students to acquire so develop a plan to increase Hector's good waiting behavior.

Begin by asking Hector how he feels when someone else cuts in front of him in line. Discuss his feelings, then ask him to tell you why he thinks it is so hard for him to wait his turn. He may or may not be able to tell you that he has too much energy, making it very difficult to relax. If he does not tell you this, suggest it as a possible reason, then teach him a relaxation technique that he can do while he is waiting his turn, such as deep breathing. Suggest that he can also use this technique when he is in his regular class and is having trouble sitting still. Perhaps also suggest that he jog in place in line or do some of the stretching exercises from his individualized program. Make sure he understands that this is acceptable in your class, but may not be in other school situations. Put "waiting for turns" on his daily self-evaluation chart so that he can keep track of this behavior. Make sure you reinforce this behavior when you catch him waiting his turn in class or when you see it on his chart. If he does cut in line, make him wait out two extra turns—a very strong punishment in his mind.

If Hector has helped develop his own physical fitness program designed to keep him very active, he probably will be too busy to wander around the gym. If, however, he does still wander, ask him if he has completed the day's activities. If he has, then his program needs to include more activities. Once an appropriate program has been chosen, establish with him a reward for finishing the activities by the end of the class period.

Perhaps Hector is simply an energetic child or maybe he is truly hyperactive. You may be able to help a team of professionals diagnose his problem (see worksheet 6 in appendix 2). If he is hyperactive, his condition may have a number of causes. One of the most likely causes is his diet. Often sugars, dyes, and preservatives seem to contribute to hyperactive behavior (see chapter 7). In your conference with Hector, ask him to recall, if he can, what he ate for the last two days. Discuss with him the fact that sugary or other junk foods might make it more difficult for him to cooperate. Then ask him if he will keep track of everything that he eats for a week by writing it in a journal. Have him also write down how he feels each day (e.g., tired, anxious, frustrated, relaxed, etc.). At the end of that week, meet again to discuss his diet. Discuss the differences in how he felt, depending on what he ate. If he can make a connection between diet and how he feels he will be more likely to change his diet. Discuss with him changes you think will help. Consider calling his parents in for a conference to enlist their support. Certainly, if keeping track is too difficult and overwhelming for Hector, you will need the parents' help in monitoring his diet. There are computer programs that help keep track of and analyze diets.

Follow up by monitoring Hector's problem behaviors of interrupting, not waiting his turn, and wandering to see if the methods you have tried are effective. Monitor his physical fitness program as well to see if he is completing his daily activities; modify the program based on his progress. Finally, monitor Hector's diet to see if any changes in it correlate with changes in behavior.

Chances are Hector will think these are good ideas and be excited to begin his new behavior management program. He probably will look forward to the opportunity to choose the game the next Friday.

*continued*

# VIGNETTE 2: FIGHTING IN THE LOCKER ROOM

Clearly, fighting is one of the most inappropriate behaviors that occurs on the school grounds. The obvious result of fighting is that it may lead to physical harm. The key—as with all inappropriate behavior—is to be proactive and prevent this type of behavior from occurring in the first place. Once it occurs, work hard to stop it from continuing or spreading.

First, if fighting and similar types of behavior that disrupt the learning process are a chronic problem, be proactive in selecting a teaching approach that is designed to prevent these types of behaviors. Strive to develop personal and social responsible behavior within a curriculum that emphasizes physical activity. Hellison's Personal and Social Responsibility Model (1995) discussed in depth in chapter 6 is an effective approach. While it takes time to design this type of program, it will be worth it. If the problem is not chronic, consider simply using the talking bench.

Second, never leave the locker room unsupervised when students are using this area. If possible, rotate the supervision responsibility with other physical educators. If you are the only physical educator and have large classes, try to purchase large mirrors to mount on the walls to enable you to see down aisles. Another proactive method is to assign the students to every other locker to keep them apart. Assigning will also keep the class in one area for easier supervision as opposed to letting the students pick their own lockers. Be aware that unsupervised locker rooms are a liability suit waiting to happen! The physical education staff must work together with the male staff in supervising the boys' locker room and the female staff in supervising the girls' locker room.

Third, post the class rules—including one related to fighting—and the consequences for breaking each rule where all can see them. Send these rules home in memo format at the beginning of the school year. Ask parents to read the rules and then sign the memo, stating they understand your rules. You can assign this task as homework and give points for returning the memo signed by the end of the week. It is always wise, particularly at the secondary level, to spot-check and call some of the parents to see who actually signed the memo. You may also wish to give a quiz at the beginning of the year, testing students' knowledge of the rules. One creative approach used by some teachers to continually reinforce and review the rules is putting the class rules into a rap song and having students sing it during the warm-up. Other teachers have developed a poem that is repeated during this time. Can't come up with a clever rap or poem? You can hold contests, cosponsored by the music or English teachers, to create and periodically revise the rap song or poem. If in your school district, the general rules and consequences have been predetermined, ensure that your rules and consequences are consistent with them.

Beyond these basic measures, work to ensure that the penalty for fighting is strong enough to deter it. For instance, in Denton (Texas) Independent School District, fighting generally results in an automatic expulsion for a duration not to exceed 10 school days. The student who is expelled is prohibited from being on the school grounds or attending school-sponsored or school-related activities during the expulsion period. The guidelines for discipline penalties related to fighting are based on a careful assessment of the circumstances of each case. Some factors that are considered are (a) seriousness of the fighting offense, (b) student's age, (c) student's attitude, and (d) potential effect of the misconduct on the school environment. Often, a parent-teacher-administrator conference is also

*continued*

held. The family's opinions and requests are taken into consideration in the final decision as to the disciplinary action.

Even with the best proactive methods in place, they may not prevent fighting. If a fight does occur, the offenders should be sent immediately to the office. Probably both should be expelled, but the length of time should perhaps be shorter for Ashante because of the circumstances surrounding the fight. Consider recommending that one or more of the following options be added to Jim's consequence: (a) Ban him from playing in a specific number of football games; (b) develop a behavioral contract that is read, agreed on, and signed by Jim, his parents, the physical educator, and a school administrator (refer to chapter 4 regarding contracts); and (c) provide long-term individual or group counseling throughout the school year.

In addition to the behavioral contract, catch Jim being good and reinforce him for this. At home, his parents may want to seek possible medical assistance if a neurological basis is a possible cause of his aggressive behavior. The behavior contract system used in physical education could also be expanded into the home to provide a more consistent behavioral approach throughout the day. In some cases, you may find it helpful to send a daily or weekly behavioral and performance report home to be signed and commented on by a parent, then returned to you. It is likely that collaboration between you and parents is not only necessary but essential to developing appropriate behavior.

## VIGNETTE 3: UNCOOPERATIVE GIRLS

Now let's examine the case of Jill and Molly, the girls who refuse to dress for physical education, taking into consideration all we've discussed in this book.

If, like us, your teaching philosophy is for all students to be as actively involved in physical education as possible so they may enjoy the lifetime benefits physical activity can bring, you must deal decisively with failure to dress. Certainly, students cannot benefit from physical education if they are not participating. So make it your long-range goal to have both girls dress for class because they are intrinsically motivated by the enjoyment physical activity brings (see chapter 6 and the section on self-evaluation). With this goal in mind, try the following different management methods ranging from lesser to greater degrees of intervention.

It is important to note that teaching philosophies vary regarding dress for physical education. So along with the rest of the physical education staff, examine current program policies and rules regarding dress. For example, are all students required to wear a uniform? Perhaps you can change the policy to allow students to dress in comfortable clothes for physical activity, including sweats, which helps some students, especially those who are shy, awkward, or obese, or who are otherwise embarrassed to be seen in shorts or a uniform.

Initially, establish a proactive behavior management plan regarding dress, introducing it to all students the first week of class. See chapter 2 for specific suggestions regarding this process.

For the majority of students in the program, these proactive management methods are enough to ensure proper dress. Since, however, they have proven ineffective with Jill and Molly, meet with both girls to discuss the importance of physical activity and have them offer you reasons why dressing for class is necessary (safety, personal hygiene, comfort, and enhanced performance).

More importantly, seek to determine the underlying reason they are not dressing for class. Be aware, however, that they may be hesitant to give their

*continued*

reasons. This is where meeting and communicating with the girls is important. If necessary, speak with Jill and Molly individually about their needs (see chapter 6). While this requires extra time, getting to know Jill and Molly and making them feel comfortable with you may help alleviate the problem. After some gentle probing, you may discover one or more reasons why the girls are not dressing, such as their parents cannot afford to purchase gym clothes, they are embarrassed to undress in front of others, they do not want to get sweaty, or are fearful of participating because they are less skilled than their peers. Some reasons for not dressing may be easier to solve than others. For example, if they cannot afford to purchase the clothes, you can probably easily remedy this by using school funds.

A good possibility exists, however, that the reason for not dressing is that Jill and Molly do not care for the activities you're offering. This is why it is important to offer a variety of appealing activities. So determine what activities Jill and Molly enjoy and explain that you will offer some of these activities as part of the curriculum later in the school year. In fact, when possible, give all students opportunities to choose activities they enjoy. For example, having the class vote on the Friday activity, allowing a student who has earned a privilege to select the activity, or offering a variety of drills from which to choose to improve in a certain sport may all be appropriate at times.

Since Jill and Molly are friends, have them work together to encourage each other to dress and participate. This encouragement or peer pressure may prove helpful. In addition, during this meeting, review your expectations, including the rules for dress and participation. Be positive but firm with them, explaining that not participating will result in not earning points for class, which will lead to failing grades. Show each student her current grade point average.

Then explain to Jill and Molly that on the days they do not dress for class they must write a report by the end of the period on the topic or unit in which the class is participating. This strategy is a constructive way to keep the students on-task so that they do not become behavior problems while sitting out because they are bored. They may want to avoid writing the report (negative reinforcement) and consequently dress for class. Do not overuse this strategy, however, as it may create in them a negative attitude toward academic work. End the meeting on a positive note by explaining to both students that you are confident they can dress and participate each day. State, "It is your choice to dress or not dress for class, and you know the consequence if you choose not to."

If after a week or two the girls are still not dressing, develop a behavioral contract (see chapter 4). Keep the contract simple. For example, if Jill and Molly dress and participate in class for so many days, they will earn a reinforcer you all agree on. The reinforcer they earn could be to choose one of the activities they earlier told you they enjoyed and have the entire class participate with them (see table 4.1 and worksheet 2 in appendix 2 for lists of different types of activities and privileges). But it is quite possible that the reinforcer they choose may not involve physical activity: They may be more interested in something unrelated to physical education, such as a poster of a rock band or a gift certificate for frozen yogurt. Remember that for a reinforcer to have meaning, it must be one the individual really desires and is willing to work toward. With your gentle but firm guidance, Jill and Molly may discover that they like physical activity after all!

# Increase the Peace

After years of dealing with anger, aggression, and confusion not only with students with behavior disorders but also with disadvantaged high-risk students, teachers could clearly see a need for change. The creative answer? "Increase the Peace" is a step-by-step program designed by music therapy and special physical education teachers to teach cooperation to elementary school students (Levis and Lininger 1994). While special educators use this approach extensively with students who exhibit behavioral disorders because it helps teachers effectively manage their classrooms, this program has been implemented in a variety of settings from individual self-contained classrooms and special instructional areas to entire campuses.

The goal of the Increase the Peace program is for students to develop and experience a clear understanding of cooperation through tools known as focus words. To implement this program, you must reward or penalize students on a daily basis, based on their abilities to understand and demonstrate a focus word. To reinforce appropriate responses, give students praise, peace chips, certificates, prizes, and celebrations called "Peacefests." To penalize inappropriate responses, give warnings, administer time-outs, and assign essays. Above all, be consistent. Once students see that making a positive change truly helps them succeed, they will meet the program's objectives every day. But this is not a competition: The goal is not win at all costs but to increase the peace and have fun doing it.

The core focus words are communication, honesty, teamwork, sportsmanship, and compromise. In the beginning, you concentrate on one focus word a week. Everything you teach should emphasize that one word in some way. By experiencing the word and expressing how it makes them feel, it becomes a part of the students' vocabularies. After introducing each of the core focus words, you teach and reteach them over time. As students demonstrate understanding of the core focus words, include these five other focus words: encouragement, maturity, composure, consideration, and patience. Then you can use and reinforce all 10 words throughout the rest of the year in every lessons.

Design cooperative learning lessons around each focus word to meet both behavioral and content objectives. Then during each class lesson, emphasize the focus word. When students do not demonstrate an understanding of the focus word, stop the lesson immediately—no matter how frequently this is required. You'll find that the competitive students become so frustrated with constant stopping that they eventually focus on the word so the activity can continue. Then you should praise students who are focused. In this way, you'll see students become more and more successful in demonstrating the focus word. Others follow suit so they too can be successful. The students enjoy the nonthreatening environment and the chance to make choices. Moreover, they stay more active, which, in turn, helps them develop skills, and most importantly, gives them the opportunity to apply and practice the new focus word—all while having fun. Let's turn, now, to the specific strategies that make "Increase the Peace" work.

Use positive reinforcements as a fun and rewarding way to build on successes. First collect data on class performance during a two-week period. Make a "peace chart" listing all students' names for each self-contained class. Use the following marks to record student performance:

• ___ Underlining the appropriate box indicates participation without problems.

• * indicates that the student had a minor problem but was able to resolve it in a "planning time." Planning time is a private second chance with minor consequences if the student chooses to discuss the problem, then rejoin the class and finish without further problems. You can have students discuss the problem among themselves, with an adult assistant, or with you when you have time. If the students involved cannot resolve the issue, consider including the entire class in solving the problem. This alone can help decrease the likelihood of other students having the same problem in the future.

• **X1** indicates the student served one time-out. Place a student who is out of control and unable to function in a planning time in a 3- to 5-minute time-out to give her time to calm down. When the student is calm enough, ask her if she is ready for a planning time. Require that the student respond verbally in an appropriate manner before discussing the problem. Once again, the planning time is a chance to develop a strategy to continue class, but now, however, the student must fill out a "peace plan." The peace plan is a written contract on which you have listed a variety of potential behavior problems. Have the student circle what she is having trouble with and what she can do to change her behavior. After she completes and signs the peace plan, allow her to rejoin the class. The student loses several points off the behavior contract, depending on the severity of the problem and how well the student cooperated during the planning time.

• **X2** indicates the student served a second time-out. This time-out should be slightly longer than the first, about 5 to 10 minutes, depending on how hard it is for the student to calm down and the problem itself. After serving the time quietly, the student must then complete another peace plan or add to the first one. Subtract several more points off the behavior contract as appropriate.

• **X3** indicates the student served a third time-out and must leave class and write an essay due the next day, discussing her peace plan in detail as appropriate for her academic level. Do not allow her to participate until she writes the essay, using physical education time to complete the task. Contact her parents to enlist their support.

• **Ab** indicates the student was absent.

• **X** indicates the student has served a suspension in the regular classroom instead of attending physical education.

Please note, however, that we do not advise classroom teachers to suspend students from special areas due to classroom behavior unless that student is a threat to others. Remember,

our goal is to keep students as active as possible. Keep a two-week daily log of each student's behavior before instituting the reward system. To streamline the process, enlist the help of squad leaders in recording the correct statistics, then you simply double-check their marks to ensure accuracy.

Students function within the Increase the Peace program on one of four levels. They all begin on level 1 and may progress to the next level every time they meet the criteria you set, such as completing a two-week period with no Xs of any kind. Make four different colors of "peace chips," one for each of the four levels out of colored paper, two inches square. Every day, give each student who performs well, earning a "_" on the chart, one to four peace chips, corresponding to the level which he has reached. Write the student's name on each peace chip and have the student drop them into the appropriate-level box, which has been decorated by students. Occasionally, choose an activity that has been especially hard for your students to complete peacefully and challenge them to earn bonus peace chips. The more peace chips a student earns, the better chance he has of winning at the end of the second week.

In the meantime, give out "Super Student" awards each Friday to each student who had no more than one * and no Xs for the week. The certificate should state that the student increased the peace that week. While students with more than one planning time or any time-outs the first week cannot have a Super Student certificate, they should still be eligible for Super Student and the drawing if they can have a good second week.

At the end of two weeks, hold a "peace day." On peace day, conduct a short lesson, 15 to 20 minutes long, reflecting on whether the students achieved peace during the two weeks. Remove the peace chips belonging to students who earned three or more Xs of any kind during the two-week period. Then draw one or two peace chips from each level's peace box. Allow these winners to each choose a prize from appropriate level's "peace bag," which contains donated or purchased T-shirts, books, magazines, school supplies, or other items the students like. The higher the level, the higher the quality of items in its peace bag. If a student has won a previous drawing and you draw her name again, award her a prize; however, draw a second name from among the students who have never won. In this way, you should be able to make sure all students win at least once a semester. After the drawing, allow all other students who were eligible for the drawing to choose a small prize (stickers, erasers, pencils, and the like). Depending on the class, you may wish to allow eligible students to earn free time as well. As you see fit, opt for a structured free time, setting up the gym with a choice of activities, or allow a less-structured general free time. During free time, insist that all students increase the peace or lose the privilege of participating.

Highlight the end of each six weeks with a celebration known as the "Peacefest," reflecting the focus words studied during the previous six weeks. This may involve a field trip with classes from all six schools served by the special physical educator and music therapist or a school-wide celebration, involving activities such as, a tennis carnival, a fun run, a holiday program, a volleyball tournament, a rap contest, a songwriting or poetry contest, an artwork show, a track and field meet, new games, or the like. You can even combine music and physical education instruction to celebrate increasing the peace. Make sure students understand they must show consistent signs of increasing the peace before they can go to a Peacefest.

How do you get started? Conduct or invite someone else to conduct an inservice for the classroom teachers, explaining exactly what is done and the steps taken toward cooperation. It really helps when regular classroom teachers use the focus words, too. Indeed, when all adults work toward the Peacefest, the chances for success are greatly increased. Your enthusiasm may even convince your colleagues and administrators to adopt "Increase the Peace" as a theme and have all students work toward a school-wide celebration.

"Increase the Peace" is continually evolving so don't be afraid to try new techniques. Some ideas will work and others will fail, and that's okay. Any concept or skill you teach with enthusiasm, fun, clear understanding, and obtainable goals will be successful. If every student leaves feeling good about herself because she was part of the group, then consider it a successful day. Remember, however, teaching has mountains and valleys. Without a plan, the valley will remain constantly flooded with anger, aggression, and frustrations. So rise above it all, climb that mountain, develop a plan that works, and you can help to increase the peace. For more information contact: Lynda Levis, 11806 Byers Cove, Austin, TX, 78753.

# Checklists for Self-Evaluation

### Checklist 1

## PERSONAL INVENTORY

Rate yourself in regard to the following statements.

|  | Consistently | Inconsistently | Never |
|---|---|---|---|
| I am tuned in to my students' needs and interests. | ❑ | ❑ | ❑ |
| I am enthusiastic when I teach. | ❑ | ❑ | ❑ |
| I am flexible in my approach to managing behavior. | ❑ | ❑ | ❑ |
| I am personable, putting my students at ease. | ❑ | ❑ | ❑ |
| I strive to know my students as individuals. | ❑ | ❑ | ❑ |

### Checklist 2

## USING POSITIVE APPROACHES

Rate yourself in regard to the following statements.

|  | Consistently | Inconsistently | Never |
|---|---|---|---|
| I catch my students being good. | ❑ | ❑ | ❑ |
| I expect students to follow my directions. | ❑ | ❑ | ❑ |
| I keep my cool and address problems quickly. | ❑ | ❑ | ❑ |
| I focus on the behavior I am correcting, not on the students involved. | ❑ | ❑ | ❑ |
| My behavior and treatment of students is consistent. | ❑ | ❑ | ❑ |
| I do what I say I'm going to do: |  |  |  |
|    I check for compliance. | ❑ | ❑ | ❑ |
|    I respond the same way to the same behavior. | ❑ | ❑ | ❑ |
|    I encourage consistency among all physical education staff members. | ❑ | ❑ | ❑ |
| I use positive tools, such as varying tasks, playing music, and using physical activity to help students relax. | ❑ | ❑ | ❑ |
| I use a continuum of styles as appropriate. | ❑ | ❑ | ❑ |

### Checklist 3

## AVOIDING NEGATIVE APPROACHES

Rate yourself in regard to the following statements.

|  | Consistently | Inconsistently | Never |
|---|---|---|---|
| I refrain from making comparisons between students. | ❑ | ❑ | ❑ |
| I avoid making idle threats. | ❑ | ❑ | ❑ |

| | Consistently | Inconsistently | Never |
|---|:---:|:---:|:---:|
| I avoid being sarcastic. | ❏ | ❏ | ❏ |
| I refrain from humiliating students. | ❏ | ❏ | ❏ |
| I avoid overstating the management situation. | ❏ | ❏ | ❏ |

## Checklist 4

## EFFECTIVE COUNSELING

Rate yourself in regard to the following statements.

| | Consistently | Inconsistently | Never |
|---|:---:|:---:|:---:|
| I seek to determine who owns the problem. | ❏ | ❏ | ❏ |
| I choose my words carefully. | ❏ | ❏ | ❏ |
| I offer guidance, rather than advice. | ❏ | ❏ | ❏ |
| I ask open-ended questions to help students solve their own problems. | ❏ | ❏ | ❏ |
| I allow students to make their own decisions as to how to meet my long-term expectations. | ❏ | ❏ | ❏ |
| I clarify what I think students are saying, rather than playing psychoanalyst and assuming reasons. | ❏ | ❏ | ❏ |
| I deal with problem behaviors as they occur, instead of using diversionary tactics | ❏ | ❏ | ❏ |

## Checklist 5

## EVALUATING YOUR PRACTICES IN PHYSICAL EDUCATION

Consider the following statements in regard to your **students**, then for each statement check the column that most accurately describes your current approach.

| | Consistently | Inconsistently | Never |
|---|:---:|:---:|:---:|
| I explain to students why certain behaviors are necessary. | ❏ | ❏ | ❏ |
| I don't view inappropriate behavior as personally threatening. | ❏ | ❏ | ❏ |
| I interact positively with students. | ❏ | ❏ | ❏ |
| I learn all students' names. | ❏ | ❏ | ❏ |
| I get students' attention quickly and effectively. | ❏ | ❏ | ❏ |
| I reinforce students who act appropriately. | ❏ | ❏ | ❏ |
| I respect students' opinions and avoid sarcasm. | ❏ | ❏ | ❏ |
| I communicate realistic expectations to students. | ❏ | ❏ | ❏ |
| I learn all I can about my students. | ❏ | ❏ | ❏ |
| I provide age-appropriate activities to my students. | ❏ | ❏ | ❏ |
| I give students clear directions. | ❏ | ❏ | ❏ |
| I identify students who have medical problems and special needs. | ❏ | ❏ | ❏ |

Consider the following statements in regard to your **professionalism** as a physical educator, then for each statement check the column that most accurately describes your current approach.

| | Consistently | Inconsistently | Never |
|---|---|---|---|
| I am knowledgeable of subject content. | ❏ | ❏ | ❏ |
| I present curriculum in a clear sequence that is easy for students to follow. | ❏ | ❏ | ❏ |
| I clearly communicate my expectations and consequences. | ❏ | ❏ | ❏ |
| I am consistent in my expectations. | ❏ | ❏ | ❏ |
| I model appropriate behavior. | ❏ | ❏ | ❏ |
| I emphasize meeting lesson objectives. | ❏ | ❏ | ❏ |
| I am tuned in to my class. | ❏ | ❏ | ❏ |
| I am enthusiastic about my teaching and my students. | ❏ | ❏ | ❏ |
| I earn the students' trust and respect. | ❏ | ❏ | ❏ |

Consider the following statements in regard to your **teaching-learning environment**, then for each statement check the column that most accurately describes your current approach.

| | Consistently | Inconsistently | Never |
|---|---|---|---|
| I provide a warm, supportive class climate that encourages learning. | ❏ | ❏ | ❏ |
| I design class activities so all students are actively involved. | ❏ | ❏ | ❏ |
| I design class activities so all students feel safe. | ❏ | ❏ | ❏ |
| I periodically check facilities and equipment for safety. | ❏ | ❏ | ❏ |
| I design activities to promote positive self-images. | ❏ | ❏ | ❏ |
| I design facilities to maximize learning. | ❏ | ❏ | ❏ |
| I have a backup plan when facilities are not available. | ❏ | ❏ | ❏ |
| I match activities to student needs. | ❏ | ❏ | ❏ |
| I orient students to management procedures, such as rules, routines, and transitions. | ❏ | ❏ | ❏ |

## Checklist 6

## PROACTIVE PLANNING DURING THE PREINSTRUCTIONAL AND INSTRUCTIONAL PHASES

Check off when you have set and initiated your policy concerning each of the following aspects of physical education management.

**Preinstructional:**

❏ Locker room procedures
❏ Attendance policies
❏ Excuses from class
❏ Dressing for class
❏ Entering and exiting the gymnasium, playground, and playing fields

**Instructional:**

- ❏ Orientation
- ❏ Class rules
- ❏ Taking attendance
- ❏ Signals
- ❏ Establishing the initial activity
- ❏ Distribution of equipment
- ❏ Organization of students into partners, groups, and teams
- ❏ Transitions between activities
- ❏ Prompting students
- ❏ Student formations
- ❏ Handling disruptions and unforeseen circumstances
- ❏ Collection of equipment

## Checklist 7

### STEPS IN DESIGNING THE BEHAVIORAL APPROACH

|  | Consistently | Inconsistently | Never |
|---|:---:|:---:|:---:|
| When selecting and defining a target behavior: | | | |
| I choose a measurable behavior (see table 3.1). | ❏ | ❏ | ❏ |
| I define precisely what I will observe. | ❏ | ❏ | ❏ |
| I prioritize the problem behaviors. | ❏ | ❏ | ❏ |
| When I observe and record the behavior | | | |
| I pinpoint the behavior, including | | | |
| event, | ❏ | ❏ | ❏ |
| duration, and | ❏ | ❏ | ❏ |
| interval. | ❏ | ❏ | ❏ |
| I use time sampling. | ❏ | ❏ | ❏ |
| I check for reliability. | ❏ | ❏ | ❏ |
| I plan the intervention to maintain, increase, or decrease the behavior using checklists 8 through 13, as appropriate. | ❏ | ❏ | ❏ |
| I evaluate intervention program effectiveness by making | | | |
| observations, | ❏ | ❏ | ❏ |
| charts, and | ❏ | ❏ | ❏ |
| graphs. | ❏ | ❏ | ❏ |

## Checklist 8

### DEVELOPING BEHAVIORAL CONTRACTS

**Writing a contract:**

- ❏ I have stated what I expect, instead of what I don't want.
- ❏ The contract is fair and suitable to all involved.
- ❏ I have designed the contract positively, stressing what will be performed rather than what will not be done.
- ❏ I have ensured that the rewards for compliance are highly prized by those involved and hard to obtain otherwise.

❏ If an initial contract, I have listed rewards for small, incremental accomplishments, gradually delaying rewards over time.

❏ I have included a bonus clause.

❏ If subsequent contract, I have made it more difficult than the previous one.

❏ The contract includes dates that the agreement begins and ends.

### Enforcing a contract:

❏ I have ensured that all involved understand the conditions of the contract.

❏ The contract is signed by all involved, possibly including parents.

❏ I have given each signing person a copy of the contract.

❏ The contract begins as soon as possible after signing.

❏ I give reinforcers immediately after students have earned them.

❏ I enforce the contract consistently and systematically.

### Following up:

❏ If the initial contract seems ineffective or I see that students cannot succeed, I renegotiate the terms accordingly.

## Checklist 9

### ADMINISTERING POSITIVE REINFORCEMENT

|  | Consistently | Inconsistently | Never |
|---|---|---|---|
| I make reinforcement contingent on the student or group demonstrating the appropriate behavior. | ❏ | ❏ | ❏ |
| I individualize reinforcers to meet the unique needs of each student. | ❏ | ❏ | ❏ |
| I am patient with my plan to increase positive behavior. | ❏ | ❏ | ❏ |
| I reinforce the student's desirable behavior immediately. | ❏ | ❏ | ❏ |
| I pair social reinforcers with tangible reinforcers so I can eventually phase out the tangible reinforcers. | ❏ | ❏ | ❏ |
| On the continuum of reinforcement methods, I choose the one that requires the least amount of intervention or, reinforcement to change a behavior. | ❏ | ❏ | ❏ |
| Once the student or class performs at the target level, I reinforce less. | ❏ | ❏ | ❏ |

## Checklist 10

### WITHDRAWING A REINFORCER

|  | Consistently | Inconsistently | Never |
|---|---|---|---|
| **Using extinction or planned ignoring:** | | | |
| I use extinction only for behaviors that are not dangerous. | ❏ | ❏ | ❏ |
| I identify what is reinforcing the student's behavor. | ❏ | ❏ | ❏ |
| I remove the reinforcer without calling attention to what I'm doing. | ❏ | ❏ | ❏ |

| | Consistently | Inconsistently | Never |
|---|:---:|:---:|:---:|
| I recognize that I cannot control all of the student's environment. | ❏ | ❏ | ❏ |
| I reinforce appropriate behaviors displayed by other students. | ❏ | ❏ | ❏ |
| I expect extinction to be gradual, staying patient. | ❏ | ❏ | ❏ |

**Using response cost:**

| | Consistently | Inconsistently | Never |
|---|:---:|:---:|:---:|
| I ensure that reinforcers for good behavior are available. | ❏ | ❏ | ❏ |
| I make sure the student in question has earned the reinforcer. | ❏ | ❏ | ❏ |
| I choose to withdraw a reinforcer that is important to the student. | ❏ | ❏ | ❏ |
| I keep the withdrawl of reinforcers to a minimum. | ❏ | ❏ | ❏ |
| I explain to the student which behavior is causing me to take the reinforcer away ahead of time. | ❏ | ❏ | ❏ |
| I refrain from warning, nagging, or threatening the student. | ❏ | ❏ | ❏ |
| I avoid trying to justify my enforcement of a response cost. | ❏ | ❏ | ❏ |
| When possible, I allow natural or logical consequences to take place instead of becoming actively involved. | ❏ | ❏ | ❏ |

**Using time-out:**

| | Consistently | Inconsistently | Never |
|---|:---:|:---:|:---:|
| I specify the period of time to be in time-out in advance. | ❏ | ❏ | ❏ |
| I inform the student specifically which behavior led to the time out. | ❏ | ❏ | ❏ |
| I administer time-out in a consistent and matter-of-fact manner. | ❏ | ❏ | ❏ |
| I wait until the disruptive behavior stops before starting to time the time-out. | ❏ | ❏ | ❏ |
| I make sure time-out is not actually reinforcing, including making sure the student is not getting out of a situation she doesn't like. | ❏ | ❏ | ❏ |
| After the time-out, I have the student state the rule broken, then tell how she'll avoid breaking the rule in the future. | ❏ | ❏ | ❏ |
| After the time-out, I reinforce appropriate behavior when the student exhibits it. | ❏ | ❏ | ❏ |

## Checklist 11

## PRESENTING AVERSIVE STIMULI

**Using direct discussion:**

| | Consistently | Inconsistently | Never |
|---|:---:|:---:|:---:|
| I first determine the cause of the misbehavior. | ❏ | ❏ | ❏ |
| I am nonthreatening. | ❏ | ❏ | ❏ |
| I show sincere concern for the student. | ❏ | ❏ | ❏ |
| If still necessary, I set and enforce a consequence for the behavior. | ❏ | ❏ | ❏ |

| | Consistently | Inconsistently | Never |
|---|:---:|:---:|:---:|
| **Using verbal reprimand:** | | | |
| I first try nonverbal reprimands, such as hand signals, whenever possible. | ❏ | ❏ | ❏ |
| I make it clear to the student that the behavior is unacceptable and why. | ❏ | ❏ | ❏ |
|    I am specific. | ❏ | ❏ | ❏ |
|    I am firm. | ❏ | ❏ | ❏ |
|    I remain calm. | ❏ | ❏ | ❏ |
|    I avoid degrading or embarrassing the student. | ❏ | ❏ | ❏ |
|    I avoid sarcasm. | ❏ | ❏ | ❏ |
|    I avoid trying to make the student feel guilty. | ❏ | ❏ | ❏ |
| I reprimand immediately after the behavior occurs. | ❏ | ❏ | ❏ |
| If the behavior is dangerous, I remove the student by giving a time-out. | ❏ | ❏ | ❏ |
| If necessary, I back up the reprimand with a loss of privilege (response cost). | ❏ | ❏ | ❏ |
| I follow through if I commit to a time-out or response cost. | ❏ | ❏ | ❏ |
| I remember that when it's over, it's over, avoiding reminding the student of the misbehavior. | ❏ | ❏ | ❏ |
| **Avoiding using corporal punishment:** | | | |
| I am aware of my school's or district's policy regarding corporal punishment. | Yes | No | |
| Regardless of the policy, I agree that it is never appropriate to hit a student. | Yes | No | |
| I get myself and others away from a violent student. | Yes | No | |
| If necessary, I use physical restraint to protect myself, the student, or others. | Yes | No | |
| **Using physical restraint:** | | | |
| I am aware of my school's or district's policy regarding physical restraint. | Yes | No | |
| I avoid touching students when I'm angry. | Yes | No | |
| I use physical restraint only when I can't get away from a violent student or to stop him from hurting himself or others. | Yes | No | |
|    • Stand behind the student. | | | |
|    • Hold the student's wrists with arms crossed over the chest. | | | |
| I hold the student firmly, not roughly, giving the feeling of protection, not punishment, until he calms down. | Yes | No | |

## Checklist 12

## REQUIRING AVERSIVE BEHAVIORS

| | Consistently | Inconsistently | Never |
|---|:---:|:---:|:---:|
| **Requiring physical activity or extra academic work:** | | | |
| I avoid physical activity as punishment, because it may give students a negative attitude toward physical activity. | ❏ | ❏ | ❏ |

| | Consistently | Inconsistently | Never |
|---|---|---|---|
| **Requiring reparation:** | | | |
| I inform parents of the misbehavior and the consequence. | ❏ | ❏ | ❏ |
| If helpful, I hold a conference with the parents and student to determine the consequence and how it will be met. | ❏ | ❏ | ❏ |
| I encourage parents to support the consequence, rather than bailing the student out. | ❏ | ❏ | ❏ |
| **Using overcorrection, both restitutional overcorrection (improving the environment, rather than simply repairing it) and positive overcorrection (forcing students to repeatedly perform the appropriate behavior):** | | | |
| I apply overcorrection immediately after the offense. | ❏ | ❏ | ❏ |
| I ensure that the consequence relates to the inappropriate act. | ❏ | ❏ | ❏ |

## Checklist 13

## GENERAL USE OF PUNISHMENT

| | Consistently | Inconsistently | Never |
|---|---|---|---|
| I establish classroom rules and consequences on the first day of school. | ❏ | ❏ | ❏ |
| When I punish, I do so immediately. | ❏ | ❏ | ❏ |
| I maintain my self-control when punishing. | ❏ | ❏ | ❏ |
| I avoid confrontations. | ❏ | ❏ | ❏ |
| I specify the behavior that warranted the punishment. | ❏ | ❏ | ❏ |
| I ensure that my use of punishment is fairly and evenly applied. | ❏ | ❏ | ❏ |
| I make sure the punishment fits the intention of the crime. | ❏ | ❏ | ❏ |
| I am consistent: What is wrong today is wrong tomorrow and the consequences remain the same. | ❏ | ❏ | ❏ |
| I return to positive methods as soon as possible. | | | |
| I avoid hitting. | ❏ | ❏ | ❏ |

## Checklist 14

## PROMOTING PERSONAL RESPONSIBILITY

| | Consistently | Inconsistently | Never |
|---|---|---|---|
| **Teacher talk:** | | | |
| I am aware of how my verbal and nonverbal language affects students. | ❏ | ❏ | ❏ |
| I send positive messages to students, seeking to enhance their senses of self-esteem. | ❏ | ❏ | ❏ |

| | Consistently | Inconsistently | Never |
|---|---|---|---|
| **Student talk:** | | | |
| I do not allow students to blame others for their own problems. | ❏ | ❏ | ❏ |
| I teach students how to rephrase their comments to reflect personal responsibility. | ❏ | ❏ | ❏ |
| **Teacher actions:** | | | |
| I determine what responsibility means to me in a situation. | ❏ | ❏ | ❏ |
| I determine why such responsibility is important. | ❏ | ❏ | ❏ |
| I have students a list of the responsible behaviors I'm expecting. | ❏ | ❏ | ❏ |
| I have students make a checklist of the responsible behaviors they are willing to take responsibility for, thereby encouraging them to evaluate themselves. | ❏ | ❏ | ❏ |
| I work with students to establish consequences for behaving responsibly and irresponsibly. | ❏ | ❏ | ❏ |
| I apply the consequences consistently. | ❏ | ❏ | ❏ |
| I encourage students to see the connection between feelings and behavior. | ❏ | ❏ | ❏ |
| I design activities that nurture personal responsibility. | ❏ | ❏ | ❏ |
| I give students choices of activities and levels of difficulty within each activity. | ❏ | ❏ | ❏ |
| I support students and encourage students to support each other in their choices. | ❏ | ❏ | ❏ |
| I assign personal responsibility projects. | ❏ | ❏ | ❏ |
| **Student actions:** | | | |
| I give students opportunities to demonstrate responsible behavior. | ❏ | ❏ | ❏ |
| I design activities that promote social responsibility. | ❏ | ❏ | ❏ |
| I use cooperative games. | ❏ | ❏ | ❏ |
| I teach conflict resolution skills. | ❏ | ❏ | ❏ |
| I show students how to deal with peer pressure. | ❏ | ❏ | ❏ |

## Checklist 15

## STRATEGIES FOR PUTTING HELLISON'S (1995) LEVELS INTO PRACTICE

| | Consistently | Inconsistently | Never |
|---|---|---|---|
| **Awareness talks:** | | | |
| I hold awareness talks as needed to increase student awareness of the levels. | ❏ | ❏ | ❏ |
| I explain the levels. | ❏ | ❏ | ❏ |
| I reinforce the levels by posting them, briefly verbally reminding students of them, and signaling with the same number of fingers. | ❏ | ❏ | ❏ |
| I periodically conduct sharing sessions so students can teach each other through discussion. | ❏ | ❏ | ❏ |

| | Consistently | Inconsistently | Never |
|---|---|---|---|
| **Levels in action:** | | | |
| I create chances for students to experience one or more levels during physical activity. | ❏ | ❏ | ❏ |
| I use direct questioning to encourage students to experience the levels. | ❏ | ❏ | ❏ |
| I incorporate self-paced activities and reciprocal teaching. | ❏ | ❏ | ❏ |
| I implement service projects. | ❏ | ❏ | ❏ |
| **Reflection time:** | | | |
| I build in time for students to reflect on the levels during lessons. | ❏ | ❏ | ❏ |
| I encourage students to complete a goal-setting checklist (p. 151 in appendix 2). | ❏ | ❏ | ❏ |
| **Individual decision making:** | | | |
| I allow students to negotiate and make choices at each of the levels. | ❏ | ❏ | ❏ |
| **Group meetings:** | | | |
| After students are familiar with the levels, I hold group meetings to allow students to share their opinions, feelings, and ideas about the physical education program. | ❏ | ❏ | ❏ |
| I facilitate these meetings by asking specific, yet open-ended questions. | ❏ | ❏ | ❏ |
| **Counseling time:** | | | |
| I reserve time for one-on-one interactions with students. | ❏ | ❏ | ❏ |
| I work closely with students who need extra guidance in applying the levels. | ❏ | ❏ | ❏ |

## Checklist 16

## APPLYING GLASSER'S (1977) 10-STEP APPROACH TO REALITY THERAPY

❏ I determine and write down current behavior management practices.

❏ I analyze my current methods, and if they aren't working, I commit to not using them anymore.

❏ I build a better personal relationship with the student.

❏ When the student misbehaves, I hold a conference with the student to focus her atttention on the problem behavior.

❏ If the disruptive behavior persists, I hold another conference with the student to review the problem and ask her what she plans to do instead.

❏ If the disruptive behavior persists, I hold a third conference with the student to ask her to write down her plan for improvement.

❏ If the student continues to misbehave, I place her in time-out during class and have her write and sign a new plan.

❏ If the student continues to disrupt, I send her to an in-house suspension, barring her from class until she comes up with a more workable plan to cooperate.

❏ If the student still misbehaves, I ask the parents to take her home, stating that she is welcome to return when she is ready to behave appropriately.

❏ If all else fails, I encourage the principal to expel the student until she is ready to cooperate.

**Checklist 17**

## USING THE SELF-EVALUATION APPROACH

| | Consistently | Inconsistently | Never |
|---|:---:|:---:|:---:|
| I teach students to evaluate their own behavior by comparing it to a set of criteria. | ❑ | ❑ | ❑ |
| I reinforce students when they meet the criteria. | ❑ | ❑ | ❑ |
| I describe and demonstrate target behaviors. | ❑ | ❑ | ❑ |
| I play alongside students to model target behaviors. | ❑ | ❑ | ❑ |
| I encourage students to model target behaviors for others. | ❑ | ❑ | ❑ |
| I ask students to reflect on their behavior at the end of class. | ❑ | ❑ | ❑ |

**Checklist 18**

## FOLLOWING THE 10 BASIC STEPS OF BEHAVIORAL MANAGEMENT

When reviewing your behavioral management strategies, check off each of the steps as you complete them.

1. ❑ I have examined my teaching and behavior management philosophy in regard to the problems I'm having.
2. ❑ I have established my teaching and behavior management goals based on my philosophy.
3. ❑ I have evaluated the effectiveness of my current teaching practices in regard to the problems I'm having.
4. ❑ I have implemented necessary changes in my teaching practices and analyzed the results.
5. ❑ After improving my basic teaching practices, I have ranked which specific behavior problems I need to deal with in order of severity.
6. ❑ I have examined the most problematic behavior, then made an earnest attempt to determine its cause.
7. ❑ I have designed an intervention to change the most problematic behavior.
8. ❑ I have implemented the intervention, then evaluated its effectiveness.
9. ❑ I have repeated steps 6 through 8 for the other problem behaviors I ranked in step 5.
10. ❑ I have repeated the first nine steps at least annually.

# Worksheets for Collecting Data

**WORKSHEET 1**

## Frequency Recording Chart

STUDENT'S NAME:                          INITIAL DATE OF OBSERVATION:

MEASURED BEHAVIOR:

DATES OF OBSERVATIONS:

---

DATES

---

| 12 | 12 | 12 | 12 | 12 | 12 | 12 | 12 | 12 | 12 | 12 | 12 |
|----|----|----|----|----|----|----|----|----|----|----|----|
| 11 | 11 | 11 | 11 | 11 | 11 | 11 | 11 | 11 | 11 | 11 | 11 |
| 10 | 10 | 10 | 10 | 10 | 10 | 10 | 10 | 10 | 10 | 10 | 10 |
| 9 | 9 | 9 | 9 | 9 | 9 | 9 | 9 | 9 | 9 | 9 | 9 |
| 8 | 8 | 8 | 8 | 8 | 8 | 8 | 8 | 8 | 8 | 8 | 8 |
| 7 | 7 | 7 | 7 | 7 | 7 | 7 | 7 | 7 | 7 | 7 | 7 |
| 6 | 6 | 6 | 6 | 6 | 6 | 6 | 6 | 6 | 6 | 6 | 6 |
| 5 | 5 | 5 | 5 | 5 | 5 | 5 | 5 | 5 | 5 | 5 | 5 |
| 4 | 4 | 4 | 4 | 4 | 4 | 4 | 4 | 4 | 4 | 4 | 4 |
| 3 | 3 | 3 | 3 | 3 | 3 | 3 | 3 | 3 | 3 | 3 | 3 |
| 2 | 2 | 2 | 2 | 2 | 2 | 2 | 2 | 2 | 2 | 2 | 2 |
| 1 | 1 | 1 | 1 | 1 | 1 | 1 | 1 | 1 | 1 | 1 | 1 |
| 0 | 0 | 0 | 0 | 0 | 0 | 0 | 0 | 0 | 0 | 0 | 0 |

Cross out a number each time the behavior occurs.

Circle the total number of times the behavior actually occurs for that particular date.

Connect the circles to form a graph.

---

Adapted from J.E. Walker and T. M. Shea (1995). *Behavior Management: A Practical Approach for Educators*, (6th ed.) New York: Macmillan.

**WORKSHEET 2**

## Physical Education Reinforcer Preference List*

NAME _____  CLASS _____

If you were to be rewarded for following class rules, what activities would you like most? From the list below choose and circle your three most favorite rewards:

1. Basketball

2. Cross-country running

3. Flag football

4. Floor hockey

5. Frisbee

6. Jump rope

7. Ladder walking (forming human ladders)

8. Poi balls (from performing art show)

9. Soccer

10. Softball

11. Sport option (a variety of equipment will be brought out and you can participate in any activity you like)

12. Volleyball

13. Water relays (requires movement of water and a water balloon toss)

14. Other:_____

*Adapted from K. Rodriques, 1996. The use of public posting and physical activity reinforcement to reduce the transition time in a middle school physical education class. Unpublished master's thesis, California State University, Long Beach.

## WORKSHEET 3

### Example of a Point Exchange Card

**WEEKLY PHYSICAL EDUCATION POINT CHART**

STUDENT'S NAME _____ CLASS _____ DATE _____

| | M | T | W | TH | F | Total |
|---|---|---|---|---|---|---|
| Class rules | ___ | ___ | ___ | ___ | ___ | ___ |
| Wearing proper dress | ___ | ___ | ___ | ___ | ___ | ___ |
| Following teacher directions | ___ | ___ | ___ | ___ | ___ | ___ |
| Performing warm-up exercises | ___ | ___ | ___ | ___ | ___ | ___ |
| Completing performance skill worksheet | ___ | ___ | ___ | ___ | ___ | ___ |
| Cooperating with classmates | ___ | ___ | ___ | ___ | ___ | ___ |
| Weekly point total | ___ | ___ | ___ | ___ | ___ | ___ |

**HOW TO USE THE POINT CARD:**

Class rules have been previously discussed and are further explained on the Class Rules Chart on the physical education bulletin board.

1. Check each blank for properly following each of the class rules.

2. Each check mark is worth one point.

3. Students who receive 20 points or better earn the privilege of participating in the Friday Sport Option Day voted on by the class.

4. Students who earn 19 points or less will participate in the physical education lesson of the day and hopefully you will work to earn the class sport option the following week!

I will periodically check point cards. Remember you are on your honor to correctly fill out your point card.

## WORKSHEET 4
## Goal-Setting Checklist for Students

DATE: _____

**GOAL #1:**

My goal is: _____.

Activities I can do to achieve this goal are:

_____

_____

_____

_____

Ways I can measure my progress toward this goal are:

_____

_____

_____

_____

**GOAL #2:**

My goal is: _____.

Activities I can do to achieve this goal are:

_____

_____

_____

_____

Ways I can measure my progress toward this goal are:

_____

_____

_____

_____

**WORKSHEET 5**

## Relaxation Training Log Sheet

NAME _____

TODAY'S DATE _____

DATE  DUE _____

Directions: Lying on your back, perform relaxation activities for the following body parts daily. Be sure to breathe correctly. Over the next two weeks spend 15 to 20 minutes daily practicing these exercises, marking Xs in the correct boxes.

| Body part | M | T | W | Th | F | M | T | W | Th | F |
|-----------|---|---|---|----|----|---|---|---|----|----|
| 1.  Knee to head | | | | | | | | | | |
| 2.  Hips | | | | | | | | | | |
| 3.  Hands and arms | | | | | | | | | | |
| 4.  Arms and shoulders | | | | | | | | | | |
| 5.  Legs and feet | | | | | | | | | | |
| 6.  Shoulders and neck | | | | | | | | | | |
| 7.  Jaw | | | | | | | | | | |
| 8.  Face and nose | | | | | | | | | | |
| 9.  Stomach | | | | | | | | | | |

**WORKSHEET 6**

## Behavioral Checklist for Students With ADD or ADHD
## (Reif 1993)

If you suspect a student has ADD or ADHD, perform an informal assessment by using this checklist to determine how many common characteristics of these problems the student exhibits. If you discover that the child exhibits several of these behaviors, suggest that a special education team, dietitian, or physician do a more formal assessment.

**Common ADD Behaviors**

_____ Easily distracted

_____ Difficulty listening

_____ Difficulty following directions

_____ Difficulty concentrating

_____ Difficulty attending to task

_____ Inconsistent performance

_____ Tunes out

_____ Disorganized

_____ Problems working independently

_____ Socially immature

_____ Easily frustrated

_____ Low self-esteem

**Additional Behaviors Seen in Students With ADHD**

_____ Constant motion

_____ Fidgets with hands or feet

_____ Plays with nearby objects

_____ Roams around

_____ Speaks out of turn

_____ Cannot wait for turn

_____ Difficulty transitioning from one activity to the next

_____ Aggressive

## WORKSHEET 7

### Nutritional Evaluation Form

Directions: Use this form daily to determine if a correlation between diet and behavior exists.

| Date/Time Behavior Occurred | Behavior | Food Consumed at Meal or Snack |
|---|---|---|
| | | |

## WORKSHEET 8

### Student Information Worksheet

Use this worksheet as a reminder of the uniqueness of your students. You can copy these questions and fill in the information for each class to help you tailor your style to the students in each class and their individual needs. To save time, make generalizations and note exceptions.

What is the age level of your students?

What grade(s) are your students in?

What is/are the socioeconomic status(es) of your students' parents?

What behavior management methods do your students' parents use?

How are your students unique in their:

learning styles?

skills?

interests?

abilities?

personalities?

How can you use this information to modify your teaching style?

# Suggested Additional Readings

## CHAPTER 1

Charles, C.M. 1992. *Building classroom discipline.* White Plains, NY: Longman.

Henderson, H.L., and R.W. French. 1993. *Creative approaches to managing student behavior in physical education.* 2d ed. Park City, UT: Family Development Resources.

Walker, J.E., and T.M. Shea. 1995. *Behavior management: A practical approach for educators.* 6th ed. New York: Macmillan.

## CHAPTER 2

Graham, G. 1992. *Teaching children physical education: Becoming a master teacher.* Champaign, IL: Human Kinetics.

Rink, J.E. 1993. *Teaching physical education for learning.* 2d ed. St. Louis: Mosby.

Siedentop, D. 1991. *Developing teaching skills in physical education.* 3d ed. Mountainview, CA: Mayfield.

## CHAPTERS 3-5

Cooper, J.O., T.E. Heron, and W.L. Heward. 1987. *Applied behavior analysis.* Columbus, OH: Merrill.

French, R., and B. Lavay, eds. 1990. *A manual of behavior management techniques for physical educators and recreators.* Kearney, NE: Educational Systems.

French, R., B. Lavay, and H. Henderson. 1985. Take a lap. *Physical Educator* 42: 180-185.

Jenson, W.R., G. Rhodes, and H.K. Reavis. 1994. *The tough kid tool box.* Longmont, CO: Sopris West.

Rhodes, G., W.R. Jenson, and H.K. Reavis. 1993. *The tough kid book: Practical classroom management strategies.* 4th ed. Longmont, CO: Sopris West.

Smith, D.D. 1984. *Effective discipline.* Austin, TX: Pro Ed.

## CHAPTER 6

Glasser, W. 1992. *The quality school: Managing students without coercion.* 2d ed. New York: Harper Collins.

Hellison, D.R. 1995. *Teaching responsibility through physical activity.* Champaign, IL: Human Kinetics.

Hellison, D.R., and T.J. Templin. 1991. *A reflective approach to teaching physical education.* Champaign, IL: Human Kinetics.

Morris, G.S.D., ed. 1993. Becoming responsible for our own actions: What's possible in physical education. *Journal of Physical Education, Recreation and Dance* 14(5): 36-75.

Stiehl, J. 1993. Becoming responsible: Theoretical and practical considerations. *Journal of Physical Education, Recreation and Dance* 64: 5, 38-40, 57-59, 70-71.

# CHAPTER 7

Davis, J.O. 1991. Sport injuries and stress management. *The Sport Psychologist* 5: 175-182.

Hackman, R.M., J.E. Katra, and S.M. Geertsen. 1992. The athletic trainer's role in modifying behaviors of adolescent athletes: Putting theory into practice. *Journal of Athletic Training* 273: 262-266.

Hewett, F.M., and S.R. Fornes. 1984. *Education of exceptional learners*. 3d ed. Needham, MA: Allyn and Bacon.

Hughes, H., and R. Davis. 1980. Treatment of aggressive behavior: The effect of EMG response discrimination biofeedback training. *Journal of Autism and Developmental Disorder* 10(2): 193-202.

Jansma, P., and R. French. 1994. *Special physical education: Physical activity, sport and recreation*. 2d ed. Englewood Cliffs, NJ: Prentice Hall.

Law, J.A. 1993. Diet and behavior: Nutrition is a better way. *New Zealand Journal of Health, Physical Education, and Recreation* 21(3): 6-10.

McGill, L.O. 1993. Progressive relaxation for athletes. *Journal of the International Council for Health, Physical Education, and Recreation* 29(4): 24-26.

Reif, S.A. 1993. *How to reach and teach ADD/ADHD children*. West Nyack, NY: The Center for Research in Education.

Tucker, B.F., and S.E. Colson. 1992. Traumatic brain injury: An overview of school re-entry. *Intervention in School and Clinic* 27(4): 198-206.

Waller, M.B. 1993. Coping with crack affected children. *People and Education* 1(1): 16-25.

Weatherred, W.S. 1996. Perceptions of pediatric endocrinologists and endocrinologists regarding the role of physical educators in the management of diabetes in adolescents. Unpublished master's thesis, Texas Woman's University, Denton.

# CHAPTER 8

Bavolek, S.J. 1996. *Child centered coaching: The philosophy behind the practice*. Park City, UT: Family Development Resources.

Charles, C.M. 1992. *Building classroom discipline*. White Plains, NY: Longman.

Levis, L., and L. Lininger. 1994. *Increase the peace: A focused approach*. Available from Lynda Levis, 11806 Byers Cove, Austin, TX 78753.

Martin, J., and J. Sugarman. 1992. *Models of classroom management: Principle, applications, and critical perspectives*. 2d ed. Calgary, Alberta: Detselig Enterprise.

McKenzie, T., and P. Rosengard. 1995. *Educational programs that work: The catalog of the national diffusion network*. 21st ed. Boston: Sopris West.

# References

Allen, J.I. 1980. Jogging can modify disruptive behaviors. *Teaching Exceptional Children* 13: 66-70.

Anshel, M.H. 1991. Relaxation training in sport: Pros and cons. *Sport Health* 9(4): 23-24.

Bavolek, S.J. 1990. *Corporal punishment: What to do instead.* Park City, UT: Family Development Resources.

Blue, F.R. 1979. Aerobic running as a treatment for moderate depression. *Perceptual and Motor Skills* 48(1): 228.

Bos, C.S., and S. Vaughn. 1991. *Strategies for teaching students with learning and behavior problems.* Boston, MA: Allyn and Bacon.

Boyce, B.A., and P. Walker. 1991. Establishing structure in the elementary school. *Strategies* 5(2): 20-23.

Brandon, J.E., R.L. Eason, and T.L. Smith. 1986. Behavioral relaxation training and motor performance of learning disabled children with hyperactive behaviors. *Adapted Physical Activity Quarterly* 3: 67-79.

Canter, L. 1992. *Seasonal motivators: Positive reinforcement activities and awards for every month of the year.* Santa Monica, CA: Lee Canter and Associates.

Carlson, T. 1995. We hate gym: Students' alienation from physical education. *Journal of Teaching in Physical Education* 14: 467-477.

Charles, C.M. 1992. *Building classroom discipline.* White Plains, NY: Longman.

Chasnoff, I.J., H.J. Landress, and M.E. Barrett. 1990. The prevalence of illicit drug or alcohol use during pregnancy and discrepancies in mandatory reporting in Pinellas County, Florida. *The New England Journal of Medicine* 322(17): 1202-1206.

Cooper, J.O., T.E. Heron, and W.L. Heward. 1987. *Applied behavior analysis.* Columbus, OH: Merrill.

Craft, D. 1995. Learning disabilities and attentional deficits. In *Adapted physical education and sport.* 2d ed. Edited by J.P. Winnick, 111-128. Champaign, IL: Human Kinetics.

Cusimanio, B.E., P.W. Darst, and H. van der Mars. 1993. Improving your instruction through evaluation. *Strategies* 7(2): 26-29.

Davis, J.O. 1991. Sports injuries and stress management: An opportunity for research. *The Sport Psychologist* 5: 175-182.

Davis, R., and R. French. 1986. Managing student behavior in physical education through a positive modified scoring system. *The Directive Teacher* 8(1): 15.

Denton Independent School District. 1996. *Student code of conduct, discipline management plan, and electronic communicating and data management policy and guidelines.* Denton, TX: Denton Independent School District.

Dougherty, N.J., and D. Bonanno. 1987. *Contemporary approaches to teaching physical education.* 2d ed. Scottsdale, AZ: Gorsuch Scarisbrick.

Doyne, E.J., D.L. Chambless, and L.E. Bentley. 1983. Aerobic exercise as a treatment for depression in women. *Behavior Therapy* 14: 434-440.

Dunn, J.M., and H.D. Fredericks. 1985. The utilization of behavior management in mainstreaming in physical education. *Adapted Physical Activity Quarterly* 2: 338-346.

Elam, S.M., L.C. Rose, and A.M. Gallup. 1996. The 28th Annual Phi Delta Kappa/Gallup Poll of the public's attitudes toward the public schools. *Phi Delta Kappa* 78(1): 41-59.

Federal Register. 1992. *Assistance to states for the education of children with disabilities and preschool grants for children with disabilities: Final rules* (September 29). Washington, DC: Department of Education.

Feingold, B.F. 1975. *Why your child is hyperactive.* New York: Random House.

———. 1979. *The Feingold cookbook for hyperactive children, and others with problems associated with food additives and salicylates.* New York: Random House.

Fishbein, D.H., and S.E. Pease. 1994. Diet, nutrition, and aggression. *The Psychology of Aggression* 213(4): 117-141.

Fluegelman, A. 1976. *The new games book.* San Francisco: New Games Foundation.

———. ed. 1981. *More new games book.* San Francisco: New Games Foundation.

Fontenelle, D.H. 1992. *Are you listening?* Bryon, CA: Front Row Experience.

French, K. 1991. Elementary teachers: Perceptions of stressful events and stress-related teaching practices. *Perceptual and Motor Skills* 72: 203-210.

French, R., and B. Lavay, eds. 1990. *A manual of behavior management techniques for physical educators and recreators.* Kearney, NE: Educational Systems.

Fronske, H., and N. Birch. 1995. Overcoming roadblocks to communication. *Strategies* 8(8): 22-25.

Gipson, M., S. Lowe, and T. McKenzie. 1994. Sport psychology: Improving performance. In *Science of coaching volleyball,* ed. C. McGown, 23-33. Champaign, IL: Human Kinetics.

Glasser, W. 1975. *Reality therapy.* NY: Harper and Row.

Glasser, W. 1977. 10 steps to good discipline. *Today's Education* (Nov-Dec): 61-63.

Glasser, W. 1992. *The quality School: Managing students without coercion.* 2d ed. New York: Harper Collins.

Gordon, T. 1994. *T.E.T: Physical educator effectiveness training.* New York: David McKay.

Grineski, S. 1996. *Cooperative learning in physical education.* Champaign, IL: Human Kinetics.

Hardy, C.J., and R.K. Croce. 1990. Relaxation training. *Sport Psychology Training Bulletin* 21: 1-7.

Hellison, D.R. 1985. *Goals and strategies for teaching physical education.* Champaign, IL: Human Kinetics.

———. 1995. *Teaching responsibility through physical activity.* Champaign, IL: Human Kinetics.

Hellison, D.R., and T.J. Templin. 1991. *A reflective approach to teaching physical education.* Champaign, IL: Human Kinetics.

Henderson, H.L., and R.W. French. 1993. *Creative approaches to managing student behavior in physical education.* Park City, UT: Family Development Resources.

Horrocks, R.N. 1978. Resolving conflict in the classroom. *Journal of Physical Education and Recreation* 48(9): 20-21.

Hughes, H.W. 1994. From fistfights to gunfights: Preparing teachers and administrators to cope with violence in school. Paper presented at the Annual Meeting of the American Association of Colleges for Teacher Education at Chicago, IL. ERIC Document Reproduction Service No. ED 366 584.

Jacobson, E. 1974. *Progressive relaxation.* 3d ed. Chicago: University of Chicago Press.

Jansma, P., and R. French. 1994. *Special physical education: Physical activity, sport and recreation.* 2d ed. Englewood Cliffs, NJ: Prentice Hall.

Johnson, H.A. 1986. Classroom management and school discipline problems: Implications for training teachers of black youth. Paper presented at the *National Conference on Preparation and Survival of Black Public School Teachers.* Norfolk, VA.

Jones, V., and L. Jones. 1981. *Responsible classroom performance.* Boston: Allyn and Bacon.

———. 1982. *Responsible classroom performance: Creating positive learning environments and solving problems.* Boston: Allyn and Bacon.

Koeppen, A.S. 1974. Relaxation training for children. *Elementary School Guidance and Counseling* 9: 14-20.

Lavay, B., and P. Bishop. 1986. Nondressing for class: A universal problem. *Journal of Physical Education, Recreation and Dance* 57(7): 52-53, 75.

Law, J.S. 1993. Diet and behavior: Nutrition is a better way. *New Zealand Journal of Health, Physical Education, and Recreation* 21(3): 6-10.

Levis, L., and L. Lininger. 1994. *Increase the peace: A focused approach.* Available from Lynda Levis, 11806 Byers Cove, Austin, TX 78753.

Loovis, E.M. 1995. Behavior management. In *Adapted physical education and sport,* 2d ed., Edited by J.P. Winnick, 75-90. Champaign IL: Human Kinetics.

Loovis, E.M. 1995. Behavior conditions. In *Adapted physical education and sport,* 2d ed., Edited by J.P. Winnick, 129-142. Champaign, IL: Human Kinetics.

Lozoff, B. 1989. Nutrition and behavior. *American Psychologist* 44(2): 231-236.

Martin, J., and J. Sugarman. 1993. *Models of classroom management: Principles, applications, and critical perspectives,* 2nd ed. Calgary, Alberta: Detselig.

McGill, L.O. 1993. Progressive relaxation for athletes. *Journal of the International Council for Health, Physical Education, and Recreation* 29(4): 24-26.

McKenzie, T.L. 1990. Token economy research: A review for the physical educator. In *A manual of behavior management methods for physical educators and recreators,* ed. R. French and B. Lavay, 102-123. Kearney, NE: Educational Systems.

Mohnsen, B.S. 1995. *Using technology in physical education.* Champaign, IL: Human Kinetics.

Morris, G.S.D., ed. 1993. Becoming responsible for our actions: What's possible in physical education. *Journal of Physical Education, Recreation and Dance* 64(5): 36-75.

Mullin, J.B. 1992. Children prenatally exposed to cocaine and crack: Implications for schools.

*British Columbia Journal of Special Education* 16(3): 282-289.

National Coalition to Abolish Corporal Punishment in Schools. 1992. *Corporal punishment fact sheet.* New York: David McKay.

Nichols, B. 1994. *Moving and learning.* 3d ed. St. Louis: Mosby.

Orlick, T. 1978. *The cooperative sports and games book.* New York: Pantheon Books.

———. 1982. *The second cooperative sports and games book.* New York: Pantheon Books.

Pangrazi, R.P., and V.P. Dauer. 1995. *Dynamic physical education for elementary school children.* 11th ed. Boston, MA: Allyn and Bacon.

Pankau, M. 1980. Teach your athletes how to relax. *Coaching Review* 3(14): 30-32.

Phillips, J.H., and J.L. Carter. 1985. Tired of being picked last: Humanistic alternatives to group division. *Journal of Physical Education, Recreation and Dance* 56(1): 96-97.

Porretta, D.L. 1995. Cerebral palsy, traumatic brain injury, stroke, amputation, dwarfism, and other orthopedic impairments. In *Adapted Physical Education and Sport,* 2d ed. Edited by J.P. Winnick, 167-192. Champaign, IL: Human Kinetics.

Premack, D. 1959. Toward empirical behavioral laws: I. Positive reinforcement. *Psychological Review* 66: 219-233.

Reif, S.A. 1993. *How to reach and teach ADD/ADHD children.* West Nyack, NY: The Center for Research in Education.

Rhode, G., D.P. Morgan, and K.R. Young. 1983. Generalization and maintenance of treatment gains of behaviorally handicapped students from resource room to regular classrooms using self-evaluation procedures. *Journal of Applied Behavior Analysis* 16(2): 171-188.

Rhode, G., W.R. Jenson, and H.K. Reavis. 1993. *The tough kid book: Practical classroom management strategies.* 4th ed. Longmont, CO: Sopris West.

Rink, J.E. 1993. *Teaching physical education for learning.* 2d ed. St. Louis: Mosby.

Rodriques, K. 1996. The use of public posting and physical activity reinforcement to reduce the transition time in a middle school physical education class. Unpublished master's thesis, California State University, Long Beach.

Rose, M.J. 1988. The place of drugs in the management of behavior disorders after traumatic brain injury. *Journal of Head Rehabilitation* 3(3): 7-13.

Sainato, D.M., P.S. Strain, D. Lefebvre, and N. Rapp. 1990 Effects of self-evaluation on the independent work skills of preschool children. *Exceptional Children* 56(6): 540-549.

Salend, S.J., C.R. Whittaker, and E. Reeder. 1993. Group evaluation: A collaborative, peer-mediated behavior management system. *Exceptional Children* 59(3): 203-209.

Sanders, A.N. 1989. Class management skills. *Strategies* 2(3): 14-18.

Sariscsany, M.J. 1991. Motivating physical education students through music. *The Physical Educator* 48(2): 93-94.

Siedentop, D. 1991. *Developing teaching skills in physical education.* 3d ed. Mountainview, CA: Mayfield.

Skinner, B.F. 1973. *Punishment and rehabilatation.* Ed. J.G. Murphy. Belmont, CA: Wadsworth.

Smith, D.J., K.R. Young, R.P. West, D.P. Morgan, and G. Rhode. 1988. Reducing the disruptive behavior of junior high school students: A classroom self-management procedure. *Behavior Disorders* 13(6): 231-239.

Smith, L.H. 1976. *Improving your child's behavior chemistry.* Englewood Cliffs, NJ: Prentice Hall.

Smith, L.H. 1979. *Feed your kids right: Dr. Smith's program for your child's total health.* New York: McGraw Hill.

Smith, M.S., and W.M. Momack. 1987. Stress management techniques in childhood and adolescence. *Clinical Pediatrics* 26(11): 581-585.

Stiehl, J. 1993. Becoming responsible: Theoretical and practical considerations. *Journal of Physical Education, Recreation and Dance* 64(5): 38-40, 57- 59, 70-71.

Summerford, C. 1996. Locker room boot camp. *Journal of Physical Education, Recreation and Dance* 57(6): 85-87.

Swager, S.M., and M.C. Mante. 1986. Three simple rules: The key to cooperation. *Journal of Physical Education, Recreation and Dance* 57(6): 85-87.

Taylor, R.D., J. Hawkins, and M.P. Brady. 1991. Extent, type, preferences, and consequences of crisis intervention training for teachers. *Educational Psychology* 2: 143-150.

Thomas, J.D., I.E. Presland, M.D. Grant, and T.L. Glynn. 1978. Natural rates of teacher approval and disapproval in grade 7 classrooms. *Journal of Applied Behavior Analysis* 11: 91-94.

Tucker, B.F., and S.E. Colson. 1992. Traumatic brain injury: An overview of school re-entry. *Intervention in School and Clinic* 27(4): 198-206.

Vogler, E.W., and P. Bishop. 1990. Management of disruptive behavior in physical education. *Physical Educator* 47(1): 16-26.

Vogler, E.W., and R. French. 1983. The effects of a group contingency strategy on behaviorally disordered students in physical education. *Research Quarterly for Exercise and Sport* 54: 273-277.

Walker, J.E., and T.M. Shea. 1995. *Behavior management: A practical approach for educators.* 6th ed. New York: Macmillan.

Waller, M.B. 1993. Coping with crack affected children. *People and Education* 1(1): 16-25.

White, M.A. 1975. Natural rates of teacher approval and disapproval in the classroom. *Journal of Applied Behavior Analysis* 8: 367-372.

Williams, E.W. 1995. Learn student names in a flash. *Strategies* 8(5): 25-29.

# Index